Made Simple

Accounting
Advanced Algebra
  & Calculus
Anthropology
Applied Economics
Applied Mathematics
Applied Mechanics
Art Appreciation
Art of Speaking
Art of Writing
Biology
Book-keeping
British Constitution
Chemistry
Commerce
Commercial Law
Computer Programming
Cookery
Economics
Electricity
Electronic Computers
Electronics
English
French

Geology
German
Human Anatomy
Intermediate Algebra
  & Analytic Geometry
Italian
Journalism
Latin
Law
Management
Marketing
Mathematics
New Maths
Organic Chemistry
Philosophy
Physics
Psychology
Rapid Reading
Russian
Salesmanship
Spanish
Statistics
Typing

COMMERCIAL LAW   Made Simple

John Parris, LL.B., Ph.D.

Made Simple Books
W. H. ALLEN   London
A Division of Howard & Wyndham Ltd.

Made and printed in Great Britain by
Butler & Tanner Ltd., Frome, Somerset
for the publishers W. H. Allen & Company Ltd.,
Essex Street, London WC2R 3JG

ISBN 0 491 00922 4 Casebound
ISBN 0 491 00912 7 Paperbound

Preface

'The common law evolves not merely by breeding new principles but also, when they are fully grown, by burying their ancestors,' remarked Diplock L.J., as he then was, in *Hong Kong Fir Shipping Co. Ltd. v Kawasaki*, [1962] 1 All E.R. 474.

The above quotation forms the basis of the present book, since it is no service to a student, or a member of the public, to set forth as a living law that which is no longer being applied in the Courts.

Throughout the book, therefore, a determined effort has been made to avoid this danger by basing the principles set out, so far as possible, on recent decisions and by ignoring some familiar cases which are no longer good law. The pretence common to many books of this nature that all the cases are reconcilable and equally enshrine the law has also been discarded.

Nevertheless, students' needs have also been taken into account, since examination questions are perhaps slowest of all to submit to change. Consequently, I have devoted sufficient space to concepts which frequently occur in examinations but which might be regarded as bearing scant relation to the realities of modern life.

The book will meet the needs of students on many academic courses ranging from the O.N.C. and O.N.D. in Business Studies to the London external LL.B and most internal university degree courses in law. It also covers the relevant parts of examinations set by a wide variety of professional bodies such as the Chartered Institute of Secretaries, the Institute of Chartered Accountants, the Institute of Cost and Management Accounts and the Royal Institution of Chartered Surveyors. Additionally, businessmen of all kinds will find the book an invaluable source of reference and guidance, for never before in the world of industry and commerce has a knowledge of the law been so necessary.

Believing, also, that nobody can learn the law solely from a textbook or without constant and critical reference to the judgments in the Law Reports, I have provided references throughout the text to the All England Law Reports (All E.R.) and All England Reports Reprints (All E.R. Rep.) as being the series most likely to be available to students and the general public. In addition, complete references of all the cases mentioned in the book are listed in a Table of Cases at Appendix Two.

I am grateful to Professor D. W. Greig of U.W.I.S.T. for reading the typescript and making a number of helpful criticisms. He has, of course, no responsibility for the text or the views expressed in it. I also owe a debt to Mrs. Jane Mayer who relieved me of much routine work, thus enabling me to concentrate on writing the book, and to Alec Spencer who prepared the three Appendices and the Index.

Finally, my thanks are due to my student, John Bates-Williams, who checked the references and to my typist, Mrs. Maureen Stanley, who wrestled with my handwriting whilst she was also in the throes of procreation.

JOHN PARRIS

Table of Contents

BOOK I: TRADING ENTITIES

CHAPTER ONE

INDIVIDUALS, CORPORATIONS AND UNINCORPORATED ASSOCIATIONS

In Britain, unlike the situation in many other countries, a man may start any business he chooses without the prior permission of the Government. Except for certain types of business for which qualifications are necessary, and others where, usually for revenue purposes, licences are required, there is a general freedom to engage in any enterprise. Indeed, as we shall see later on page 124, ever since the early 17th century it has been a principle of the English Law that *prima facie* restraints on trade are void.

Trading may take place:

1. By Individuals.

2. By Corporations. In addition to natural persons—real live human beings—the law recognises other *personae* as they are called; that is to say, artificial persons, recognised in law as having an identity separate from the individual human beings who comprise them. They are usually termed corporations and these corporations may consist of different types:

(a) **The corporation sole.** The one-man corporation is something recognised as separate from the individual who holds the office for the time being. For example, the Rector of a Church of England parish is a corporation sole—unlike a Methodist minister, or a Roman Catholic Priest. So, too, is a Bishop of a Church of England diocese, unlike his Roman Catholic counterpart.
The Crown. This is a corporation sole, as is the Public Trustee. Property vested in a corporation sole belongs to the corporation and not to the person who for the time being holds the office.

(b) **Corporations aggregate.** These are of various kinds and the most familiar is the Limited Liability Company. They, once again, are artificial persons recognised as having an identity in law separate from the individuals who comprise the corporation.

3

3. **By Partnerships or Firms.** These are groups of persons who associate together for the purpose of carrying on a business with a view to profit.

4. **By Unincorporated Associations.** These are collections of people who come together, but whose primary purpose is not to make profit but to pursue some interest they have in common—whether it be a sport, a religion or the promotion of a special breed of cat or cattle. But many of these often engage in trading activities. The religious bodies may publish books and magazines, and frequently do; the tennis club will inevitably enter into contracts and own property; and the rabbit breeding clubs may buy and sell serum or stock; and almost every other type of club with premises of its own will probably buy and sell liquor.

Trading by Individuals

No permission from anybody is required to start most forms of business, though, if premises are to be used, planning permission will invariably be necessary before, say, a private dwelling house can be used as a shop or offices.

Nor is there any age limit at which a person can commence trading. 'There is nothing except the commonsense of his customers to prevent a six-year-old setting up business' pointed out the Latey Committee on the age of majority.

Particular care, however, is required in dealing with *minors*—persons under the age of 18—as these are not liable on their trading contracts. Money paid to them for goods which are not received cannot—in the absence of deliberate fraud by the minor—be recovered, nor can they be made to pay for goods received or made to return the goods. They cannot be made bankrupt in respect of trading debts, since, as we shall see later on page 108, these are not debts in law. Otherwise, of course, an individual trading as such is liable to the full extent of all his assets for the trading debts of his business.

The Business Names Register

If an individual uses a name in business which differs *in any way* from his true name, he is required to register the trading name with the Registrar of Business Names, Companies House, City Road, London EC1 Y1BB. He is using his true name if he trades:

    (i) under his surname alone.

    (ii) under his surname or fore (or christian) name or names.

    (iii) under his surname and initials.

But if he uses anything else—such as Bill Jones & Co.—he is required to register.

Registration of business names is a simple matter, consisting of filling up the appropriate form and sending the fee (currently £1) to the Registrar. Registration does not give any exclusive right to use that name and in general any name can be registered, whether it is that of an existing business or not, though the Registrar has power to refuse to register names which are misleading.

Non-registration has two effects:

1. It is a criminal offence, punishable with a maximum penalty of £5 a day for so long as the default continues—except that the Registrar rarely bothers to prosecute since magistrates regard the offence as so trifling that the penalties are contemptuous.

2. If the *Registration of Business Names Act, 1916* is not complied with, contracts are unenforceable by the unregistered business though all the rights of the other contracting parties exist. However, the Court has a wide power to grant relief to the party in default if satisfied the default was due to inadvertence.

The *Registration of Business Names Act* applies in a similar fashion to companies and to partnerships as it does to individuals.

Statutory Corporations

These may be created by Act of Parliament as, for example, the British Railways Board and the Post Office Corporation, and are subject to what is termed the *ultra vires* rule. That is, if they make contracts 'outside their statutory powers' the contracts are not binding on them. This is dealt with more specifically later on pages 103 *et seq.* in so far as it relates to companies but the same principles apply to this type of corporation.

In some cases, too, there is difficulty in knowing whether they contract at all where they merely carry out their statutory duty to supply consumers. The same problem applies to companies specifically created by special statute—such as gas and water undertakings—and is discussed more fully on page 77.

Corporations may also be created under the prerogative of the Crown by **Royal Charter**. The Pharmaceutical Society is a body of this nature, as is the Hudson Bay Company. Such corporations are not subject to the *ultra vires* rule and they have the full capacity to do anything that an ordinary individual can. But if they exceed the powers given them in their charter of incorporation, they may be liable to forfeit the charter, and for this reason any member of such a corporation will be granted an injunction (see page 67) by the Courts to restrain the chartered corporation from exceeding its powers: *Jenkins v Pharmaceutical Society* (1921).

The Difference between Limited Liability Companies and Partnerships

The difference between these two concepts can conveniently be tabulated, though there are exceptions, which will be noted later.

Partnership	Company
1. Has no separate legal personality	Is a 'persona' apart from the members (i.e. 'shareholders') comprising it

A partnership is a relationship which subsists between persons carrying on business in common with a view to profit and it is never anything more than the sum total of all the individual partners, even though known as 'a firm'. By a concession, however, the Rules of the Supreme Court 1965, Order 81 (1) allow a partnership to sue or to be sued in the name of the firm.

A limited liability company, however, is something quite different from its shareholders. Mr. Salomon held most of the shares in a public company called Salomon and Co. Ltd., and he also held debentures (a secured loan) charged against all the assets of the company. When the company became insolvent and went into liquidation, he claimed that his debentures entitled him to payment in priority over any other creditor of the company. The rest of the creditors protested that this was unfair since the company was never anything more than Mr. Salomon wearing different clothes so to speak. The Courts held that the company had a separate identity in law from Mr. Salomon, so he was entitled to have his debentures paid out in full before any other creditors got anything: *Salomon v Salomon and Co. Ltd.* 1897, [1895–99] All E.R. Rep. 33. This is a fundamental principle of the law, but it must be said that there has been some considerable erosion of it in recent years, not least of all by the Inland Revenue.

2. Partners have unlimited liability	The liability of shareholders of a company is limited

If a partnership is unable to pay its debts, all the members of the partnership can be made to discharge them to the full extent of their personal fortunes. But shareholders of a company who have paid up the nominal value of their shares are not liable for the debts of the company (see page 18 for limited partners).

3. Numbers in a partnership are limited	The number of shareholders in a company is not limited

By the *Companies Act, 1967,* the maximum number of partners in a banking or trading partnership is limited to 20 but the number in a professional partnership is unlimited. No such limits apply to a company and it can have as many shareholders as it has shares, though the number of shareholders may have some effect on whether it is a private or a public company.

4. Partnerships can come into   Companies only come into
    existence informally   existence on registration

From time to time, there have been cases where the Courts have found a partnership to exist even though there had never been any formal documentation and often where its existence was denied by the persons concerned. Companies can be formed in accordance with the *Companies Acts, 1948* and *1967* and only come into existence on registration.

5. There is no restriction on the   A company's powers are
    powers of partnership   limited by its Objects Clause

The *ultra vires* doctrine, in short, has no application to partnership. For a full explanation of this doctrine see page 103.

6. One partner can bind all the   A shareholder cannot bind the
    others   company

The acts of one partner within the normal course of his trade, even though entirely unauthorised by the other partners, binds all the others (see page 14). A shareholder of a company has no power to make a contract or to bind the company in any way whatsoever.

7. A partnership is a private   Companies' accounts have to be
    concern   filed with the Registrar

Partnerships can arise in a number of different ways, but their accounts and revenues are private matters between the partners (and the omnipotent taxman, of course). All companies have to file their accounts with the Registrar, and these are open to public inspection.

8. A new partner means a new   The company continues
    partnership   however often the shares change
                           hands

If a partner leaves, or dies or a new one joins, the old partnership comes to an end and a new one comes into existence. A company continues whoever holds the shares.

9. Profits can be divided amongst   The profits have to be
    the partners in any agreed   distributed amongst the
    proportion   shareholders by dividend
                           in accordance with the rights
                           attached to their shares

Partners can divide the profits amongst themselves by agreement in any way they choose, but the dividend paid out on a company's shares must be in accordance with the rights attaching to the shares, i.e. preference shares coming before ordinary shares.

10. A partnership can be dissolved instantly by agreement, or by a variety of other methods	A company is dissolved by liquidation in accordance with the *Companies Acts*

How a partnership comes to an end is dealt with in detail later (see page 17).

The Difference between Partnerships and Co-Ownership

People can be joint owners of property without being partners and the essential differences between the two concepts in law are:

1. Partnership has to be carried on with a view of profit	Co-ownership may sometimes be with a view to profit, but does not always have to be

The very essence of the whole idea of partnership is this concept of profit; so that other concepts of law and other relationships, such as unincorporated associations like clubs, are excluded even though they may trade and may incidentally make profits. The test is: What is the fundamental purpose of the relationship?

2. Partnership is always the result of agreement, express or implied	Co-ownership may result from acts other than agreement

If a father leaves a house by will to his two sons jointly they will become co-owners. This clearly has nothing whatever to do with agreement between the two of them, and they are not partners.

3. A share in a partnership cannot be transferred to a third party without the consent of the other partners	One co-owner can always divest himself of the rights in the property without the permission of the other

Even if the property is land and the co-owners are joint owners in land, one can sell his share without even consulting the other; but a partner cannot sell his interest in a partnership to another person without the agreement of all the other partners.

4. The acts of one partner bind all the others	There is no implied authority on the part of one co-owner to bind the other

The law on all this is set out expressly in s. 2 of the *Partnership Act, 1890.*

'Joint tenancy, tenancy in common, joint property, common property, or part ownership does not of itself create a partnership as to anything so held or owned, whether the tenant or owners do or do not share in any profits.'

Unincorporated Associations

'A club' may mean a business owned by an individual, a partnership or a limited company, as are most 'night clubs', 'country clubs' and 'football clubs', etc. In all three cases they are known as 'proprietary clubs'. Most professional football clubs are owned by limited liability companies and are therefore proprietary clubs, but a local football or cricket team will almost inevitably be a members' club and therefore an unincorporated association.

The points to note about such bodies are:

1. They are not persons in law and cannot therefore sue or be sued

There are exceptions by Acts of Parliament to this (such as Trade Unions and Trustee Savings Banks)—but this is the general principle. There is provision made under Order 15 Rule 12 of the Supreme Court Rules for a Representative action 'where numerous persons have the same interest in any proceedings', but where there is a changing membership, as with most unincorporated associations, this is not applicable.

2. There is often a contract between each member and all the other members, in which the rules of the association constitute the terms

This is dependent on the interpretation of all the circumstances and it may well be that there is evidence that there was no contractual intent (see page 74). Where there is, however, the Courts will intervene by declaration and by injunction to restrain the wrongful expulsion of members, or actions against them which are contrary to natural justice.

3. Contracts with third parties purporting to be made on behalf of an unincorporated association do not bind the members so as to make them personally liable

This applies unless the member has expressly or impliedly pledged his personal credit.

4. Members of the Committee of an unincorporated association may be liable both in contract and tort in respect of contracts or acts which they have personally authorised

In *Bradley Egg Farm v Clifford*, [1943] 2 All E.R. 378, a member of the Lancashire Utility Poultry Society—an unincorporated association—sued for damages for negligent tests carried out by the Society for white diarrhoea in hens. Judgment was given against the Executive Council.

5. Land and buildings, etc., can only be held by trustees on behalf of the members of incorporated associations

This is because the association itself is not a *persona*.

6. In the event of dissolution of the association, property held in trust for the association is divisible amongst the existing members at the date of dissolution

An allotment association purchased land for £210 which was conveyed to trustees but the money was raised by what were termed 'shares' of £1 each; in addition, allotment holders were members of the association and paid a small subscription. From 1961, the association became inactive, but in 1967 the land was sold for £70,000. The Court held that this sum had to be distributed equally amongst all members in 1961, whether allotment holders or 'shareholders', after the shareholders' money had been refunded. *Re St. Andrew's Allotment Association Trusts*, [1969] 1 All E.R. 147.

It will be apparent from the above that there are considerable dangers for traders dealing with clubs and similar unincorporated associations, and also for members of executive committees who authorise transactions—though members of unincorporated associations may sometimes come in for unexpected windfalls.

CHAPTER TWO

PARTNERSHIPS

How Partnerships Come into Existence

The formation of limited companies and their administration and dissolution amounts to a formidable body of law and is outside the scope of this book.

Partnership has already been defined in the words of the *Partnership Act, 1890* as '*the relation which subsists between persons carrying on business in common with a view to profit*' (s. 1).

As a basic principle it can be said that a partnership can come into existence only by agreement between the parties, but this agreement can be expressed or implied. There are many circumstances and cases where the Courts have found partnerships to have existed even though one of the parties has denied the fact. For the essence is, as we have seen, that a partner is fully liable for all the debts of the partnership and it is often therefore convenient if the Court can be persuaded to accept that one was not a partner. Some prudent business men are willing to finance a business and to share in the profits but are reluctant to be fully liable for its losses if it becomes insolvent. Many cases, therefore, have been devoted to determining whether, on a particular set of facts, a partnership existed or not.

Express Partnerships

In practice, these are often concluded in the form of a deed, although this is not necessary. In fact, there is no need at all for any written document to constitute a partnership. Where such documents exist they are usually known as **Articles of Partnership.**

Most of the *Partnership Act* is devoted to laying down principles to apply where the partnership agreement is silent about the matters dealt with, so it is important that any document which does come into existence should be drafted only after detailed examination of that Act.

Implied Partnerships

In the absence of express agreement, whether the partnership exists between two or more persons or not is an issue of fact, but s. 2 (3) of the *Partnership Act* gives some guidance.

'The receipt by a person of a share of the profits of a business is *prima facie* evidence that he is a partner in the business.'

Prima facie evidence means, of course, that there is presumption to this effect, but this can be rebutted or refuted by evidence to the contrary. The result is that people can be held to be partners who never had the intention of being. But the sharing of *gross takings* is not even *prima facie* evidence of a partnership; the Act refers to *profits*.

The Act itself then goes on to specify five circumstances where the receipt of a share of profits does *Not* by itself amount to evidence of a partnership. These are:

1. Receipt of a debt by instalments out of profits

'The receipt by a person of a debt or other liquidated amount by instalments or otherwise out of the accruing profits of a business does not of itself make him a partner in the business or liable as such.'

2. Contract of employment with remuneration linked to profits

'A contract for the remuneration of a servant or agent of a person engaged in a business by a share of the profits of the business, does not of itself make him a partner in the business or liable as such.'

So if a man is employed as a salesman with all or part of his earnings related to the profits of a business, he is not to be taken as partner by means of that fact alone. And the same applies to an agent who is an independent contractor and not a servant of the business. If his commission is linked to the net profits of the business this is not, without something more, evidence of being a partner.

3. Annuities in favour of widows or children of a former partner charged on the business and related to profits

'A person being the widow or child of a deceased partner and receiving by way of annuities a portion of the profits made in the business in which the deceased person was a partner, is not by reason of such receipt a partner in the business or liable as such.'

4. Loans where the rate of interest is related to profits, provided the contract is in writing

'The advance of money by way of loan to a person engaged or about to engage in any business on a contract with that person whereby the lender shall receive a rate of interest varying with the profits, or shall receive a share of the profits arising from carrying on the business, does not of itself make the lender a partner with the person or persons carrying on the business or liable as such.'

'Provided that the contract is in writing and signed by or on behalf of all the parties thereto.'

This is perhaps the most important of the five qualifications. For if a person lends money to a business and agrees either that the rate of interest shall be related to the profit or that in return for the loan he shall have a share of the profits, 'the presumption is that he is a partner and liable for the partnership debts' (s. 3).

To rebut this:

(i) it is necessary to have an agreement *in writing*;
(ii) the agreement must be signed by all the parties.

It is a prudent course to recite in such a document that by reason of the agreement the lender is not nor shall he be deemed to be a partner in the business, or liable for its debts.

The Statute attempts to incorporate and improve on the principle laid down in the House of Lords in the leading case of *Cox v Hutchinson* (1860). Until that date, receipt of a share in the net profits was taken as *conclusive* proof of partnership, with the result that any person who shared in the profits became liable for all the debts of the business to the full extent of his personal assets.

In the above-mentioned case, the House of Lords held that where a trader who was insolvent entered into an agreement with his creditors whereby he would, under their supervision, carry on his business and out of the profits pay off his debts, he was not in partnership with the creditors. This decision was much to the surprise of the legal profession of the time and seemed to represent a heads-I-win tails-you-lose agreement so far as future creditors were concerned.

But on the present construction of the Act, if the creditor or lender:

(i) has a say in how the business is to be run and or
(ii) acquires an interest in the capital assets and
(iii) is to be repaid *only* out of the profits (not the gross takings),

then it may well be that he would be considered a partner and liable for partnership debts.

Further, the Act also provides by s. 3 that the person who lends money in return for a share of the profits is to be deferred as a creditor in the event of bankruptcy, death or a composition with creditors for less than the full amount, until all the other creditors have been paid.

5. Portion of profits received in consideration of sale of the business

'A person receiving by way of annuity or otherwise a portion of the profits of a business in consideration of the sale by him of the goodwill of the business is not by reason only of such receipt a partner in a business or liable as such.'

So if a man sells a business under an arrangement whereby the purchase price for goodwill shall be paid by instalments based on the net profits, he is not to be considered a partner by reason of that fact alone. This section apparently is restricted to *goodwill* and not to other and more tangible assets of a business; if the price of them or the payment of the agreed price is related to the profit, the presumption that he is a partner may still arise.

Partnership by Estoppel

If a person holds himself out as being a partner, with the result that credit is given or the one to whom the representation is made acts to his detriment by relying on the representation, even if he is not a partner the person making the representation may be precluded from denying the fact. For a full explanation of this principle of estoppel see page 32.

S. 14 (1) of the *Partnership Act*, puts the position clearly:

'Everyone
who by words written or spoken or by conduct
represents himself or who knowingly suffers himself to
be represented
as a partner in a particular firm
is liable as a partner
to anyone who has on the faith of any such representation
given credit to the firm
whether the representation has or has not been
made or communicated to the person so giving
credit by or with the knowledge of the
apparent partner making the representation
or suffering it to be made.'

The Relationship between Partners

Relationship between partners is a **fiduciary** one, as it is called, in which the partners must exercise complete frankness and good faith one to another.

Subject to the express terms of any agreement the *Partnership Act* lays down the duties and the rights of partners as follows:

The Duties of Partners One to the Other

1. **To provide full information and accurate accounts of all matters affecting the partnership, s. 28**

2. **To account to the other parties for any benefit received from transactions affecting the partnership, s. 29 (1)**

In an old case there were three partners in a business. One of them obtained in his own name, and for his own benefit, a renewal of the lease of the premises where the business was carried on. It was held that the lease belonged to the partnership: *Featherstonehaugh v Fenwick* 1810, [1803–13] All E.R. Rep. 89.

Similarly where one partner sold his own goods to the partnership at the market price but without disclosing that they were his, he was held liable to account to his partners for the whole profit he had made: *Bentley v Craven* (1853).

3. **Not to compete with the partnership business, s. 30**

One partner cannot take part in or run any business which is in competition with the partnership. If he does so, he will be liable to account to his partners for any profit made.

The Rights of a Partner

1. **To take full part in the management of the partnership business**

2. **To have the books of the partnership kept at its principal place of business and to have access to them at all times and to copy them if he so desires, s. 24**

Moreover, he is entitled to have the books examined by an accountant or any other agent he may care to appoint.

3. **To be indemnified by the other partners for payments made and liabilities incurred in the ordinary course of the business or for the preservation of its interests, s. 24 (2)**

4. **Not to have new partners introduced without his consent**

But if the Articles of Partnership made provision, for example, for sons of existing partners joining the firm on attaining their majority, he will, of course, have to agree since he has already by that document given his consent.

5. **Not to be expelled from the partnership by the others, s. 25**

Although a partner cannot be expelled by the other partners, there is no way in which one partner can stop the others dissolving a partnership by notice, unless the Articles of the partnership expressly provide that the partnership shall last for a fixed period or be dissolved only if all the partners are agreed upon it.

6. Not to have the fundamental nature of the partnership business changed without the consent of all partners

For all other matters arising out of the partnership business, a majority of the partners are entitled to decide.

7. To share equally in the capital and the profits of the business, in the absence of any agreement to the contrary

Most partnership agreements do, of course, provide that senior partners shall receive a greater share of the profits than junior partners and the Act does nothing to restrict any form of agreement between the partners as to the distribution of profits or assets.

8. To have interest at 5% per annum on any money advanced to the partnership over and above the sum he has agreed to subscribe, s. 24 (3)

The Relationship between Partners and the Outside World

The firm is liable on all contracts made by any one of the partners. 'As between the partners and the outside world . . . each partner is the unlimited agent of every other in every matter connected with the partnership business.' But this applies only to transactions which are in the ordinary course of the firm's business.

And there are some important qualifications:

1. The power to borrow money in the name of the partnership is limited to trading firms. Trading firms are those which buy and sell goods. It does not apply to other partnerships—for example, to professional ones. Even where two men were in business as cinema proprietors and one borrowed money in the firm's name, in breach of the Articles of Partnership, the firm was held not bound and not liable for the debt: *Higgins v Beauchamp* 1914, [1914–15] All E.R. Rep. 937.
2. Negotiable instruments. Trading partnerships are liable for negotiable instruments such as Bills of Exchange and cheques issued in the firm's name by one partner. But so far as other partnerships are concerned, the firm is only liable if on the particular facts it is usual for firms of its nature to issue negotiable instruments of the class concerned.
3. In old cases, before the *Partnership Act*, it was held that no partner could bind a firm without express authority:

    (a) by executing a deed.
    (b) by submitting a dispute to arbitration, or
    (c) by giving a guarantee on behalf of the partnership.

4. Finally, no partner can bind his firm if he has no express authority provided that *the other contracting party knows this perfectly well.* Nor does he bind the firm if the other person does not know he is a partner.

The firm is also liable for any torts committed by a partner in the course of the firm's ordinary business (s. 10); and also when the wrongful act itself, not being in the ordinary course of business, was expressly authorised by other partners.

There is, however, a difference between the firm's liability for the act of a partner in contract and in tort. In contract, the liability is *joint* (s. 9). That means that if one partner only has been sued, and judgment has been obtained against that one, other partners cannot be sued. But for torts the liability is both joint and *several* (s. 12), with the result that if judgment is obtained against one partner and it is not satisfied, all the other partners can be sued subsequently. In both cases, of course, if the partnership is sued in the firm's name, and judgment given against the partnership, all partners are liable to the full extent of their personal fortune.

The Dissolution of Partnerships

The method of dissolution of a partnership is to some extent dictated by the Articles of Partnership:

1. Where the Articles of Partnership provide for it to last a fixed period, it is dissolved at the end of that period (s. 32).
2. If entered into for a specific venture, it ends when that venture ends.
3. If set up under an agreement that provides that it shall subsist until put an end to 'by mutual arrangement only', then the consent of all the partners is necessary for dissolution: *Moss v Elphick* (1910). If the Articles contain a clause that permits the partnership to go on even though one retires provided the other purchases his shares, this too is valid. Otherwise it is dissolved by notice or by somebody else joining.
4. But most partnerships are what is termed **partnerships at will,** which means they can be dissolved simply by notice being given to the others by one of the partners. If the partnership was set up originally by a deed, notice in writing is necessary. But if otherwise, then oral notice is sufficient.
5. A partnership is automatically dissolved by the death of any one partner.
6. Likewise, it is automatically dissolved by the bankruptcy of any one partner.
7. If, as the result of the outbreak of war, one partner becomes an enemy alien, then the partnership is automatically dissolved.

8. Although some of the partners may oppose such a course, the Court has power to order the dissolution of a partnership:

   (a) if the defendant partner has persistently been in breach of his obligations.
   (b) if the business can only be carried on at a loss.
   (c) if one of the partners becomes subject to the *Mental Health Act, 1959* and deprived thereby of contractual capacity (see page 105).
   (d) if any partner for other reasons becomes incapable of fulfilling the obligations of the partnership.
   (e) for conduct by a partner which—although outside the obligations of the partnership agreement—is detrimental to the partnership—as where one partner has been convicted of a crime involving dishonesty.

Finally, there is a just and equitable clause if the Court arrives at the decision that it is right that the partnership should be dissolved. This applies in cases where the partnership, though profitable, is carried on by partners between whom such bitter enmity exists that the business becomes deadlocked.

Limited Partnerships

The *Limited Partnerships Act* of 1907 provided for some partners to have their liability for the firm's debts limited.

Such partnerships can only exist provided there is at least one general partner with unlimited liability.

A limited partner is not liable for the firm's debts beyond the amount of his subscribed capital. Such a partnership must be registered at Companies House with specific details of the sum contributed by each limited partner and of the agreement.

A limited partner is precluded from taking part in the management of the firm's business, although he has the right of access to the books. He cannot dissolve the partnership by notice, nor does his death, bankruptcy or his leaving on notice act as a dissolution of the partnership.

CHAPTER THREE

AGENCY

'He who does something by another does it himself' (*Qui facit per alium, facit per se*) is the maxim of the law. Whenever, therefore, one man allows another to make a contract for him it is as binding as if he had made it himself. The man who acts for another is termed 'the agent'.

The word is, however, loosely used in conversation in other senses. The 'agent for Renault cars' is not an agent in law at all. Usually, he is an independent contractor who buys cars from the manufacturer and sells them on his own behalf to his customers. The essence of agency is the establishment of contractual relationships between the agent's principal and a third party. There is no contract of sale between the motor car manufacturer and anybody who buys one of his cars from a so-called 'agent'.

The relationship of agent and principal can come about in a number of different ways:

1. **By express authorisation.** There may or may not be a contract between the agent and principal, but a man can authorise anybody to do what he can do himself in law. Normally no formalities are necessary. Even if the agent is to enter on his principal's behalf into a contract which must be expressed in writing (see page 113), the authorisation can be oral. Another exception to this is where the contract is to be made under seal. In that case, as a result of the *Powers of Attorney Act, 1971*, the appointment must also be made under seal. A general *power of attorney* which confers unlimited authority on an agent to do everything that his principal could do by way of dealing with contractual obligations also has to be under seal.

2. **By implied authority.** Where one is placed in a position so that 'according to the ordinary usages of mankind he is understood to represent and act for the person who has so placed him' he will be an agent. A common situation is that of the manager who has apparent authority to make contracts on behalf of his employers.

3. **By ratification.** If an apparent agent acts on behalf of a

19

principal without authority or exceeds his authority, the principal can later adopt the contract so made.

But to ratify a contract the principal must have been **in existence** and **ascertainable** at the time when the contract was made. For that reason, as we shall see on page 103, a limited liability company cannot ratify contracts made on its behalf before the company was formed, for the simple reason that it was not then in existence. Ratification has the effect of making the contract as good as if there had been prior authorisation.

4. **Of necessity.** Agency by necessity can arise where one man is in possession of the goods of another and it becomes necessary to do something to preserve that property.

A horse was sent by rail and there was nobody present at the station to receive it. The railway company were forced to incur charges by putting the horse in stables for the night. It was held that they could recover their expenses as agents of necessity: *G. N. Railway v Swaffield* 1874, [1874–80] All E.R. Rep. 1065.

A ship's captain always has authority to pledge the credit of her owners and can borrow money without the owner's consent to complete a voyage where the vessel needs repair.

But it is essential before a man can become an agent of necessity that he be unable to communicate with the owner. If he fails to do so, he will be liable to the owner, as where the Great Western Railway sold a consignment of tomatoes which were going bad without consulting the owners. It was held that they were not agents of necessity, and were liable for conversion of the goods and breach of contract: *Springer v G.W. Railway* 1921, [1920] All E.R. Rep. 361. In these days of telephone and telex, the opportunity for agents of necessity to come into existence must be rare.

5. **By estoppel.** Where one person, by acts or words, leads others to believe that another has authority to act on his behalf, he is estopped from denying the agency. It follows that if a person is endowed with apparent or ostensible authority, the one who puts him in that position is bound by his acts, whether they be authorised or not. The owner of a public house sold it and stayed on as manager. In that capacity he ordered cigars although he was expressly forbidden to do so. It was held that the new owner was liable as he had placed the former owner in a position where he had ostensible authority.

The Implied Warranty of Authority

If a man expressly holds himself out as being the authorised agent for a principal and he is not, he is liable to anybody who has relied on that statement and incurred loss. So, too, is the agent who has limited authority and exceeds it. The principle behind this is that there is a collateral contract of warranty whereby the agent impliedly warrants he has authority. In effect, he says to everybody he deals with: 'I promise you I have my principal's authority to do this.'

An agent bought a ship for £6,000. His principal repudiated the contract as being outside the agent's authority. The seller eventually had to accept £5,500 for the ship. The agent was held liable to pay the difference.

It is immaterial whether the agent has acted knowingly or not, or fraudulently or not. He is liable even though he was a properly authorised agent but ceased to be as a result of some event of which he has no knowledge. A firm of solicitors were instructed by a Mr. Toynbee to defend an action against him and they entered a defence on his behalf. Unknown to them, he had been certified insane, one effect of which was to cancel their authority to act as his agents. They were held liable to pay the costs on the grounds that it was a breach of warranty of their authority: *Yonge v Toynbee* 1910, [1908–10] All E.R. Rep. 204. In addition to this contractual remedy the agent may also be liable for the tort of deceit, if he acts fraudulently.

The Duties of an Agent

All agents are under a duty to behave **honestly** in their dealings with their principals. So that if they do receive bribes, illicit commissions or make a secret profit, they are liable to account for them to their principal—quite apart from the principal having the right to terminate the agency without notice. It was on this basis, amongst others, that the Court held an Army Sergeant to be liable to account to and pay the Crown the profits made out of black market activities in Cairo during the last war. He had made use of his uniform and rank to see that lorries carrying contraband goods on which he rode were not searched by the police: *Reading v A.G.*, [1951] 1 All E.R. 617.

The agent is also required to exercise his best **skill and judgment** in his principal's interests and to obtain the best prices he can for him.

He is also under a duty of **obedience** and must carry out his instructions. If he fails to do so, he has forfeited his right to remuneration and may lose his right to an indemnity for expenses incurred.

An agent is also under a duty not to have **interests conflicting with those of his principal.** Therefore where a stockbroker was employed to buy shares and sold his own to his client, the contract was rescinded.

An agent must keep his principal's monies separate from his own and must **account for all monies received.**

B

The Rights of an Agent

Although an agent can work without remuneration and can be appointed non-contractually, even if no remuneration has been discussed, the Court will readily presume that the services of an agent should be remunerated, provided the circumstances are such that people normally expect to be paid for the services. There is a valid contract notwithstanding no express remuneration has been fixed and it is subject to an implied term that it will be reasonable. This is an example of a contractual *quantum meruit* (see page 49).

There is no implied term in a contract of agency, where the agent works on commission, that the principal will do nothing to prevent him earning his commission. In *Luxor (Eastbourne) Ltd. v Cooper*, [1941] 1 All E.R. 33, it was argued before the House of Lords that there should be such an implied term where estate agents were entrusted with the sale of property, but this was rejected. Where a person was appointed sole agent to sell his principal's coal for seven years and before that date the principal sold the colliery, it was held that there was no implied term that the colliery would not be sold in the period: *Rhodes v Forwood* 1876, [1874–80] All E.R. Rep. 476.

If, however, the contract is really a contract of employment, with the agent accepting salary on a commission basis alone and there is a term of years specified, damages will lie for a breach of it: *Turner v Goldsmith* (1891).

The agent is entitled to an indemnity against all liabilities incurred in the course of acting as agent. This includes compensation for any loss suffered and not just for expenses incurred. Where a cotton broker was employed to buy cotton for speculation by a client and suffered heavy losses in consequence, he was entitled to an indemnity: *Christoforides v Terry* 1924, [1927] All E.R. Rep. 815.

The Undisclosed Principal

An agent may contract with a third party in his own name and apparently on his own behalf. If he does so for an undisclosed principal, the principal has the right of coming forward and taking over the contract, accepting both the burden and the benefits. But where a principal does so, the agent may still remain liable, for the other party has a choice whether to hold the agent, the original contracting party, liable or whether he will elect to hold the principal liable.

Even if the undisclosed principal resides abroad this does not affect the position.

The right of the undisclosed principal to intervene may be lost if there is a term in the contract that expressly or by implication indicates that the contract is personal to the agent. It has been held earlier that an undisclosed principal cannot take over a contract of sale of land where the agent was described as 'owner' or 'proprietor', but in more recent cases the principal has been allowed to intervene even though the agent has been described as 'landlord' or 'charterer'.

There are some contracts which are so personal to the parties that no substitution is possible.

To be effective, this right only arises where the agent was acting within his authority from the principal at the time he made the contract.

Ratification

But where an agent purports to contract on behalf of a principal, but in fact has no such authority or where he exceeds his authority, the named principal can later adopt the transaction—even though the agent never intended that he should. And if the principal ratifies such an agreement, then this relates back to the time when the contract was originally made.

Termination of Agency

The relationship between agent and principal may be determined:

1. **by express revocation by the principal.** Even if the relationship between agent and principal is a contractual one and for a term of years, the principal is entitled to revoke the agent's authority at any time and without cause. The agent, of course, may have grounds for an action for damages but the Courts will do nothing to preserve a relationship which the principal does not wish to continue.

   There is an exception to that rule: if the principal has granted the agent authority joined together with a proprietary interest, the authority cannot be revoked. An example would be where a man sells a business and authorises the buyer to collect outstanding debts. In that case the seller is in law the principal for the collection of those debts and the buyer becomes the agent coupled with a proprietary interest.

   Another exception is to be found in sections 126 and 127 of the *Law of Property Act, 1925*. A power of attorney by deed if (a) expressed to be irrevocable and (b) given for valuable consideration, *or* for a fixed period of less than one year, is not revocable so far as a third party who is 'a purchaser' from the agent is concerned.

2. **by renunciation by the agent.** The agent may, as the principal may, bring the agency to an end by a unilateral renunciation; subject to being liable for damages where the agency was for a fixed time which has not expired.

3. **by the death of the principal.** The death of the principal at once puts an end to the authority of the agent, unless there are specific

terms in a contract of agency to the contrary. The power of attorney, subject to sections 126 and 127 of the *Law of Property Act, 1925*, may continue, however (see above).

4. **by the insanity of the principal.**
5. **by the bankruptcy of the principal.** Bankruptcy of the agent does not necessarily revoke his authority.
6. **by illegality** including either party becoming an enemy alien as the result of the outbreak of war. Stevenson & Sons Ltd. were sole agents in Britain for the sale of machinery made by German manufacturers. The outbreak of war automatically terminated the agency: *Stevenson & Sons Ltd. v Akt für Cartonnagen-Industrie* (1917).
7. **by expiration of the period agreed or completion of the performance agreed.** If an agent is employed to find a buyer, the agency comes to an end by the successful performance; similarly, if the agency is for a limited period, the expiration of that period terminates the appointment automatically without notice.

BOOK II: CONTRACTUAL OBLIGATIONS

CHAPTER FOUR

THE NATURE OF CONTRACTUAL OBLIGATIONS

What is a Contract?

Ask the first man you meet in the street what a contract is and he will probably reply: 'It's a piece of paper on which are certain conditions the people have agreed to.'

There are, however, only a few contracts which have to be expressed in writing and every day of our lives all of us assume contractual obligations without writing, and often without words. We do it every time we get on a bus, buy anything, or take part in a business transaction.

Like the elephant, a contract is easier to describe than define. An early attempt at definition, made about a century ago, was that of Sir Frederick Pollock: 'A contract is a promise . . . that the law will enforce.' Anson, writing shortly afterwards, defined a contract as 'a legally binding agreement made between two or more persons'. Both definitions are unsatisfactory, for various reasons which will appear later, but of these two, that of Pollock is to be preferred. However, one can only agree with the present editor of the important book on the subject which still bears Anson's name, who says 'It is better to eschew the idea of defining a contract altogether.'

The reason, although he does not mention it, is that there is really no such thing as 'a contract'.

That is, there is nothing which has a separate and independent existence apart from the obligations imposed by the law on persons. It is therefore not strictly correct to speak of 'a contract' at all, and it is correct only to refer to 'contractual obligations'; grammatically, the word 'contract' should be used only as an adjective to describe a type of obligation imposed by law—never as a noun. Naturally, it is impossible to define accurately the non-existent; but it is perfectly possible to describe with accuracy the circumstances in which the law will impose obligations of the class called 'contractual' on persons.

However, though it may not strictly be semantically correct to speak of 'a contract', it is a convenient piece of shorthand, and it is now too late, after judges and lawyers have been referring to 'contracts' for centuries, to seek to establish purity of language. The

27

present author will, therefore, like all those before him, make use of this familiar but inaccurate expression, even as he pedantically insists that there is no such thing.

The Action of *Assumpsit*

The enforcement of contractual obligations by the King's Court came only late in English legal history. Nearly two thousand years ago the Romans had a highly sophisticated system of Contract Law, but the author of the book we know as 'Glanvill' could write around A.D. 1187: 'Private agreements are not usually enforced by the Courts of our Lord the King.' A promise made in solemn form under the seal of the man who made it (usually in relation to the holding of land) might be enforced against him in the King's Court by the Writ of Covenant; but other promises were not. However, the Royal Courts were not then, as they are now, the only courts in England. There was an enormous number of other courts and in some of these, such as the Court of the City of London, a Covenant not under seal could be enforced. A merchant therefore could be held to a promise without his seal—but not by an action in the King's Court; not, that is, at Common Law. (Similarly, it was actionable in the City of London Court to call a woman 'a whore', but not in the King's Courts.)

When the enforcement of promises not under seal did begin in the King's Court it was in an indirect fashion. A man who had suffered loss by relying on the promise of another could by the middle of the 16th century sue in the King's Bench Court. But he had to rely on an action called *Assumpsit*, which was what we would now call an action in tort—that is, for a civil wrong whereby damage had been suffered. Assumpsit means 'he undertook' or 'he assumed the obligation', and to succeed the plaintiff had to prove:

(i) that the defendant undertook to do something (or, for that matter, not to do something);

(ii) that the defendant had failed to do it (or had done what he promised not to do); and

(iii) that he, the plaintiff, had suffered loss in consequence.

Even in the 18th century, contractual obligations were not regarded as an important part of English law, and Blackstone, writing in 1756, devoted only twenty-eight pages to them in his vast work (in contrast to three hundred and eighty pages on the subject of property) and then only to contracts as a means of transferring the ownership of property.

The *Consensus ad idem* Theory

English ideas about contractual obligations were therefore in a very uncrystallised state when, in 1805, there was translated into

English a massive and comprehensive *Treatise on the Law of Obligations* written more than forty years earlier in French by Pothier (1699–1772). Few books have had greater influence and it is to be regretted that all reference to this author has disappeared from the latest edition of the *Encyclopaedia Britannica*. The English Law of Contract without Pothier is like Hamlet without the ghost; without him the tortuous evolutions and convolutions of the 19th century are barely explicable, but without him too there might well have been no play at all. Unwisely English theorists and judges accepted many of Pothier's ideas and tried to incorporate them into the English Common Law; and that in spite of the fact that Pothier had not been writing about the Common Law at all, but about the type of adapted Roman law that applied in France before The French Revolution. Only in the last decade has our law on contractual obligations begun to free itself from these imported ideas and revert to earlier native concepts.

From Pothier stems the idea that there could be no contractual obligation unless the parties had arrived at *consensus ad idem*, once defined as 'a concurrence of intention of two parties, one of whom promises something to the other, who on his part accepts the promise'. Hence, sentences appear in earlier textbooks to suggest that *consensus* is essential to a valid contract, i.e. 'if there is no true agreement between the parties . . . if the parties are not *ad idem*, there is no contract'. This concept, however, is now widely recognised as erroneous and obsolete. As Harriman pointed out years ago, 'This consensual theory is insufficient to explain the law of contract. It derives its chief force from the vigour with which two leading English writers have endorsed the theories of continental jurists.' (He referred of course, to Pollock and Anson.) In the vast majority of cases where contractual obligations are assumed in real life, there is nothing remotely like *consensus ad idem*, at least in the sense of complete identity of the minds of the parties on all material terms.

The doctrine of consensus is, however, still not without influence when the effect of mistake on a contract is under consideration. Even here, however, it has been superseded to a large extent by the Court looking to see whether it would be fair and equitable to hold a party to obligations he has assumed when he was under a serious mistake at the time when he undertook them (see page 158).

Linked to the consensus theory is the idea that the agreement is arrived at by a process called 'offer' and 'acceptance' and that these are essential. Unhappily for this theory, there are numerous cases where the Courts have held that contractual obligations existed even though it was impossible specifically to identify anything which could be called an 'offer' or anything which could be called 'acceptance' (see page 149).

In many other cases the so-called 'offer' is an entirely artificial concept. What logic is there in the law that when an intending passenger asks at a railway booking office for a ticket to Victoria, that does not constitute an offer but when the railway clerk pushes a piece of pasteboard towards him, that does? As Lord Denning has said: 'In those cases the issue of the ticket was regarded as an *offer* by the company. If the customer took it and retained it without objection, his act was regarded as *acceptance* of the offer. . . . These cases were based on the theory that the customer, on being handed the ticket could refuse it and decline to enter into a contract on those terms. He could ask for his money back. That theory was, of course, a fiction. No customer ever reads the conditions. If he had stopped to do so, he would have missed the train or boat.'

In other similarly familiar circumstances, no court has yet said what constitutes the offer. When a bus carries a passenger there can be no doubt that both the bus owners and the passenger have assumed contractual obligations, but the Courts have yet to decide exactly when and how. In a case in 1947, the then Master of the Rolls, Lord Greene, discussed this topic and suggested that the contract was made either when the passenger got himself on to the platform or, perhaps, when he got inside the bus: *Wilkie v L.P. Transport Board*, [1947] 1 All E.R. 258. But this raises interesting and so far unresolved questions as to whether there can be a concluded contract when a passenger gets on a bus believing it is going to Liverpool Street when in fact it is travelling the opposite way. If he travels two miles in the wrong direction, is he liable to pay the fare?

These are subjects that will be fully discussed later (see page 149) and it is sufficient at the moment to observe that contractual obligations can exist when there is no *consensus ad idem* and nothing that can be specifically identified as 'offer and acceptance'. Neither can therefore be fairly described, as they are in most elementary textbooks, as 'essential to a valid contract'.

Express Promises

When Sir William Blackstone, the first Professor of English common law, came to write his masterly treatise in the 18th century, before dealing with the action of *assumpsit* he first described the Writ of Covenant available for promises contained in a document under seal, and then went on: 'A promise is in the nature of a verbal covenant and wants nothing but the solemnity of writing and sealing to make it absolutely the same. If, therefore, it be to do any explicit act, it is an express contract, as much as any Covenant and the breach of it an equal injury.'

We may say, therefore, that the first ground on which contractual obligations are imposed on a person by the law is where he has made an express promise.

But not every express promise is enforceable as a contractual obligation and there are numerous promises which the law will not enforce for a variety of reasons, including:

(i) UNCERTAINTY: where the promises were not sufficiently specific to enable a Court to enforce them (see page 71).

(ii) NO CONTRACTUAL INTENTION: where there was no intention to enter into a contractual obligation (see page 74).

(iii) WITHOUT CONSIDERATION: because the promise was not made under seal and the man who made it got nothing in return for it. In other words, it was what lawyers term 'a parol promise without consideration' (see page 81).

(iv) WITHOUT CONTRACTUAL CAPACITY: because there was a want of contractual capacity on the part of the person who made the promise. For example, if he were under 18, and therefore in law a minor, and if the promise were one which the Courts will not enforce against minors (see page 105).

(v) FOR WANT OF FORM: because the promise was one which the law requires to be in a special form, e.g. in writing, and it was not (see page 113).

(vi) FOR ILLEGALITY: because the promise was to do some thing illegal. No-one would expect the Courts to enforce a promise by bank robbers to share the proceeds of their crime equally; though long ago an enterprising highwayman did once try to collect his share of the proceeds through the Courts by suing on an unspecified 'agreement' (see page 121).

(vii) MISREPRESENTATION: because the promise has been induced by the false statements of the person to whom it has been given (see page 137).

(viii) MISTAKE: the Courts may in some circumstances also release a person from the obligations of his promise, if it was given because of an important mistake (see page 158).

These exceptions are all considered in more detail later, in the pages indicated above.

It must also be pointed out that whereas in common speech, 'a promise' normally means an undertaking to do something in the future, in law there can also be a promise about the condition of a thing or its quality or as to the existence of a present set of facts.

Implied Promises

Blackstone also went on to say that in addition to express contracts (where the promisor has in fact given a promise in words) there were also implied contracts. That is where the party had not in fact made a promise but where the law would impute or ascribe one to him 'such as reason and justice dictate'.

He gave two instances:

Quantum meruit (literally: 'as much as he deserves'). 'If I employ a person to transact any business for me or perform any work, the law implies that I undertook to pay him so much as his labour deserves.' So if a motorist takes his car into a garage and asks them to mend a puncture, even though he does not expressly say 'I will pay you a reasonable price for your services,' the law attributes such a promise to him. Garage owners, like other people, do not work for nothing and there is an implied understanding that they shall be paid for what they do and that this shall be at a reasonable rate—whatever is fair in the circumstances. If, however, a young lady were to suffer a puncture by the roadside and a young man were to appear and mend it for her, there would be no implied promise. The law would not, in those circumstances, impute a promise to her to pay anything, since 'according to the common usages of mankind', as the old books charmingly describe it, such services are normally rendered for nothing; or for such rewards as gratitude alone may suggest.

Similar to this, is what Blackstone termed *Quantum valebant* (literally: 'as much as they were worth'). 'There is also an implied *assumpsit* in a *quantum valebant* very similar to the former; being only where one takes up goods or wares of a tradesman without expressly agreeing the price.' This common law principle has in part now become statutory: section 8 of the *Sale of Goods Act, 1893* reads:

(i) 'The price in a contract of sale may be fixed by the contract or may be left to be fixed in a manner thereby agreed, or may be determined by the course of dealing between the parties.'

(ii) 'Where the price is not determined in accordance with the foregoing provision the buyer must pay a reasonable price. What is a reasonable price is a question of fact dependent on the circumstances of each particular case.'

It follows that if two people agree, the one to buy, and the other to sell a particular article ('a chattel'), without naming a price, binding obligations have been assumed on both sides (see page 71). But it is otherwise where the purchase and sale is of land or a house, for each piece of land has a unique quality and there is therefore no 'reasonable price' that can be implied, and hence there is no contract, since an essential term—namely the price—has not been determined.

Contracts by Estoppel

But in modern times the law has imposed contractual obligations where there has been no express promise in situations where one could not be implied in the way contemplated by Blackstone, and in circumstances where there certainly has been no agreement or anything approaching consensus between the parties.

Serjeant A. M. Sullivan, K.C. (the last of the old Common Pleas serjeants), was interested in buying a yacht called the *Ailsa*. The owner, a Mr. Constable, was selling the yacht 'as she lies', which was well understood in yachting circles to mean that he was making no promises and giving no warranty as to her condition. The buyer had to take her as he found her. But Mr. Constable did tell the Serjeant that she was '. . . sound and good . . . and makes no water'. When the Serjeant agreed to buy he sent a cheque to the owner's agents with a letter which read: 'I want to be sure that he (Mr. Constable) understands that . . . I rely upon his word and not upon inspection or survey.' The cheque was cashed without comment. The hull of the *Ailsa* turned out to be crumbling from dry rot and Serjeant Sullivan sued Constable and obtained damages for breach of a contract containing a term that the yacht was sound: *Sullivan v Constable* (1932).

Clearly, Constable never intended *as a term of the contract of sale* to give a promise that the yacht was sound. In fact, he thought he was doing the exact opposite and had made it plain that he intended to sell the boat 'as she lies'. Yet he was held by the Court to have assumed a contractual obligation.

The principle of law upon which this decision was arrived is known as estoppel. A person is not allowed to deny the truth of a statement formerly made by him or the existence of facts he has by words or conduct induced another to believe in. It is of much wider application than contract law, but in this sphere the principle was set out early in the last century by Baron Parke in *Freeman v Cooke*, [1848] All E.R. Rep. 185. A man is not allowed to deny the fact (which is what 'estoppel' means) that he had given a promise if he makes a representation which 'he means to be acted upon and it is acted upon accordingly'.

Strictly speaking, the principle of estoppel only applies where four conditions are fulfilled. A man is prevented (or stopped or 'estopped') from denying the truth of something he has previously asserted if:

    (i) it was an assertion of present existing fact and not of future performance. There cannot therefore strictly be such a thing as estoppel by a promise to do something in the future (see page 96, however, for the modern doctrine of *equitable* or *promissory estoppel*);

    (ii) the assertion of fact was intended to be acted upon by the other party to whom it was made;

(iii) it was *in fact* acted upon by that party; and
(iv) that party suffered detriment in consequence of the falseness of the assertion.

Those are the rules of estoppel and a few judges have therefore found technical difficulties in applying the term to the position where a man has behaved in such a fashion as to lead the other party to believe he was giving a promise; they therefore fall back on saying that he is 'precluded by his conduct from denying' that he gave such a promise—as Mr. Constable was. 'The vendor and his agent, having kept that cheque without comment, the vendor could not be allowed to say that there was no such term in the contract';—which all comes to the same thing really: a contract by estoppel.

Contractual Obligations by the Objective Test

The question in contracts by estoppel is a subjective one: did one party make a statement which he intended the other to rely upon, and did the other in fact rely on it? More favoured nowadays is a test for contractual obligations which might fairly be termed the objective test.

As an alternative to the situation above, where a man makes a representation he means to be acted on, in *Freeman v Cooke* Baron Parke also considered a further situation: 'If, whatever a man's real intention may be, *he so conducts himself that a reasonable man* would take the representation to be true and believe that it was meant that he should act upon it and he did act upon it as true.'

Here the test is an external one: what would a reasonable man have concluded? If a reasonable man would conclude that the parties have accepted certain contractual obligations, then the law imposes such obligations on them—whatever their real state of mind. 'The law is content with the outward manifestation of agreement and is not concerned with whether the parties are really agreed.'

A firm of boiler makers were asked by the defendants to machine certain parts for a malting drum and, not really wishing to undertake the work, they quoted a very high price of '30 shillings a cwt.'. This offer was accepted under the impression that it was '30 shillings *a ton*'. The defendants, when sued by the boiler makers, contended that there was no express contract since one had meant 30 shillings *a cwt.* and the other 30 shillings *a ton* and therefore there was no agreement between them; hence, the defendants' only liability was to pay a reasonable sum—*a quantum meruit*—on the basis of an implied obligation. This argument was rejected by the Courts. The plaintiffs, the boiler makers, were entitled to be paid at 30 shillings a cwt.: *Ewing & Lawson v Hanbury & Co.* (1900). Clearly there was the outward manifestation of agreement and it was immaterial that there was no real consensus. 'The parties are to be judged not by what is in their minds, but by what they have said or written or done', as Cheshire and Fifoot put it: or, as Lord Denning put it, 'Once the two parties, whatever their inmost states of mind, have *to all outward appearances* agreed with sufficient certainty in the same terms on the same subject matter, then the contract is good.' What he really meant was that the law will allow neither party in those circumstances to deny that they have assumed those contractual obligations.

Contracts of Adhesion

The full operation of the principle can be seen in what are today the most common forms of contracts—those where one party, usually a member of the public, has no opportunity of negotiating the terms but must accept or reject those offered by the other party. If you want to buy a new motor car, it is highly probable that you will be allowed to do so only on the terms dictated by the manufacturers. If you want to hire purchase it, you must most certainly accept the terms offered by the finance companies—or go without. If you want to take a package holiday, go on a cruise or cross the Channel with your car, all you can do is to accept the terms imposed by the other contracting party; often by a piece of paper which, as Lord Devlin aptly put it, is 'the sort of document . . . not meant to be read, still less understood'.

Such contracts are sometimes termed contracts of adhesion (from the French, who first recognised them as *contrats d'adhesion*) because one party can only adhere to them or reject them completely. Sometimes they are called 'Standard Form Contracts'.

Often the terms of such contracts are, to put it bluntly, iniquitous. One famous holiday camp will only accept guests on terms that the person who makes a reservation for his family or party undertakes to recompense them if it, the camp, has to pay compensation to any member of his family or party injured by its negligence! And a car ferry firm only carries cars on terms that the owner of the car is entirely responsible for any damage or injury caused by that car, even if caused by their negligence. And their parent company only carries passengers on cruises under a condition which purports to exclude all liability for all negligence by the company *or any of its servants*; so that, on the face of it, if a drunken ship's doctor castrates you instead of removing your appendix, you can sue neither him nor the company.

The Courts have shown a regrettable lack of courage in dealing with such contracts, on the ground as Lord Reid put it, that 'the general principle of English law (is) that the parties are free to contract as they may think fit'; in that, they have not followed the

Elizabethan and 17th-century Court of Chancery which did not hesitate to set aside contracts, such as commodity loans, on the grounds that the terms were unfair; and right up to the middle of the last century cases are to be found in which Equity would grant relief for 'unconscionable bargains'. However, when we come to deal in detail with exemption clauses such as those described above (see page 168), it will be found that the Courts have invented some methods of circumventing them and in fact all the conditions specifically mentioned in the contracts above are probably quite valueless provided the injured party has the financial resources and determination enough to sue.

Apart from such devices invented by the Courts, the only protection for those entering contracts of adhesion is the publicity afforded by the Press and the Consumers' Associations, to shame the inventors of such contracts into abandoning the more extreme of them; and the inadequate protection afforded by Statute.

To some extent the position has been mitigated so far as railway passengers are concerned, by the *Transport Act, 1962*, s. 43, which provides, that so far as the British Railways Board, London Transport Board, British Transport Dock Board and British Waterways Board are concerned, all terms or conditions which purport to exclude or limit the liability to passengers for death or bodily injury shall be 'void and of no effect'. This does not extend to other bodies or private companies nor to goods or to a person who enters railway premises on a platform ticket.

Apart from that, the legal position is clear; contracts of adhesion are binding, irrespective of whether both parties accept all the terms or not; but there is some difference between those documents which are signed and those 'common form' documents, such as railway tickets, which are not.

Standard Contracts that are Signed

The general rule of law is that a person is bound by a written or printed contract which he has signed whether or not he read it, understood it or accepted it. Miss L'Estrange bought a cigarette vending machine from Graucob Ltd. under a 'Sales Agreement' which she signed without reading. The agreement was printed on brown paper and in 'regrettably small print', and one term excluded all liability for the condition of the machine. It never did work, but the Divisional Court held that the suppliers were protected by the clause in small print. As Lord Justice Scrutton put it: 'When a document containing contractual terms is signed . . . the party signing it is bound and it is wholly immaterial whether he has read the document or not.' So much for the necessity of consensus, offer and acceptance, etc.: *L'Estrange v F. Graucob Ltd.*, [1934] All E.R. Rep. 16.

The reason why a person is bound by a document he has signed but not read is that set out on page 34. If a person signs a document, a reasonable man would conclude that he had, so far as the other contracting party is concerned, accepted all the terms of it. 'The law is clear, without any recourse to the doctrine of estoppel, that a signature to a contract is conclusive,' Lord Devlin said. A defendant can say that the terms are unfair and unreasonable, that he never voluntarily agreed to them, that it was impossible to understand or even to read them and that if he had tried to negotiate any change the other party would not have listened to him . . . in vain. He has signed the contract, and a reasonable man would conclude that he had accepted the terms, whether he knew them or not, and the law therefore imposes those contractual obligations on him.

There are, however, exceptions to this principle. The Court may in appropriate circumstances relieve one party from the obligations where his signature has been obtained by fraud or by the misrepresentation, however, innocent, of the other party; and his signature may not be binding even as against third parties in the limited circumstances where the plea of *non est factum* ('It is not my deed') can be raised successfully (see page 160).

Unsigned Common Form Documents

With unsigned documents the law is slightly different. Here, the law states that a man must be given reasonable notice that there are conditions annexed to the issue of the ticket. He need, however, be given no notice as to what the conditions are; apparently it is enough if he is told there are terms and, if he takes the ticket with that knowledge, he is then bound by those terms. 'If in the course of making a contract one party delivers to another a paper containing writing, and the party receiving the paper knows that the paper contains conditions which the party delivering intends to constitute the contract, I have no doubt that the party receiving the paper does, by receiving and keeping it, assent to the conditions contained in it, although he does not read them and does not know what they are.'

In the distant and happier days when issues of fact were decided by a jury, a Mr. Parker left a bag in the left luggage office of the South Eastern Railway. For that privilege he paid 2d and received a ticket on the face of which were the words: 'The company will not be responsible for any package exceeding the value of £10.' The bag was lost and Mr. Parker claimed its value of £24 10s. The Court of Appeal held that the jury should be directed to answer three questions:

(i) Did the plaintiff know there was writing on the ticket?

(ii) If he knew there was writing, did he know the writing contained conditions?

(iii) Even if he did not know the writing contained conditions, was, in the opinion of the jury, reasonable notice given him that the writing contained conditions? *Parker v S.E. Railways*, [1877] All E.R. Rep. 166.

If the answer to (i) was 'Yes' and either (ii) or (iii) were answered affirmatively, the railway company was protected by the limitation clause.

From being an issue of fact for the jury to decide, over the years the question whether there was reasonable notice or not turned into a question of law, so that by 1923 Mr. Justice Swift could say: 'I am of opinion that the proper method of considering such a matter is to proceed upon the assumption that where a contract is made by the delivery, by one of the contracting parties to the other, of a document in a common form stating the terms upon which the person delivering it will enter into the proposed contract . . . if the form is accepted without objection by the person to whom it is tendered this person as a general rule is bound by its contents . . . whether he reads the document or not.'

In law and practice, the question has now resolved itself into the simple formula: as far as contractual tickets are concerned does the document on the face of it bear the words 'For Conditions See Back'? If it does, it would appear that reasonable notice has been given that there are conditions and that is sufficient to make them part of the contract.

The effect can be seen in a case of importance. A Mrs. Thompson, who could not read, gave her niece the money to buy an excursion railway ticket from Manchester to Darwen. On the face of the ticket appeared the words 'For Conditions See Back', and on the back were the words: 'Issued subject to the conditions and regulations in the company's timetables and notices and excursion and other bills.' Mrs. Thompson was injured through the negligence of the railway company's servants. One condition amongst that multifarious crowd of documents excluded liability to the ticket holder for injury, however caused.

The jury at the trial found that reasonable notice of the conditions had not been given to Mrs. Thompson, but the Court of Appeal reversed this verdict, holding that the fact that a considerable search had to be made before the conditions could be discovered was immaterial. 'The mere circuity which has to be followed to find the actual condition does not prevent a passenger having notice that there was a condition.' *Thompson v L.M.S.*, [1929] All E.R. Rep. 474.

No attempt has been made in any of the long line of judgments to justify this position on the basis of principle and the only grounds on which these decisions can be upheld is that a reasonable man would conclude that a person who accepts such a ticket must be taken to indicate to the other that he accepts all the conditions whether he knows of them or not, and is therefore precluded from denying it. And apparently, according to Chitty, the leading text-book on Contract Law, 'It is immaterial that the party receiving the document is under some personal, but non-legal, disability such as blindness, illiteracy or an inability to read our language.'

But what if that disability were in fact known to the other contracting party? On this point there is as yet no decision of the Courts and it is one of the debating points that examiners at degree level delight in asking students.

And what if the conditions annexed by reference are totally un-reasonable? If, for example, the condition in Parker's case had in-cluded a term that if he left his bag in the left luggage office for more than twenty-four hours, he should have to pay the railway company £10,000? One of the judges in the Court of Appeal in Parker's case was prepared to hold that such a condition would not be binding, on the ground that there was an unexpressed and unwritten term that none of the unknown conditions would be unreasonable. But in none of dozens of the 'ticket cases', as they are called, has any con-dition been held void because it was unreasonable; and surely for a cruise company or a railway company to exclude all liability for their own negligence might well be considered by some people as utterly unreasonable; as would a motor car manufacturer who dis-owned all liability in law for a vehicle he had just manufactured and allowed an innocent purchaser to put on the road. Yet both are the sort of exemption clauses which have repeatedly been held binding.

In 1956 Denning L.J., as he was then, was prepared to hold that the more unreasonable the condition, the greater notice must be given of its existence. 'Some clauses which I have seen would need to be printed in red ink on the face of the document with a red hand pointing to it before the notice could be held to be sufficient.' And in 1970, as Master of the Rolls, he seems to have been able to per-suade a Court of Appeal to agree that what is necessary before a term can be part of the contract is not merely reasonable notice that there are conditions, but reasonable notice of *the* condition exempting from liability. As Megaw L.J. said, 'The question here is of the particular condition on which the defendants seek to rely and not of the conditions in general.'

This is a recent trend and a radical departure, which of course undermines the force of the decision in *Thompson v L.M.S.*; and if reasonable notice in fact must be given of *the* exempting clauses, it would appear that the blind and those who do not speak our language may well not be bound by notices they cannot read.

It may, however, be doubted whether these observations by Denning M.R. and Megaw L.J. are a binding part of the decision in the case which follows in which they were spoken: *Thornton v Shoe Lane Parking Ltd.*, [1971] 1 All E.R. 686.

The plaintiff, 'a trumpeter of the highest quality', parked his car in a multi-storey car park in the City of London, where there was no attendant. Having driven his car to a barrier, a ticket was issued by a machine and bore the words: 'This ticket is issued subject to the conditions of issue displayed on the premises.' The conditions of issue were, needless to say, only visible in another part of the garage, and after the ticket had been issued, one of them, buried away under a mound of verbiage, included a clause excluding liability for injury to the customer. The trumpeter was injured partly through the company's negligence.

The point of the case, as it has been in others of this nature, is whether the liability clause was a term of the contract; and the decision was that the time when the contract was made was when the ticket popped out of the machine, so that the conditions on the notice formed no part of the contract. As Lord Denning said, none of the earlier ticket cases had any application to a ticket issued by an automatic machine. 'The customer pays his money and gets his ticket. He cannot get his money back. He may protest to the machine, even swear at it; but it will remain unmoved. He is committed beyond recall.' His Lordship seems not to know how an automatic car park works, because of course the plaintiff did not in fact pay his money before he got his ticket, but would have paid when he called to collect the car; but that is perhaps not material to the real basis of the decision. The contract was completed when the ticket popped out of the machine. Why? Because the Court of Appeal decided that it was. In other words, in this particular case it was held that the motorist made the offer by driving up to the machine and his offer was accepted by the emergence of the ticket. Contrast the railway ticket cases where it is the booking clerk who makes the offer by pushing a piece of pasteboard towards the traveller.

Unilateral and Synallagmatic Contracts

Basically, all contractual obligations may be divided into two kinds: unilateral and bilateral, sometimes termed 'synallagmatic', since there may well be more than two parties to a contract.

If the reader does not know the word 'synallagmatic', can't find it in the dictionary and considers it 'gratuitous philological exhibitionism', he will not be alone. The word was but recently imported into the English language from the French Civil Code, by

Lord Diplock. A synallagmatic contract is a contract of mutual obligation—a situation, in fact, where all the parties are subject to contractual obligations.

A unilateral contract on the other hand is the situation where only the man making the promise is under a contractual obligation. If I promise £1,000 to you should you swim the Irish Channel, that creates no contractual obligation on you to do so—not even if you express to me your intention of performing the feat. But should you do so, I am obliged by law to pay to you the £1,000.

'Under contracts which are only unilateral (the "if" contracts) . . . the promisor undertakes to do or to refrain from doing something on his part if another party ("the promisee") does or refrains from doing something. But the promisee does not himself undertake to do or refrain from doing that thing. The commonest contracts of this kind in English law are options for good consideration to buy or to sell or to grant or take a lease, competitions for prizes . . .' 'In its more complex and more usual form, as in an option, the promisor's undertaking may be to enter into a synallagmatic contract with the promisee . . .'

'It never gives rise to any obligation on the promisee to bring about the event by doing or refraining from doing that particular thing': Lord Diplock in *United Dominions Trust v Eagle Aviation*, [1968] 1 All E.R. 104.

There are numerous questions that must be discussed in relation to unilateral contracts but they are postponed until later in this book (see page 145).

In the synallagmatic contract which, of course, is the more common variety, and the one in which the fact of agreement may well be a material factor, all the parties are under contractual obligations —'Each party undertakes to the other party to do or refrain from doing something and in the event of failure to perform his undertaking, the law provides the other party with a remedy': Lord Diplock.

In some contracts of mutual obligation of this kind, it is possible to identify an offer by one party and an acceptance by the other which leads to obligations on both. But anybody who has had to read the often voluminous correspondence and minutes of negotiations leading to a contract of the ordinary commercial type will know that frequently it is impossible to isolate any particular moment when one side makes an offer and the other accepts it. In very simple situations it may, however, be possible. For this purpose therefore an offer may be defined as a conditional promise to accept certain contractual obligations provided the other party signifies that he also is willing to do so. And the general rule of law is that, in circumstances where this is applicable, the offer must be communicated

to the offeree and there are no obligations on either party until
the offeree has communicated his acceptance to the offeror.

'Suppose, for instance,' said Lord Denning in one case, 'that I
shout an offer to a man across a river but I do not hear his reply
because it is drowned by an aircraft flying overhead. There is no
contract at that moment. If he wishes to make a contract, he must
wait till the aircraft is gone and then shout back his acceptance so
that I can hear what he says.'

Acceptance by Post

There is, however, one unusual situation where the law imposes
contractual obligations against the will of one of the parties and with
neither real nor apparent agreement nor estoppel of any kind to
justify it.

This is where the offer is made by post and the offeree is expressly
invited to reply by post or might be said impliedly to be invited to
reply by post. Here, the contract is completed when the letter of
acceptance is posted, not when it reaches the offeror; indeed the
contract is binding even if the letter of acceptance *never* reaches the
offeror.

The contractual obligations become binding on both parties even
though the offeror may in the meantime have withdrawn his offer.

A Mr. Fraser, on 7th July, made an offer to Mr. Henthorn to sell
him certain houses in these terms: 'I give you the refusal of the
Flamank Street property at £750 for fourteen days.'

The very next day, Fraser posted a letter at 1 p.m. revoking this
offer, as he was entitled to do in spite of the promise to keep
it open for fourteen days (for the reasons see page 81). At
3.50 p.m. the same day Henthorn posted a letter accepting the offer,
and at 5 p.m. the same day Fraser's letter of revocation was delivered
to him. It was held there was a binding contract for the sale of the
property, made at 3.50 p.m. on 8th July when Henthorn posted his
letter of acceptance: *Henthorn v Fraser*, [1892] 2 All E.R. Rep. 908.

Poor Mr. Fraser was therefore saddled by law with a contractual
obligation to sell his house, an obligation that he did not want and
from which he had expressly withdrawn. The reason for this extraordinary situation is explained in the case of *Household Fire Insurance v Grant* (1879), where the letter of acceptance (a letter of allotment of shares) was never delivered at all but where the unfortunate
intended recipient was held liable to pay for shares he didn't then
want. 'The contract . . . is actually made when the letter (of acceptance) is posted . . . There is no doubt that the implication of a complete, final and absolutely binding contract being formed, as soon as
the acceptance of an offer is posted, may in some cases lead to inconvenience and hardship. But such there must be at times in every

view of the law . . . At the same time I am not prepared to admit that the implication in question will lead to any great or general inconvenience. An offeror may, if he chooses, always make the formation of the contract he proposes dependent on the actual communication to himself of the acceptance. If he trusts to the post he trusts to a means of communication which, as a rule, does not fail . . .': Thesinger L.J.

The Post Office in Lord Justice Thesinger's day and in 1892, when Mr. Fraser was able to post a letter in Liverpool at 1 p.m. which was delivered in Birkenhead at 5 p.m. the same day, must have been a very different thing from the Post Office of today. It has been suggested that the theory behind this legal doctrine is that the offeror has expressly or impliedly made the Post Office his agent to receive acceptance on his behalf. It would be interesting to have Mr. Grant's views on that subject, as he paid the full price for shares which were by then worthless bits of paper.

The only real justification advanced for this doctrine is that it is a matter of business convenience.

A Definition of a Contract

It is now possible to summarise the nature of contractual obligations and perhaps, with great hesitation, to put forward a definition of a contract.

Situations where contractual obligations have been found by the Court to exist include:

(i) where there is an express promise intended to have legal consequence (see page 30).

(ii) implied promise where there is no express promise but the law will imply such a one as justice requires (see page 31).

(iii) no promise but estoppel, where a person is precluded from denying that he has given a promise (see page 32).

(iv) where a reasonable man would conclude a promise had been given and, again, where a person is precluded from denying that he has given a promise (see page 34).

(v) where the law, as a matter of business convenience, imposes the obligation. As, for example, in the contracts by post situation (see page 42).

A fair definition therefore would perhaps be, to adopt somewhat satirical words used by the American Judge Learned Hand in *Hotchkiss v National City Bank* (1937): 'A contract is an obligation which the law will attach to certain acts or words of the parties which ordinarily are considered to have a contractual intent.' And if it be suggested that such a definition is circuitous, it is no more so than any of the other definitions quoted above.

The Difference between Contracts and Torts

The distinction between a tort and a contract lies in the fact that:

(i) in contract, the obligation is imposed by law only as the result of an act or words by the persons concerned, whereas in tort the obligation is imposed by law on everybody, even though liability may only be incurred when some act is done or some words uttered; and,

(ii) in contract, the duty lies only to a specific person or persons, whereas in tort it lies towards everybody.

Often in practice it is difficult to distinguish between the two, and indeed the same act may be both a tort and a breach of contract. For example, a fare-paying passenger may be able to sue for an act of negligence which is a breach of the general duty to take care (i.e. a tort); which act is also a breach of the obligation to take care assumed contractually.

But the distinction between contract and tort is of practical importance for the following reasons:

(i) The measure of damages recoverable for tort (at least, for a deliberate one) is greater than for a breach of contract (see page 53).

(ii) The right to an action starts in contract when the breach takes place, not when the loss is suffered; whereas in tort (apart from trespass) the cause of action arises when damage starts, not when the wrongful act was done. So that although the *Limitation Act* of 1939 provides for the same period of limitation of right of action, namely six years, for 'actions founded on simple contract or tort', those six years may expire earlier in a claim based on breach of contract than for a claim based on a tort.

(iii) A claim for damages arising out of a breach of contract can be proved for in a bankruptcy, whereas a claim arising out of tort usually cannot be. This means that for a breach of contract a dividend may be recovered, whereas in tort it may not be.

(iv) A contractual right, including a right of action arising out of a breach of contract, can usually be assigned to another person, whereas a right of action arising out of a tort cannot be.

(v) A person under 18 ('a minor') may be liable at almost any age for his torts, whereas he is not liable on contracts except in special circumstances (see page 105).

There are also important differences in procedure in actions in the Courts.

The Difference between Contractual Obligations and Trusts

In most cases, contractual obligations are imposed by law upon persons as a result of their voluntary words or acts. There are, however, other obligations of a different character which people commonly assume by their voluntary acts or words. These are known as **trusts.** A trust has been defined as 'an equitable obligation binding a person (called **'the trustee'**) to deal with property over which he has control (**'the trust property'**) for the benefit of a person or persons (**'the beneficiaries'**) . . . any one of whom may enforce the obligation.

One of the principles applicable to contractual obligations is that a person who is a stranger to a contract—that is, one to whom the promises were not given—can neither sue on the contract nor be made subject to the obligations of it (see page 99).

That is so even though the contract is made expressly for the benefit of the stranger, i.e. Tom and George promise one another to each pay £100 to John. John cannot sue either if they fail to pay him.

But where there is a trust, the person for whose benefit the trust has been created, the 'beneficiary', *can* sue the persons who have undertaken the obligation of the trust. That is, if Tom and George set up a fund and make themselves trustees of £200, £100 of which each has contributed, for the benefit of John, he can sue them for the money.

The dividing line between contract and trust until recently was disturbingly vague and even now the position is not absolutely clear. However, in general terms, the following may serve to distinguish the two:

   (i) There is no trust except where the parties have indicated that it was their intention to create one. 'It is not legitimate to import into the contract the idea of a trust when the parties have given no indication that such was their intention': Greene M.R. in *re Schebsman*, [1943] 2 All E.R. 387, 768, 779.

   (ii) There must be a fund or property which is subject to the trust and there is no trust unless the donor acknowledges formally that he holds property in trust or the property has been validly transferred to trustees. Even a valid contract to create a trust does not give a right of action to the person intended to benefit; he can only sue when property has become subject to the trust.

   (iii) If there is a trust, the parties who have created it cannot later vary it by agreement between themselves, whereas in all contractual situations the parties can alter the terms by agreement whenever they wish, and even cancel the obligations or rescind the contract if they so desire.

There is also a further class of obligations from which it is important to distinguish contractual ones. Confusingly, these are called 'quasi-contractual' obligations.

Quasi-contractual Obligations

The term 'quasi-contractual' obligations derives from the Roman law expression *obligatio quasi ex contractu*. But, as often happens when a Latin expression is adopted into English law, a completely different meaning is attached to it. In Roman law if a storm blew off the roof of your neighbour's house while he was away from home and you, uninvited but as an act of charity, spent money in putting a tarpaulin over and protecting his property, you could recover your expenses from him *quasi ex contractu*. English law, however, apparently thinks nothing of charitable acts, and in similar circumstances no such expense could be recovered from your neighbour— not even if he promised later to reimburse you (see page 83).

The English so-called 'quasi-contractual obligation' is quite different, and the only possible justification for the use of the term is that one theory of the origin of these obligations, current as late as 1914, was that they rested on a notional promise. This theory, for which there was some historical foundation, is not now generally accepted and it would be more appropriate to refer to this class as **'the equitable obligation of restitution and recompense'**.

For example, if I owe Harry some money and by mistake pay it to his twin brother Tom, there is no contractual obligation on Tom to repay me; yet it is obviously unfair that he should be allowed to retain it. It is an **'unjust enrichment'** for which equity will impose on Tom an obligation to restore. '. . . It lies for money paid by mistake; or upon a consideration which happens to fail; or for money got through imposition (express or implied) or extortion; or oppression; or an undue advantage taken of the plaintiff's situation, contrary to the laws made for the protection of persons under those circumstances. In one word, the gist of this kind of action is that the defendant, upon the circumstances of the case is obliged by the ties of natural justice and equity to refund the money'; so said Lord Mansfield in 1760.

A rather startling extension of this doctrine was made by the Court of Appeal when it held that a man who, believing himself to be the owner of a damaged car, which, in fact, had been stolen, spent £226 repairing it, was entitled to recover this sum from the true owner before the car was returned to him: *Greenwood v Bennett* (1972).

This is a topic to which it will be necessary to refer again in detail later in connection with the contracts of minors (see page 107) and non-contractual *quantum meruit* (see page 50).

CHAPTER FIVE

HOW THE LAW ENFORCES CONTRACTUAL OBLIGATION

Contractual obligations can be enforced in a number of ways by the Court:

Debt. Sums of money due under a contract will be ordered to be paid.

Damages. The invariable remedy of the Common Law Courts for failure to perform contractual obligations was an award of a payment of money as 'damages'. As we have seen on page 28 the action of *assumpsit*, which was the means whereby contractual obligations in general were enforced, was essentially an action for the compensation of a civil wrong by an award of damages; but there can be no damages unless there has first been a breach of contract.

Quantum Meruit. The Courts may also award a sum by way of *Quantum Meruit*—'as much as they deserve'. This is described in detail later (see page 49).

Specific Performance (see page 65). The old Court of Chancery had other and sometimes more persuasive methods. An order for the specific performance of a contract was an order that some positive obligation of a contract should be carried out; and the defendant who refused to obey such an order might remain in prison until he did. In addition the Court of Chancery would award:

Injunctions (see page 67). These might be either:

Prohibitive Injunctions (sometimes also termed 'restrictive' or 'preventive' injunctions). A specific order that a certain thing shall not be done, or

Mandatory Injunctions (sometimes called 'compulsive' injunctions). An order that something shall be done.

The essential difference between specific performance and a mandatory injunction is that the first requires the performance of a positive obligation while the second requires some positive act to be done to fulfil a negative stipulation. For example, if there were a contractual obligation *not* to build on certain land, which is a negative stipulation, and the defendant proposed to build on it, a prohibitive injunction would be issued to stop him; if however, he had already built on it, a mandatory injunction might be granted to make him pull down what he had erected. Whereas if the obligation were to convey the land to a buyer—that is a positive act—the appropriate remedy would be an order for specific performance.

These remedies still exist today and are known as **equitable remedies** since they were in use by the Court of Equity—that is to say the Court of Chancery. They are always discretionary. The plaintiff may be entitled to them if the Court sees fit, but an award of damages is something that the plaintiff was entitled to as of right for breach of a contract, even though the sum received may only be nominal.

Equitable remedies were only available from the Court of Chancery and it had no power to award damages, until that power was given it by what is popularly termed 'Lord Cairn's Act', the *Chancery Amendment Act, 1858*. That Act itself has been repealed by subsequent legislation, but the power is still vested in the High Court and an interesting use of it has been made in recent times by the grant of damages for Breach of Confidence. It is also possible that the Act may allow a Court to award damages in lieu of an injunction even *before* there has been a breach of contract, but there appear to be no recorded instances of this happening.

In addition to these equitable remedies, others granted by the Court of Chancery were:

Rescission. This is an order that contractual obligations on all parties shall be discharged; or to put it another way, the revocation of a contract (see page 140).

Restitution. This is closely related to rescission and is an order that the parties should be restored to their original position. It has a wider application in that it may be used outside contract to make a person part with property wrongfully in his possession or to follow or trace assets which have been dispersed (see page 46).

Rectification. The Courts have never rectified contracts as such, but an order for rectification is an order for the correction of a written document, so that it truly expresses the intention of the parties (see page 69).

Since the *Supreme Court of Judicature Act, 1873* there has, of course, been only one High Court and all these remedies, both damages and equitable remedies, are available in all the Courts in the same action. Nevertheless it can be important when reading reported cases before 1873 to look carefully to see which Court was hearing the case and what remedy was being sought. An example of the mistakes which can be made by neglect of this is to be found in

Lord Wright's judgment in *Norwich Union v Price*, [1934] All E.R. Rep. 352, where his Lordship referred to the famous case of *Cooper v Phibbs* (1867), where a man entered into a 30 years' lease of fishing rights which in fact he himself owned. Lord Wright was under the impression that the decision meant that the Court had held that the contract was void, 'The mere *simulacrum* of a contract', at common law; whereas in reality that case was an application to the Court of Chancery to set aside the lease on terms and the Court would only have acted in so doing if it were satisfied that the contract was not void at common law. In other words, the Court could only grant the equitable relief of setting aside the lease, if satisfied that the contract was valid at common law.

The Action for Debt

Debt may, of course, arise in many other ways than out of contractual obligations—by a gratuitous promise to pay in a deed or by obligations imposed by law, such as rates and taxes.

But in so far as money is due under a contract, this must be distinguished from damages. If a man has promised contractually to pay a sum of money, however excessive it may be, the Courts have no option but to condemn him in the sum to which he has agreed.

This essential difference has been made clear in some Hire Purchase contracts. If the hirer breaks the contract and the contract provides for a certain sum as damages as a result, the Court has a discretion to decide whether the sum named is liquidated damages or a penalty (see page 52). If, on the other hand, the contract allows him to terminate the contract on terms that he pays a certain sum, then the Court has no discretion but to order that sum to be paid: *Associated Distributors Ltd. v Hall*, [1938] 1 All E.R. 511. The result may be that he may be worse off if he performs the contract than if he breaks it.

There are circumstances where Statute, however, has intervened to relieve from payment of money due under a contract, as in the case of the *Infants' Relief Act, 1874* (see page 109), the *Moneylenders Acts* and the *Hire Purchase Acts* (page 212).

Quantum Meruit

Unhappily, this term '*quantum meruit*' is used in three distinct senses:

1. **As a contractual obligation.** Where there is a contract and an agreement that a reasonable price should be paid for work done or services rendered, the term is used as Blackstone used it (see page 31) to mean the reasonable price.
2. **Following a breach of contract.** The innocent party has the option of

suing either for damages or for the value of work done. This latter applies particularly to lump sum contracts where nothing is due until the whole of the work has been completed. This is sometimes termed the rule in *Cutter v Powell*, [1795] All E.R. Rep. 520. The second mate of the ship *Governor Parry* had contracted for the sum of 30 guineas to sail from Jamaica to Liverpool. He served for seven weeks, but the week before the ship arrived at Liverpool, he died. His widow was held entitled to nothing, since the voyage had not been completed. So, too, in *Huttman v Boulnois* (1826), where a servant engaged for a year for a fixed sum left before the year had ended. He was entitled to nothing.

But where the innocent party is prevented from earning the lump sum by virtue of a breach of contract by the other party, he is entitled to a *quantum meruit* for the work done. In *Planché v Colburn*, [1831] All E.R. Rep. 94, the plaintiff was engaged to write a book about armour for the sum of £100. Before he could complete it, the project was abandoned by the publishers. He was held entitled to the £50 the jury had awarded him for the work already done, as a *quantum meruit*.

But this does not apply to the guilty party. Even if he has done most of the work under a lump sum contract before he abandons it he is entitled to nothing. Sumpter was a builder who contracted to build a house for £565. Halfway through the job, he abandoned the work. It was held he could recover nothing for what he had done: *Sumpter v Hedges* (1898); but the other party was liable to pay a reasonable price, a *quantum valebant*, for materials Sumpter had brought on to the site, and which had been used by the other party to complete the work, since he had an option as to whether he used these or not. (The law regarding building contracts has, however, since been substantially modified by the doctrines of 'divisible contracts'—see *Hoenig v Isaacs*, [1952] 2 All E.R. 176—and 'substantial performance'—see *Dakin v Lee* (1916) and page 172.)

3. **Quasi-contractual *quantum meruit*.** If work is done under a contract which, although believed to be valid at the time, in fact proves to be void, the party who has done the work may be awarded a *quantum meruit* for his services. In *Craven-Ellis v Canons Ltd.*, [1936] 2 All E.R. 1066, the plaintiff became director of the defendant company and was awarded remuneration subsequently by a resolution which, for technical reasons, was void. The Court held he had no claim on a contractual basis, but for the services rendered, on a quasi-contractual basis (see page 46), he was entitled to remuneration on the same scale.

But, as has been mentioned earlier, in the absence of an implied or express promise, services rendered do not have to be paid for, except in the exceptional cases of salvage at sea and agency of necessity (see page 20). It is extremely doubtful also whether in English law, a doctor who intended to charge for his services could recover for medical attention unsuccessfully rendered to a suicide; unlike a case which happened in Canada under French Canadian law. English law is based on promise, express or implied, not upon benefit.

The Different Kinds of Damages

The law knows of various sorts of damages, arising out of the breach of contractual obligations.

Nominal damages are those awarded in cases where the plaintiff has proved a breach of contract by the defendant but has suffered no loss. In *Staniforth v Lyall* (1830), the defendant failed to provide a cargo for a ship he had chartered but the plaintiff shipowner suffered no loss because he immediately found another charterer. The defendant was held liable only for nominal damages.

In the old days, nominal damages were generally in the sum of forty shillings; no more than 'a peg on which to hang costs'. The costs, of course, might well amount to a substantial sum and up to 1954 were invariably awarded to a successful plaintiff even if he only recovered nominal damages. In recent years, however, the Courts have shown a disinclination to award costs in such cases and any plaintiff who has suffered a breach of contract but has not lost thereby is well advised to restrain any enthusiasm he may feel for litigation.

General damages are those which follow the failure to perform the contractual obligation and the principles on which they are assessed are discussed in the next section of this chapter.

Special damages are specific items of loss which the plaintiff is required to set out in detail in his Statement of Claim.

Exemplary damages are damages in excess of the loss actually suffered, which are intended to have a punitive element—to teach the defendant not to do it again. Whatever the position in tort, it seems clear that there are now no circumstances in which exemplary damages are recoverable for breach of contractual obligations.

The only circumstance approaching the recovery of exemplary damages in contract is where a trader (but not a private individual) has a cheque dishonoured by a bank when he has funds available to meet it. Then the Court will presume that he has suffered substantial damages without requiring him to prove it: *Gibbons v Westminster Bank Ltd.*, [1939] 3 All E.R. 577. (A private individual, however, may be able to sue for libel.)

But damages are not recoverable in contract for a grossly insulting manner of breach nor (since the abolition of breach of promise actions) for injury to 'feelings, affections or for wounded pride'. Mr. Addis was given six months' notice as manager for the Gramophone Company Ltd. and a new manager immediately appointed in his place. A jury awarded him £600 damages for the humiliation suffered by the manner of his dismissal, but the House of Lords set this aside: *Addis v Gramophone Company Ltd.*, [1909] All E.R. Rep. 1. On the other hand, according to Lord Denning in *Cook v S*, [1967] 2 All E.R. 299, damages for nervous shock or anxiety state caused by breach of contract are recoverable—provided they were reasonably foreseeable.

Liquidated damages are those which have been fixed in advance of the breach by agreement between the parties (see page 62).

Unliquidated damages are those which fall to be assessed by the Court, i.e. the ordinary case of breach of contract where the parties have not agreed as a term of the contract what the damages should be if such a breach takes place.

The Principles on which Damages are Assessed

Before approaching the general principles it is perhaps worthy of note that there is one exceptional circumstance in which no damages whatsoever are recoverable for breach of contract. This is where a seller of land, without any fault on his part, is unable to provide a good title. This, it is said, is because of 'the peculiar difficulty of making a title to land in England'.

Apart from that, the object of damages for breach of contract, in the words of Parke B., immortalised by constant repetition:

'A party sustaining a loss by reason of a breach of contract, is, so far as money can do it, to be placed in the same situation . . . as if the contract had been performed.'
> *Robinson v Harman* 1848, [1843–60] All E.R. Rep. 383.

In spite of their immortality, however, these words should not be taken at their face value and must be qualified by two principles:

(i) The duty on the injured party to mitigate (reduce) his loss by such means as are within his power.

'In assessing the damages for breach . . . a jury will, of course, take into account whatever . . . a prudent man, ought in reason to have done whereby his loss . . . would have been diminished.'
> Cockburn C.J. in *Frost v Knight*, [1872] All E.R. Rep. 221.

(ii) The rules regarding remoteness of damages (see page 58). If Baron Parke's dictum were literally applied the defendant would be liable for all sorts of uncontemplated, improbable and utterly unpredictable damages. The man who sold defective colour films might find himself with the entire cost of an

expedition up the Nile to film Wild Life for television. Therefore the Courts have evolved the principle:

'In cases of breach of contract the aggrieved party is only entitled
to recover such part of the loss actually resulting as was at the
time of the contract reasonably foreseeable as liable to result from
the breach.'
Asquith L.J. in *Victoria Laundry v Newman Industries*, [1949] 1 All
E.R. 997.

Since the same act may be both a breach of contract and also a
tort, it is necessary to point out here that the tests of the amount of
damages recoverable in tort are different. For a tort (a deliberate one,
such as deceit, at any rate):

  (i) the aggrieved party is to be placed, so far as money will do it,
      in the same position as if the tort had never been committed.
 (ii) so far as remoteness of damages is concerned, the test in tort
      is more in favour of the injured party than in contract.
(iii) the conduct of the defendant and his motives may be taken
      into account, as also may the conduct of the plaintiff.

The difference between the two standards is well illustrated by the
case of *Doyle v Olby*, [1969] 2 All E.R. 119. Doyle bought an iron-
mongers' business from Olby as the result of misrepresentations
which the Court held to be fraudulent and a conspiracy, as well as a
breach of contract. If treated as a breach of contract, by Baron
Parke's definition, the plaintiff was entitled to be placed in the same
position as if the contract had been performed. In other words, he
was entitled to the difference between the value of the business as it
was in reality and the value of the business as it was held out to be.
The sum so assessed was £1,500. But since the misrepresentations
were also the torts of Deceit and Conspiracy, he was entitled to be
placed in the same position as if these torts had never taken place.
He could therefore recover all losses and expenses incurred in the
three years before he was able to dispose of the business and this
sum was assessed as £5,500.

The breach of contract must have caused the loss, and not merely have been the occasion for it, before damages can be awarded

The problem of causation is one of the most difficult that any legal
system has to face; sometimes expressed (probably fallaciously) by
drawing a distinction between *causa causans*—the immediate cause—
and the *causa sine qua non*, some precedent event but for which the
causa causans would not have operated.
  If a burglar breaks into a house and escapes on to a rooftop, and

c

a police officer chasing him falls off the roof and breaks his neck, is the burglar the cause of the constable's death? This may well be a *causa sine qua non* but not a *causa causans*.

The plaintiff in an action for damages for breach of contract must prove that his loss was caused by the breach. How difficult this is to define may be seen by two cases, within a year of one another, which are not easy to reconcile.

In *Weld-Blundell v Stephens*, [1920] All E.R. Rep. 32, the defendant was under a contractual obligation to the plaintiff to maintain confidential all correspondence received from the latter. In breach of that duty, he left lying about a letter which was defamatory of X and this letter was seen by a third party. The third party communicated the contents to X, who immediately sued the plaintiff for libel. The House of Lords held that the plaintiff was entitled only to nominal damages and could not recover all the damages and costs he himself had to pay out in the libel action. The loss was not caused by any breach of contract, but by the action of the third party, i.e. it was a *causa sine qua non*.

But in *London Joint Stock Bank Ltd. v MacMillan*, [1918] All E.R. Rep. 30, the defendant, in breach of his contractual duty to the bank, drew a cheque in such a way that it could be easily altered, and it was altered by the criminal act of a third party. It was held that the breach of contract was the cause of the loss suffered by the bank. (In both cases, the Courts held that the act of the third party was reasonably foreseeable.)

A similar problem arose when a building firm, in breach of their contractual obligations to the plaintiff, failed to provide him with any suitable equipment to carry out his trade. He, therefore, had to make use of improvised equipment and was injured as a result. The Court of Appeal held that these injuries were not caused by the defendant's breach: *Quinn v Burch Bros. (Builders) Ltd.*, [1966] 2 All E.R. 283.

But what if the loss is caused by both parties to the contract? This appears to have been the situation which arose in *Government of Ceylon v Chandris*, [1965] 3 All E.R. 48, where a cargo of rice was contaminated and damaged, by the defendant not providing a proper ship and by the plaintiff not shipping the goods in suitable containers. The Court fell back on the normal proposition of the law that whoever alleges a thing must prove it and that damages can only be awarded where the burden of proof on the part of the plaintiff is discharged by showing that the loss was caused by the defendant. So unless the plaintiff could prove that the damage was caused by the breach, he could not recover.

Finally, can a plaintiff's damages be reduced under the *Law Reform (Contributory Negligence) Act, 1945* for breach of contract if the damage has been caused 'partly by his own fault and partly by the fault of some other person'? This is an interesting problem set by the legislature for the Courts; on a strict reading of the Statute, it would appear applicable to both contract and tort and all negligence arising out of either.

Damages are to be awarded in compensation solely for what the party in default was under a contractual obligation to do, and not what he would probably have done. The manager of a shop was on a five-year contract at a salary of £4,000 a year. In addition, for the first three years, he received a bonus. He was then wrongfully dismissed and claimed damages, not only for the loss of salary—about which there was no dispute—but also for loss of the bonus or the increase in salary into which it had been commuted. It was held by the Court of Appeal that since there was no contractual obligation on the employers to pay the bonus or grant him an increase in salary—even though they almost certainly would have done had he remained in their employment—he could not recover these sums: *Laverack v Woods*, [1966] 3 All E.R. 683.

On the other hand, expenses incurred before a contract was entered into are recoverable if they have been spent to no purpose as a direct result of the breach of contract: as, for example, where a television company incurred heavy expenses in preparing a programme for a certain artist who contracted to appear in it and then broke the contract. The artist was held liable for them, even though they had been incurred before he entered into the contract.

In assessing damages, the incidence of taxation must be taken into account (*Parsons v B.N.M. Laboratories*, [1963] 2 All E.R. 658, following the tort case of *B.T.C. v Gourley*, [1955] 3 All E.R. 796, where damages of £37,000 awarded to the plaintiff for loss of earnings were reduced by the House of Lords to £6,000, as a result of the income tax they calculated he had saved).

The fact that damages are difficult to assess will not deter the Courts from determining them; and they have been willing to price the lost chance of winning a beauty contest in *Chaplin v Hicks*, [1911] All E.R. Rep. 224, as well as the loss of publicity to an artist in *Clayton v Oliver*, [1930] All E.R. Rep. 414.

There is a duty on the innocent party to mitigate or minimise his loss

The law 'imposes on the plaintiff the duty of taking all reasonable steps to mitigate the loss consequent upon the breach and debars him from claiming any part of the damage which is due to his neglect to take such steps', said Lord Haldane in *British Westinghouse v Underground Electric*, [1912] All E.R. Rep. 63. The classic illustration of this principle is the case of *Brace v Calder*, [1895] All E.R. Rep. 1196. The plaintiff was employed by a partnership of four which came to an end, thereby wrongfully terminating his contract of employment. Two partners immediately offered him the same post and at the same salary but, out of pique, he refused. The Court held that all he was entitled to were nominal damages of 40 shillings, because he had failed to mitigate his loss by acceptance of the post offered him.

The test, however, is 'what a prudent person ought reasonably to do in order to mitigate his loss' and in this connection status and salary are both relevant factors where the cause of action arises from wrongful dismissal. The former managing director is not expected to mitigate his loss by taking a job as a lavatory attendant. Indeed, in *Yetton v Eastwood Froy Ltd.*, [1966] 3 All E.R. 353, a former joint managing director was held to be entitled to refuse to accept the post of *assistant* managing director at the same salary of £7,500; nor was he unreasonably failing to mitigate his loss by neglecting to follow up the offer of a post at £2,500 a year.

Similarly, a client who had bought a house with a defective title as the result of the negligence of his solicitor was not to be expected, as a reasonable and prudent man, to engage in litigation against the vendor to reduce his loss: *Pilkington v Wood*, [1953] 2 All E.R. 810. A prudent man could not be expected to engage in prolonged and expensive litigation for the purpose of mitigating his loss.

But the duty to mitigate only arises when there has been a breach of contract

The proposition above may appear self evident, but complications are introduced by what the judges have, most misleadingly, christened **'anticipatory breach'**; misleadingly, for an anticipatory breach is not necessarily a breach of contract.

Anticipatory breach is a repudiation of the contractual obligations before the time has come for their performance. It may be by words—as where a party expressly says he does not intend to do what he has promised to. Or it may be by an act, as in the case of *Frost v Knight* 1872, [1861–73] All E.R. Rep. 221, where the defendant had promised to marry the plaintiff after his father's death but, before that event happened, married somebody else. So if a person places it outside his power to perform the contract, as by selling a cruiser he has undertaken to hire out later, that is a repudiation of, or, as it used to be called earlier, 'a renunciation' of his obligations.

But a repudiation is not necessarily a breach of contract. It only becomes such if the other party accepts it as a breach; but not otherwise. 'An unaccepted repudiation is writ on water.'

Two courses are open to the promisee:

(i) 'If he pleases, he may treat the notice of intention as inopera-

tive and await the time when the contract is to be executed
and then hold the other party responsible for all the consequences of non-performance.'

(ii) 'If he thinks proper, he may treat the repudiation of the other
party as a wrongful putting an end to the contract and may at
once bring his action as on a breach of it.'

Cockburn C.J. in Frost v Knight.

Two cases will illustrate Lord Cockburn's first proposition. Mr.
McGregor was the Scottish proprietor of a garage and in his absence from the premises one day his sales manager was persuaded
to sign a contract with White and Carter (Councils) Ltd. for three
years of advertisements on litter bins which that company had
attached to lamp-posts in the neighbourhood.

When Mr. McGregor returned to his garage and found out what
his manager had signed on his behalf he wasn't pleased. The very
same day he wrote repudiating the agreement. The Company chose
to ignore this and went ahead and prepared the necessary plates for
the bins and exhibited them. They then sued Mr. McGregor, not for
damages, but *in debt* for the whole amount of rentals due under the
contract; and in the House of Lords they succeeded: *White and
Carter (Councils) Ltd. v McGregor*, [1961] 3 All E.R. 1178.

The case has aroused a lot of controversy amongst academic
lawyers; firstly, because it was argued that it was contrary to the
duty to mitigate the loss flowing from a breach. That is answered
simply: 'It cannot be said that there is any duty on the part of the
plaintiff to mitigate his damage before there is any breach which he
has accepted as a breach.' The duty to mitigate only arises when there
has been a breach of contract, i.e. in the circumstances set out in
Lord Cockburn's second proposition above. The other and main
objection is that the doctrine is from an ethical point of view absurd.
Is an architect really entitled to spend two years preparing drawings
for a town hall which he has been told will never be built? Or, to
quote an example given by Lord Reid in the case above: if a company
engages an expert to go abroad and prepare an elaborate report
and before he sets off, they tell him they no longer want it, is he
really entitled to waste thousands of pounds on a trip to Australia,
say, and in preparing a report, and then charge the company his
full fee, when a much smaller sum by way of damages would give
him full compensation for his loss? Is a printer entitled to go on and
print wedding invitations even if he is told the wedding will no
longer take place? It would appear so. In *Anglo-African Shipping of
New York v Mortimer Ltd.* (1962), the plaintiffs agreed to supply
the defendants with a quantity of rubber sheeting. Before the time
for delivery, the defendants cancelled the order. The plaintiffs ignored

the cancellation and went ahead and delivered the goods. The Court of Appeal held they were entitled to.

There are, however, some qualifications of this remarkable doctrine. The manager of the pop group known as 'The Kinks' was discharged by them. He claimed to have rejected their repudiation of his services and that he was entitled to his full percentage of their earnings, right up to the end of his contract, years later. He did not claim damages, because to have done so would have been inconsistent with this claim, since he would first have to accept the repudiation as a breach of contract. He, in spite of the doctrine, lost his case in the Court of Appeal. A majority of the Court, basing themselves on early 19th-century cases such as *Smith v Hayward* (1837) held that contracts of personal service are in a class of their own (*'sui generis'* is the legal expression) and that repudiation, even if unaccepted, ended the right to wages and converted it into a right to damages only: *Denmark v Boscobel*, [1968] 3 All E.R. 513.

But this is an evasion based on an exception rather than a solution of the problem, and it may well be that the true law is that the right to refuse to accept a repudiation only exists where the injured party *can go on and perform his own obligations without the co-operation of the other party*. In other words, that performance by the innocent party and not mere willingness to perform is necessary. Unfortunately there is a great deal of authority against this suggestion including, of course, that of Lord Cockburn quoted above where he said the innocent party was entitled to 'await the time when the contract is to be executed'.

There is some basis for it, however, in building law. A builder who is told to stop work on a project is bound to accept these instructions; but this may be because he requires the licence of the building owner to go on the land.

And in the sale of goods, there is some authority in *British Westinghouse v Underground Electric*, [1912] All E.R. Rep. 63, that where a buyer has repudiated a contract for the sale of goods before the time for delivery has arrived, the seller is not entitled to reject the repudiation and hang on to the goods in a falling market until the day of delivery and so enhance the damages. But this proposition may have to be looked at again in the light of the later House of Lords decision in *White and Carter v McGregor*.

Damages are not recoverable if they are not reasonably foreseeable at the time when the contract was made

The question of the extent to which damages are recoverable is termed that of *Remoteness of Damages*. In spite of thoroughly unsatisfactory reports of the case, the law is based on the decision in *Hadley v Baxendale*, [1854] All E.R. Rep. 461.

That case appears to have laid down two propositions, per Alderson B.:

'Where two parties have made a contract which one of them has broken, the damage which the other party ought to receive should be such as may fairly and reasonably be considered to arise naturally, i.e. according to the usual course of things' (*The so-called 'first rule'*)

or

'such as may reasonably be supposed to have been in the contemplation of both parties, at the time they made the contract as the probable result of the breach of it'. (*The so-called 'second rule'*).

Anson believed that a careful reading of the judgment as a whole suggested that in the so-called second rule, the Court merely intended to express in other words, for the sake of greater clarity, what they had already said in the so-called first rule; i.e. that the damages which can fairly and reasonably be considered as arising 'naturally' were those which 'may reasonably be supposed to have been in the contemplation of the parties at the time when they made the contract'. Lord Denning apparently adopted this view once when he quoted this judgment but substituted for the word 'or', the words 'that is to say'.

Another difficulty about the case was that there is some confusion as to the findings of fact. The plaintiffs' mill was stopped by the breakage of a crankshaft and the broken crankshaft had to be sent to the original manufacturers as a pattern. The carriers, in breach of their contract, delayed delivery of the shaft and in due course the plaintiffs sued for £300 loss of profits which they would otherwise have made if the mill had been working. The reports of the case state that the defendant's clerk was told that the mill was stopped and that the shaft must be delivered immediately. In which case, one can only presume that loss of profits must have fallen under the second rule as being within the contemplation of the parties, and therefore should have been recoverable. However the Court held that they were not. Later decisions proceeded on the basis that special losses of this nature could only be recovered if there were circumstances to show that the defendant not merely knew but had also accepted liability for such losses (*Horne v Midland Railway* (1873); *Bostock v Nicholson* (1904)).

However, the whole matter was reviewed by the Court of Appeal in *Victoria Laundry v Newman*, [1949] 1 All E.R. 997, in which the judgment was delivered by Asquith L.J. He accepted that there were in fact two distinct rules in *Hadley v Baxendale* and proceeded to reformulate them in a series of propositions, three of which are material:

(i) 'In cases of breach of contract the aggrieved party is only entitled to recover such part of the loss actually resulting as was at the time of the contract reasonably foreseeable as liable to result from the breach'

(ii) 'What is reasonably foreseeable depends on the knowledge of the parties at the time'

(iii) 'This knowledge may be:

    (a) *imputed,* that is to say what everyone as a reasonable person is taken to know *in the ordinary course of things.* (This, Lord Justice Asquith equated to the first rule in *Hadley v Baxendale.*) or

    (b) *actual,* where in a particular case there is knowledge which the defendant actually possesses of *special circumstances* '*outside the ordinary course of things*'

(And, this, his Lordship believed to be the same as the second rule in *Hadley v Baxendale.*)

In *Victoria Laundry v Newman* the defendants agreed to supply and instal a large boiler for the plaintiff's laundry on the 5th June. It was not in fact delivered until the 8th November. The plaintiff claimed two items of damage:

1. £16 a week as loss of profits from new customers they could have taken on.
2. £262 a week as loss of profits under a special contract they had with the Ministry of Supply for dyeing battledresses.

The trial judge refused them both, finding as a fact that the special objects for which the boiler was required had not been drawn to the defendant's notice.

The Court of Appeal allowed the first item of £16 a week under the imputed knowledge rule. 'Reasonable persons in the shoes of the defendants must be taken to foresee without any express intimation that a laundry which, at a time when there was a famine of laundry facilities, was paying £2,000 odd for plant and intended to put such plant into use immediately, would be likely to suffer in pocket from five months delay.'

But the claim for the £262 a week under the contract with the Ministry of Supply was rejected as these were 'special circumstances outside the ordinary course of things'.

This decision of the Court of Appeal was subsequently approved of by a majority in the House of Lords in the *Heron II,* [1967] 3 All E.R. 686 with some minor verbal qualifications. For ninety years, ever since *The Parana* (1877), the rule of law had been that if a shipowner diverted a ship for his own purpose and so prolonged a voyage in breach of contract, the only damages a charterer could recover was interest on the value of the cargo for the period of the delay. The *Heron II*, under charter, loaded a cargo of three thousand tons of sugar in Constanza and carried it to Basrah and in breach of the contract was nine days late on arrival. Had the ship arrived on the due date the charterers would have received £32 10s a ton for their sugar; as it was the market had slumped, and they only got £31 2s 9d, a total loss of £4,011. Interest on the cargo would have been in the region of £134. The House of Lords held the total loss was recoverable since the shipowner knew there was a sugar market in Basrah and must therefore be imputed to know that prices rise and fall on such markets.

Damages for Non-delivery or Non-acceptance of Goods

Goods usually fall into three classes, according to the purpose for which they are bought. They may be:

(i) profit-earning chattels, as the boiler in the *Victoria Laundry* case, or
(ii) goods bought for resale, or
(iii) goods bought for consumption.

Damages for non-delivery is dealt with by s. 51 (2) of the *Sale of Goods Act, 1893*.

'The measure of damages is the estimated loss directly and naturally resulting in the ordinary course of events, from the seller's breach of contract.
Where there is an available market for the goods in question the measure of damages is *prima facie* to be ascertained by *the difference between the contract price* and the *market price* of the goods at the time or times when *they ought to have been delivered*, or, if no time was fixed, then at the time of the refusal to deliver.'

In other words, the buyer, when he knows he can't get the goods he has contracted to buy, ought to go to another seller and obtain them from him and sue for any difference in price. If the goods are not available elsewhere, as happened in *Patrick v Russo-British Grain Exports*, [1927] All E.R. Rep. 692, where the commodity was Russian wheat, provided the seller knows that the buyer requires them as profit earning or to resell, then the measure of damages is the loss of profit.

Damages for wrongful non-acceptance. These are dealt with in s. 50:

'The measure of damages is the estimated loss directly and naturally resulting in the ordinary course of events, from the

buyer's breach of contract. Where there is an available market for
the goods in question the measure of damage is prima facie to be
ascertained by the *difference between the contract price* and the
market or current price at the time or times when the *goods ought
to have been accepted*, or, if no time was fixed for acceptance, then
at the time of the refusal to accept.'

In other words, the seller has to go out and find another buyer, and
sue for the difference in price, if any.

If he is selling for profit and can sell all he can get at the price, he
has suffered no loss and therefore is entitled to only nominal damages, as happened in *Charter v Sullivan*, [1957] 1 All E.R. 809, when
the buyer refused to take delivery of a Hillman car when these were
in short supply and the seller therefore sold it to somebody else. If,
however, the seller loses a sale as the result of the buyer's refusal to
accept delivery, as happened in *Thompson v Robinson*, [1955] 1 All
E.R. 154, where the retailers could not sell the car to any other of
their customers but managed to get the wholesalers to take it back,
they are entitled to their loss of profit in the sale.

Damages for delay in delivery of goods is said to be the difference
in price at the time when the goods ought to have been delivered and
the time when they actually were: *Elbinger v Armstrong* (1874); but
this fails to draw the crucial difference between profit-earning
chattels and chattels for resale, and goods for consumption. It may
apply to goods for resale and for consumption but, as we have seen
on page 60, very much greater damages may be awarded for delay in
delivery of profit-earning chattels.

Damages Fixed by the Terms of the Contract

Where the contract specifies the sum to be paid in respect of any
particular breach, as is quite common in building, shipping and
many other contracts, these may be:

1. **Liquidated damages.** A genuine pre-estimate, so far as one is
   possible at the time when the contract was made, of the loss
   likely to be suffered. In which case this sum, no more and no
   less, is recoverable, whatever the damage suffered.
2. **A penalty.** A sum named to intimidate the other party into
   performing the contract (to put him *in terrorem* is the legal
   jargon) and not as a genuine pre-estimate of the loss likely
   to be suffered. Equity would grant relief against penalties and,
   in that event, the aggrieved party could recover the actual
   damage he could prove—and no more.
3. **Limited damages.** This happens where both parties realise that
   the damages may well be in excess of the sum named but one
   contracting party is not willing to accept any greater liability

and the other agrees to this. That was the position in *Cellulose Acetate v Widnes*, [1932] All E.R. Rep. 567, where the contract limited damages to £600 but the plaintiff's loss was in fact £5,850. It was held they could recover no more than the sum named in the contract. But a limited damages clause may not protect a party in the event of a fundamental breach of contract (see page 171).

It is important to distinguish these three categories from *sums payable on the happening of a certain event*, i.e. under the contract. In all the cases above, a breach of contract had first to occur. In *Alder v Moore*, [1961] 1 All E.R. 1, the defendant, a professional footballer, was insured against permanent total disablement. He was injured and the insurer accepted that this was permanent and total and paid him £500. He signed a form that he would take no part in professional football again and 'in the event of infringement of this condition he will be subject to a penalty of the amount paid him'. Two members of the Court of Appeal decided that 'there was no *contractual* obligation on the defendant not to play professional football again'—therefore this was simply a sum of money repayable under the terms of the contract on the happening of a certain event, and therefore recoverable. Devlin L.J. dissented.

Sums payable where a hirer under a Hire Purchase agreement exercises an option to terminate the contract were held in *Associated Distributors Ltd. v Hall*, [1938] 1 All E.R. 511, by the Court of Appeal to be unrelated to the law regarding liquidated damages or penalties, since the sums were not payable on breach of contract. But in *United Dominions Trust v Ennis*, [1967] 2 All E.R. 345, Lord Denning found a neat way round that one, by holding that a hirer is not to be taken to exercise an option to terminate unless he does so consciously, knowing of the consequences. The *Hire Purchase Act, 1965* deals, of course, now with this position in so far as the goods in question are within the scope of that Act (see page 212).

How to Distinguish Liquidated Damages from Penalties

As has been seen, when a sum has been named in a contract as damages for any particular breach if it is in law liquidated damages, that sum—no more and no less—is recoverable for that breach of contract, irrespective of the loss actually incurred. Whereas if the fixed sum is held to be in law a penalty, the sum named is not recoverable and the aggrieved party can only recover such actual damage as he can prove to the satisfaction of a Court.

How does the law decide which of the two is a fixed sum named in a contract as payable in the event of a breach?

The leading authority is to be found in the judgment of Lord

Dunedin in *Dunlop v New Garage*, [1915] All E.R. Rep. 739, which was a case where tyre manufacturers tried to maintain fixed retail prices; this time by naming a sum of £5 damages for every tyre which was sold below their listed price.

The propositions advanced by Lord Dunedin are accepted as the basis of our modern law. Paraphrased, they are:

1. It doesn't matter what the parties themselves call the fixed sum—that is by no means conclusive. In the building trade, for example, the liquidated damages clause is invariably known as 'the penalty clause'. Usually it is not that at all. But on the whole, the parties may be presumed to know what they are doing, so that if they call a thing 'a penalty' there may be a disposition on the part of the Court to treat it as such.

2. The essential element of a penalty is that it is an attempt to intimidate the other contracting party into performing the contract because of the threat; to hold him '*in terrorem*' as the lawyers like to call it.

3. By contrast, liquidated damages is an attempt to pre-estimate the loss which a particular breach may occasion. It doesn't matter that the parties may be way out in their calculation; provided that, *when the contract was made*, it was a reasonable attempt, it will be liquidated damages.

   In *Dunlop v New Garage* the House of Lords accepted:

   (a) that some damage would result to Dunlops if people to whom they had sold tyres resold them below the manufacturer's fixed retail price list. (A quaint finding in view of our modern views about retail price fixing).

   (b) that the actual damage from any particular sale was impossible to forecast.

   (c) therefore it was one of those cases where it was reasonable for the parties to estimate the damage at a certain figure.

   (d) that £5 a tyre was not an extravagant sum and was therefore recoverable.

4. In deciding whether or not the sum named is an honest attempt to pre-estimate the damage likely to result from a particular breach, the Court will have regard to the following:

   (a) If a larger sum of money is payable in default of payment of a lesser, then this is inevitably a penalty, i.e. if you don't pay me £10 by the 1st June, you then have to pay me £20—this latter sum is not recoverable.

   (b) If the sum named is likely to exceed any possible loss and is extravagant, it is obviously a penalty.

(c) If the same sum is payable in respect of minor breaches of contract and major ones, there is a presumption—but no more—that it is a penalty.

For example, a Hire Purchase agreement provided that in default the hirer should pay 75% of the value of the car as 'agreed compensation for depreciation'. This was held to be a penalty because it applied whether the default was in payment of the first monthly instalment—when the depreciation would have been small—or the last. Moreover, on the particular facts of the case the H.P. Company would be better off by £136 by a default than if the contract had been fulfilled. This was, in the words of Denning L.J., 'not a genuine pre-estimate of damage, but an extravagant and extortionate sum held *in terrorem* over the head of the hirer': *Landom Trust v Hurrel*, [1955] 1 All E.R. 839 (which report prints the plaintiff's name incorrectly as Lando*n*); and in *Lombank v Excell*, [1963] 3 All E.R. 486, the Court of Appeal also held a so-called agreed 'sum for depreciation' to be a penalty because it was a standard form clause applicable to all types of goods, new or second-hand. In *Ford Motor Co. v Armstrong* (1915), another price-fixing agreement, the sum of £250 was payable for any breach of the contract including such trifling infringements as exhibiting the plaintiff's cars without their written consent. This was held to be a penalty and therefore irrecoverable.

The Equitable Remedy of Specific Performance

This, as has been noted earlier, is a remedy formerly given by the Court of Chancery, but there is also statutory provision for it, so far as the delivery of goods is concerned, in s. 52 of the *Sale of Goods Act, 1893*. The wording of that Statute appears to give the Courts an unfettered discretion to order specific performance of contracts for the sale of specific goods, but in fact they have exercised jurisdiction under the section strictly in accordance with the old Chancery ideas.

Specific performance will only be ordered where damages are an inadequate remedy

In practice, this results in orders being made only:

(i) where the contract relates to the sale of land, which is always regarded as something unique. Both buyer and seller are entitled to such an order, but only if the seller already has the title vested in him;

(ii) where the contract is for a unique chattel. A set of Heppelwhite chairs was not held (*Cohen v Roche* (1927)) to be sufficiently unique to justify an order, but an Adam style door was so regarded in *Phillips v Lamdin*, [1949] 1 All E.R. 770, but only because it had been taken from a particular house where it had been ever since the house had been built and was to be restored there;

(iii) where a third party might otherwise be deprived of a benefit due under a contract. As will be seen (page 98) no person can take a benefit under a contract to which they are not a party and for which they have given no consideration. But the House of Lords ordered specific performance at the instance of one of the parties for payments to be made to a third party in *Beswick v Beswick*, [1967] 2 All E.R. 1197, because damages otherwise would be nominal (see page 51).

Old Peter Beswick sold his small coal merchant's business to his nephew on terms that he himself should have £6 10s a week so long as he lived, and thereafter his widow should have £5 a week. Shortly afterwards he died, and the nephew made one payment of £5 to Mrs. Beswick the widow and then ceased.

Mrs. Beswick sued in two capacities:

(a) in her personal capacity, and
(b) since her late husband had left no will, she was able to take out Letters of Administration and thus become his administratrix, vested with all the rights of the deceased.

She failed in the House of Lords in her personal capacity, since she was not a party to the contract, but an order of specific performance was made in her favour as administratrix, for the nephew to pay the annuity of £5 a week to her in her personal capacity.

A party aggrieved by a breach of contract has no *right* to an order of specific performance; it is essentially a discretionary remedy which the Court may award if it sees fit.

But specific performance will never be awarded:

(i) unless the obligations of the contract are mutually enforceable. For that reason a minor will never be granted specific performance for a contract which is voidable at his option (see page 109);

(ii) where the contractual obligation would require constant supervision by the Court. The earliest cases are all concerned with the cultivation of land, as where a tenant farmer covenanted in his lease to observe a certain rotation of crops. The Courts would not give specific performance in such circumstances. More recent cases include the obligation to provide porterage for flats (*Ryan v Mutual Tontine* (1893)), and the obligations of a shipowner under a charter-party;

(iii) for contracts of personal services. The Courts will not force a man to work under an employment contract or an employer to keep him on. In either case, damages are regarded as the appropriate remedy.

Specific performance may be refused:
(i) if the party claiming it has not behaved fairly himself;
(ii) if he is in breach of his own obligations under the contract, as in *Australian Hardwoods v Railway Commissioners*, [1961] 1 All E.R. 737, where the plaintiffs sought specific performance of an option to purchase in a lease, but were greatly in arrears with their rent;
(iii) if it would cause undue hardship to the defendant, as where the defendant purchased a plot of land to which there was no lawful access over the surrounding property. *Denne v Light* (1857);
(iv) if the contract has been induced by duress, misrepresentation or mistake.

Injunctions—Prohibitive and Mandatory
Although prohibitive injunctions (see page 47) are also discretionary, it was said by Cairns L.C. in 1878 in *Doherty v Allman* that 'if the parties for valuable consideration, with their eyes open, contract that a particular thing shall not be done, all that a Court of Equity has to do is to say by way of injunction that which the parties have already said by way of covenant—namely . . . the thing shall not be done'.

But where contracts of personal service are concerned prohibitive injunctions will not be granted unless:

(i) there is an *express* negative stipulation. If Tom promises to sing at the Deadbeat nightclub, that may possibly imply that he will not sing the same night at the principal rival establishment, the Beatdeads. But no injunction will be possible, unless there is an express promise *not* to appear anywhere else that night;
(ii) the effect of the injunction would not be the same as specific performance of the contract, i.e. to compel the person to perform the contract.

Bette Davis made a contract with Warner Bros. which included express terms that:

(i) she would not act for anybody else, and
(ii) she would *not* engage in any other occupation, without their consent in writing.

In breach, she entered into an agreement to make a film for some-body else. The Court granted an injunction to restrain her from acting for anybody else but was not prepared to grant an injunction to restrain her from engaging in any other profession. So she was free, if she chose, to earn her living as a waitress or a chambermaid. To deprive her of all opportunity of earning a living in some other capacity might have the same effect as an order of specific perform-ance: *Warner Bros. v Nelson*, [1936] 3 All E.R. 160.

But when an injunction was sought against a pop group called 'The Troggs' for an express negative stipulation that they would not employ anybody but the plaintiffs as their managers one was refused. Without a manager they would have been unable to have continued in their chosen profession and this would, the judge held, have had the same effect as an order of specific performance—in spite of the fact that they were free to find other employment: *Page One Records v Britton*, [1967] 3 All E.R. 822.

Prohibitive injunction may be refused when it would be contrary to public policy to enforce the covenant, e.g. where the promise is in restraint of trade (see page 124).

Mandatory injunctions are granted most reluctantly, and in a recent case where a part of an orchard was sold with an express negative covenant that a roadway would not be raised, and it was, the Court was unwilling to order the destruction of the roadway and adjourned the proceedings for another possible solution to be found: *Charring-ton v Simons & Co. Ltd.*, [1971] 2 All E.R. 588.

Rectification

Documents which fail to express the true intention of the parties will be rectified—corrected—by the Court and this has been done with conveyances, policies of marine insurance and bills of quantities in building contracts, amongst other documents.

The conditions under which the Court will rectify a document are:

(i) The error must be of fact and not law.

(ii) The Court must be satisfied by 'irrefragable evidence' that there was a mistake in the expression of the contract; that means there must be no doubt whatever about it.

(iii) The mistake must be that of both parties and not merely that of one. In *Higgins v Northampton Corporation* (1927) the Corporation put its seal to a document that correctly ex-pressed their intentions but not that of the plaintiff contractor. There was no power to correct it.

(iv) Until *Joscelyne v Nissen*, [1970] 1 All E.R. 1213, it was com-monly said that the Courts could only rectify a document if there was 'an antecedent binding contract' and not just a common intention to enter a written contract in certain terms. But in that case the Court of Appeal rejected this view and rectified a written agreement even though there was no previous binding contract but only a common intention to make a contract in certain terms.

Mr. Joscelyne entered into an agreement with his daughter whereby he transferred to her a house and his car hire business on consideration of her paying him a pension for life and also all his gas, electricity and coal bills. The written document, however, merely recorded an agreement to 'discharge all expenses' of the house, which clearly was not wide enough to include the father's bills for gas, etc. The daughter did in fact pay all such bills until she quarrelled with the father. The Court held that it was sufficient that both parties intended to incorporate such a term in the written agreement, in spite of the fact that there was no prior binding contract before the written agreement came into existence. It therefore rectified that document by writing in an obligation to pay the bills named.

CHAPTER SIX

PROMISES THE LAW WILL NOT ENFORCE

Before there can be contractual obligations enforceable by the Courts it is essential that the obligations are specified with sufficient precision for the Courts to be able to enforce them. This of course is obvious; it is no use the parties making promises to one another which are of such a nature that no Court can tell definitely what they mean or when they have been broken. The parties must make their own agreement and specify the terms with sufficient certainty to enable them to be enforced if necessary by the Courts. If the terms are too vague, there is no contract. As Lord Maugham put it: 'In order to constitute a valid contract, the parties must so express themselves that their meaning can be determined with a reasonable degree of certainty.'

The force of this requirement can be seen from a case which is usually classed under another heading in most textbooks. Two merchants entered into an agreement, the one to sell and the other to buy a cargo of cotton 'ex *Peerless* from Bombay'. One merchant had in mind a ship called *Peerless* sailing from Bombay in October. The other was referring to another ship, also called the *Peerless*, which was sailing from Bombay in August. The Court held that there was no contract between the two; clearly there were no obligations that any Court could enforce, in the absence of further indication as to which '*Peerless*' was intended. Therefore the buyer could not recover damages for non-delivery. Cases of this nature, where there is a latent ambiguity in what the parties have agreed, have nothing really to do with the doctrine of mistake (see page 162). The reality of the situation is that no Court could possibly decide what to enforce: *Raffles v Wichelhaus* (1864).

The Law Reports abound in cases where parties have not specified their agreement with sufficient particularity. In *Guthing v Lynn* (1831), the defendant promised to pay the plaintiff a further sum of money, in addition to the purchase price, 'if the horse proves lucky'. The Court declined to enter into speculation as to what was or was not 'a lucky horse'. In *Davies v Davies* (1887), one partner promised to retire from a business 'in so far as the law allows'. In *Montreal Gas v*

70

Vasey (1900) one term of the contract was that 'favourable consideration' would be given to its renewal. All these words were held to be
too vague to be enforceable.

The difficulty of deciding what exactly the parties meant arises
particularly where they refer to terms or conditions not specifically
set out and of which there are several forms in current use. An agreement was made to buy a van 'on hire purchase terms' (*Scammell v
Ouston*, [1941] 1 All E.R. 14). This was held to be too vague to impose contractual obligations since there were numerous hire purchase
terms in common usage. Words, therefore, which are capable of
having a number of different meanings cannot bind the parties at all.
'Subject to strike and lock-out clauses' (*Love & Stewart v Instone*
(1970)), 'Subject to . . . war clause' (*Bishop & Baxter v Anglo Eastern*,
[1943] 2 All E.R. 598), 'Subject to . . . *force majeure* conditions'
(*British Electric v Patley*, [1953] 1 All E.R. 94) are similar examples.
No Court could possibly say what strike clauses, what war clauses
or what *force majeure* conditions were incorporated in these agreements.

On the other hand it is said that the Court may ignore a clause
which is not one that has a number of possible meanings, but is one
that is completely meaningless—provided the meaningless words can
be deleted from the agreement and still leave a perfectly valid and enforceable contract. In *Nicolene v Simmonds*, [1953] 1 All E.R. 882,
there was an agreement to buy and sell a quantity of iron reinforcing
bars. The seller failed to deliver and when sued for damages set up the
defence that there was no binding contract because the agreement
contained the words 'we are in agreement that the usual conditions of
acceptance apply'. There were no usual conditions of acceptance;
and hence this was not an obligation which the Court could enforce.
But the Court of Appeal refused to accept that argument. 'A distinction must be drawn between a clause which is meaningless and a
clause which has yet to be agreed . . . a clause that is meaningless can
be ignored, whilst still leaving the contract good, whereas a clause
which has yet to be agreed may mean there is no contract at all,
because the parties had not agreed on all the essential terms' said
Denning L.J.

No Agreement to Make an Agreement

It is for the parties themselves to make their own agreement on all
essential points; and if they fail to do so there are no contractual
obligations. 'A concluded contract is one that settles everything that
is necessary to be settled and leaves nothing to be settled by subsequent
agreement between the parties,' said Lord Dunedin in *May and
Butcher v R* (1934). The parties had entered into what they no doubt
thought at the time of making it was a binding agreement for the

purchase of First World War surplus tents; but the agreement read 'the price to be paid . . . shall be agreed upon from time to time between the Commission and the purchasers'. The Court of Appeal held that this meant that a reasonable price was to be paid, and therefore there was an enforceable contract since, in the absence of an agreement between the parties as to what was reasonable, the Court could decide. But the House of Lords reversed this decision and held there were no binding obligations at all. As the parties had yet to agree the essential element of price, there was no contract. In that, the House of Lords followed an earlier decision. An actress made an agreement with a producer for her engagement 'at a West End salary to be mutually arranged . . . between us'; it was held, there was no contract: *Loftus v Roberts* (1902).

Certum est quod certum reddi potest

But these principles are subject to the important qualification, that is expressed in the maxim: *Certum est quod certum reddi potest*—'That is certain which can be made certain'.

If in *May and Butcher v R* for example, instead of leaving the price to be settled by future agreement between themselves, the parties had elected to allow the price to be fixed by a third party, there would have been a valid contract. Although Lord Buckmaster, dissenting, in the House of Lords, in that case said: 'I find myself unable to understand the distinction between an agreement to permit the price to be fixed by a third party and an agreement to permit the price to be fixed in future by the two parties themselves', the difference in fact is quite clear. The two parties may never agree on the price.

If an arbitration clause is included in the agreement it may have the same effect as reference to a third party, for it provides machinery whereby such details can be decided in the absence of agreement. A Mr. Foley sold land to Classiques Coaches Ltd. for the erection of a motor coach garage and, in a separate document, the company agreed to buy all their requirements of petrol from him at a price 'to be agreed by the parties from time to time'. One clause provided for an arbitrator to be appointed to settle disputes arising out of the contract. It was held that this was a binding contract for the supply of petrol of reasonable quality at a reasonable price and the provision regarding an arbitrator provided a method of arriving at this, even when the parties, as it in fact had happened, failed to agree the price: *Foley v Classique Coaches Ltd.*, [1934] All E.R. Rep. 88.

Similar reasoning was applied when Fine Fare Ltd. entered into an agreement for the supply of broiler chickens from F. & G. Sykes (Wessex) Ltd. for a period of five years. The agreement provided for the supply of between 30,000 to 80,000 chickens each week during the first year but failed to specify how many chickens were to be supplied in subsequent years. There was an Arbitration Clause and the Court held that there was a binding contract because the number could be decided by the arbitrator: *F. & G. Sykes (Wessex) Ltd. v Fine Fare* (1967).

Also, of course, if in *May and Butcher* the agreement allowed *one* of the parties to fix the price in future, there would have been a valid contract, since a certain method of arriving at the price would have been specified.

The absence of expressed agreement between the parties on *all* essential terms of a contract is not always fatal. 'The general presumption is that the parties have expressed every material term which they intended should govern their agreement, whether oral or in writing.' But if there are gaps, the Court may be able to close these by reference to either:

(i) previous dealings between the same parties, or
(ii) an implied term, which may be imported by the custom and usage of a trade, or by statute, or to give commercial effect to the intention of the parties (see page 167).

Somewhat surprisingly, the House of Lords found itself able to complete a contract for the parties in *Hillas v Arcos*, [1932] All E.R. Rep. 494. There was an agreement between the plaintiffs to buy from the defendants, the Trading Agency of the Soviet Government, 22,000 standards of timber in one year with an option to take 100,000 in the following year. The Court of Appeal held the option too vague to be enforceable at law, 'considering the number of things left undetermined: kinds, sizes and quantities of goods, times and port and manner of shipment . . .'—but the House of Lords reversed this decision. The absence of agreement about the *details* of the second year's trading could be completed by reference to the terms of the first year's.

Even where an agreement is entirely silent about price, it is not fatal unless the contract relates to land or an interest in land. For the Court must imply in the agreement, a promise that a reasonable price shall be paid. So far as the sale of chattels is concerned the *Sale of Goods Act, 1893* enacts:

S. 8 (i) 'The price in a contract of sale may be fixed by the contract, or may be left to be fixed in manner thereby agreed, or may be determined by the course of dealing between the parties.'
   (ii) 'Where the price is not determined in accordance with the foregoing provisions, the buyer must pay a reasonable price.'

So, if in *May and Butcher*, the parties had not said a word about the price of the goods, there would have been a good contract because by reason of this section, the price would have to be a reasonable one. And if the parties could not themselves agree on what was a reasonable price, the Courts would do it for them.

The present position, therefore, in regard to the sale of goods appears to be:

Price to be fixed in future by third party
—GOOD CONTRACT.
Price to be fixed in future by one of the parties
—GOOD CONTRACT.
No method of fixing price specified
—GOOD CONTRACT.
Price to be fixed in future by agreement between both of the parties with Arbitration Clause
—GOOD CONTRACT.

It is only where the price is to be fixed in future by agreement between both of the parties that there is NO CONTRACT.

It is not surprising therefore that the decision of the House of Lords in *May and Butcher v R* has not received universal approbation. As Scrutton L.J. observed dryly about that case and *Hillas v Arcos*, 'The two decisions of the House of Lords are not easy to fit into one another.' He, of course, was one of the judges of the Court of Appeal which had been over-ruled in both cases.

The tendency nowadays, when the parties have made a business agreement intending it to impose contractual obligations, is to uphold it wherever possible. *Verba ita sunt intelligenda ut res magis valeat quam pereat*: 'Words are to be so understood that the object may be carried out and not fail.'

The principles that are applied by the *Sale of Goods Act, 1893,* and by the Common Law for centuries before that, to chattels, have been applied to contracts of service. In *British Bank v Novinex,* [1949] 1 All E.R. 155, there was a term that an agreed commission should be paid on certain transactions. This, the Court held, meant that there was an implied term that the defendants would pay a reasonable commission and what was a reasonable commission the Court itself was able to decide in the light of previous dealings between the parties. Similarly, a promise to a secretary to pay her a bonus if she undertook extra duties was held to carry the implication that it would be a reasonable sum and what that sum was the Court itself decided: *Powell v Braun,* [1954] 1 All E.R. 484.

Absence of Contractual Intent

It will have been apparent from page 27 *et seq.* that there are many promises made by people which do not give rise to contractual obligations and that, to quote Atkin L.J. in *Balfour v Balfour,* [1918–19]

All E.R. Rep. 860, 'there are agreements which do not result in contracts within the meaning of that term'.

The problem faced by every legal system that has ever existed is what tests to apply to distinguish promises which should be enforced as contractual obligations and those which should not. The Romans solved the problem by recognising certain common situations as giving rise to contractual obligations, or, in the alternative, requiring a minor ceremony to make the promisor realise he was assuming legal obligations. Before promises of this latter sort were binding, the person to whom the promise was made had to check with the promisor and make him consider the seriousness of what he was doing by asking formally: '*Spondesne ?*' That is usually translated as 'Do you stipulate?' But its real force was: 'Do you promise that as a contractual obligation?' The promisor was only bound if he solemnly replied '*Spondeo*'—'I stipulate—I promise it as a contractual obligation.' The question did two things, as Sir Henry Maine points out in his *Ancient Law*: 'By breaking the tenor of the conversation (the question) prevents the attention from gliding over a dangerous pledge' and it 'provided an opportunity for withdrawal from an improvident undertaking'.

English law solved the problem of what promises to enforce in a slightly different way. Originally, it would enforce promises by the action of *assumpsit* (see page 28) only where the promisor got something in exchange for his promise—which is no doubt how, in spite of the diverse theories of legal historians, the doctrine of consideration (see page 81) first became embedded in the English law of contract. Later the law required not only that, but also a specific contractual intention; so that today it is said that no promise is enforceable as a contract unless that was the intention of the promisor. 'An intention to affect legal relations is essential to the formation of a contract in English law' is how the proposition is put in the current edition of Anson on *The Law of Contract*.

But judges are not mind readers who can peer inside skulls, so that in reality what matters is 'not the parties' actual intention but the intention the Court imputes to them', as Denning L.J., dissenting, pointed out in *Gould v Gould*, [1969] 3 All E.R. 728. There is, however, a further proposition: 'There is one golden rule which is of very general application: namely, that the law does not impute intention to enter legal relationships when the circumstances and the conduct of the parties negatives any intention of the kind.' Greene M.R.

Business Agreements

Generally speaking, therefore, business deals may be presumed to be intended to be contractual obligations, whatever the real intention of the parties, and even if they use words which might possibly be taken to convey the contrary. In *Edwards v Skyways Ltd.*, [1964] 1 All E.R. 494, a redundant pilot was promised an approximate sum of money as an '*ex gratia* payment', and the Court held, in spite of these words, that the promise created a contractual obligation. If, in business transactions, the parties wish to ensure that the agreement is not to be taken as a contractual obligation it is always open to them to say so in language which is unmistakable. The Court will then respect their intentions, as it did in *Rose & Frank v Crompton Bros.*, [1924] All E.R. Rep. 245. The plaintiffs entered into an agreement for exclusive distribution of carbon tissue paper in the United States of America, and (possibly to evade the monopoly laws of that country) agreed with the defendants that 'this arrangement is not entered into as a formal or legal agreement and shall not be subject to legal jurisdiction in the law courts'. The Court held there was no contract.

Similarly, every time a man fills in a football coupon he expressly agrees with the promoters that the agreement is 'binding in honour only' or some such words, that are carefully chosen to exclude contractual obligations. It follows that even if he claims to have won the first prize and the promoters refused to pay it to him, he cannot sue them successfully; as a Mr. Appleson discovered when he brought an action against Littlewoods for £4,335 which he alleged was due to him: *Appleson v Littlewoods Ltd.*, [1939] 1 All E.R. 464.

The use of words such as 'subject to contract' or 'subject to the preparation and approval of a formal contract' indicate clearly enough that the parties do not intend to be bound at that stage even though they may have agreed all the essential details. It is common practice in England (though not in Scotland) to insert these words in the preliminary agreements for the purchase and sale of houses. One result is that the seller may change his mind about selling or raise the selling price later or accept a better offer, without the buyer having any redress in law against him; conversely, of course, it enables the buyer to opt out of the bargain if he finds he is unable to sell his own house, raise the necessary mortgage, or if he simply changes his mind.

Words other than those mentioned above have to be interpreted according to the view the Court takes of the parties' intentions. 'I accept your offer and have asked my solicitors to prepare a contract' was held to have created immediate contractual obligations, even though no formal contract was ever prepared: *Rossiter v Miller*, [1878] All E.R. Rep. 465.

More recently, when a Mr. Cobarro agreed to sell a mushroom farm to a Mr. Branca the parties signed a document which read: 'This is a provisional agreement until a fully legalised agreement, drawn up by a solicitor and embodying all the conditions herewith stated, is signed.' On the true construction of the document the Court of Appeal held that it was intended to be a contractual obligation from the moment it was signed, and binding until a later document of the character described had been executed. But the Court was at pains to stress that each case of this character was one of the true interpretation to be placed on the document in question by the Court as an expression of the intention of the parties: *Branca v Cobarro*, [1947] 2 All E.R. 101.

Agreement between trade unions and employers or associations of employers were held not to be contractual in *Ford Motor Co. v A.U.E.*, [1969] 2 All E.R. 481, partly on the ground that most of the promises were too vague to enforce—'mere pious aspirations'— but more because in the light of the opinions expressed to the Donovan Commission on Trade Unions by both trade union officials and employers neither party ever intended that such agreements should be actionable as contracts. This authority was reversed by the *Industrial Relations Act, 1971*, so that the presumption now is that such agreements are intended as contracts unless the parties specify otherwise—as they invariably do.

Statutory Undertakings and Contractual Intent

A more debatable development within recent years is seen in a number of cases in which the Courts have held that corporations created by Act of Parliament and charged with specific duties, such as the supply of water, gas or electricity, are merely fulfilling their statutory obligations when they supply their customers, and have no intentions of making contracts with them.

The earliest case of this kind appears to be *Milnes v Huddersfield Corporation*, [1886-90] All E.R. Rep. 350, where it was held that there was no contractual obligation by a water company created by Act of Parliament towards those it supplied.

The same thing was said in relation to a gas company later in *Clegg Parkson and Co. v Earby Gas Co.* (1896): 'the obligation of the Company if any, depends on Statute and not upon contract'.

So when, in October 1937, the Croydon Corporation distributed to consumers, through its mains, water that was contaminated by typhoid germs and started an epidemic in which over 300 people became infected and 43 died, the Corporation succeeded in escaping liability in contract. Had it been a contract, those injured would have been entitled to damages under the *Sale of Goods Act, 1893*, since water (like milk) is a chattel. Damages would have been recoverable whether or not the Corporation had been negligent, since the water was clearly not fit for the purpose required. But Stable J. held that the relationship was not a contractual one, but 'a relationship between two persons under which one is bound to supply water and the other, provided he has paid the equivalent rent, is entitled to receive it': *Read v Croydon Corporation*, [1938] 4 All E.R. 631.

This principle was apparently regarded as so axiomatic that none of these cases appears even to have been discussed in *Willmore v South Eastern Electricity Board* (1957). Mr. and Mrs. Willmore started in business as poultry farmers rearing chicks by infra-red heat and the South Eastern Electricity Board promised them an adequate and persistent supply of electricity to maintain lamps for that purpose. This the Board failed to do, with the result that the lamps chilled, the chicks died and Mr. and Mrs. Willmore were ruined financially. The judge held that the representations about proper supply of electricity were not made *animo contrahiendi*, as he put it,—'with contractual intent'—and there was no contract at all between the South Eastern Electricity Board and the unfortunate consumers. 'I have come to the conclusion that the plaintiffs, having failed to prove a contract, can have no cause of action for damages for breach of contract.'

Presumably on the basis that it is best to ignore what you disapprove of, none of these cases finds mention in the leading practitioners' monograph on the Law of Contract; but with the creation of new statutory bodies coming into existence all the time, if this is the law—as it appears to be—then it is time it was not. No judge yet seems to have considered that what Parliament intended may well have been to charge these bodies with the duty to accept contractual obligations to their customers.

Long before this principle was invented, it had been held that no contractual obligations arose out of the carriage of letters by post—a principle that extends as far back as 1701. You cannot therefore sue the Post Office Corporation if they lose a valuable letter—as Triefus and Co. Ltd. discovered with the G.P.O. in 1957, when registered packages of diamonds dispatched to New Zealand disappeared in the course of transmission, thanks to the activities of a light-fingered member of the post office staff: *Triefus v General Post Office*, [1957] 2 All E.R. 387.

Domestic Arrangements

There is one class of case in which the law almost invariably presumes that the parties do not intend to contract. These are cases where members of one family are the parties. A civil servant employed in Ceylon left his wife behind in the United Kingdom and (in 1915) promised her housekeeping money of £30 a month until he returned. He never did return, and eventually the wife obtained a *decree nisi* of divorce and then sued for the sum outstanding on the promise to pay her £30 per month. She was unsuccessful, the Court holding that such agreements are not sued upon 'because the parties never intended that they should be sued upon': *Balfour v Balfour*, [1919] All E.R. Rep. 860.

The same presumption applies where husband and wife make an arrangement between themselves about a joint bank account (*Cage v King*, [1960] 3 All E.R. 62). And even where a husband bought his wife a car in the vain hope that it would improve relations between them, and allowed her to register it in her own name, it was held to be still his property, i.e. there was no contract making her the owner: *Spellman v Spellman*, [1961] 2 All E.R. 498.

A different situation may arise between husband and wife where the parties have separated or are about to do so. Then any arrangements they come to about their assets may well be assumed to have been intended as contractual. In *Merritt v Merritt*, [1970] 2 All E.R. 760 the husband had deserted his wife and he came to an agreement in writing with her about the house they jointly owned. 'In such a case, where an agreement is reached as to the ownership of the matrimonial home . . . the supposition is that a legal relationship is intended,' held Stamp J., finding that there was a contract between the two.

The presumption that there is no contract intended between members of the same family can be rebutted in other circumstances as well. For example, where relatives gave up their own house and in reliance on promises, moved into a joint household, in *Parker v Clark*, [1960] 1 All E.R. 93 it was held there was a contract and so too where a number of people living in the same house, two of whom were related, formed a syndicate to enter newspaper competitions: *Simpkins v Pays*, [1955] 3 All E.R. 10. Obviously, in circumstances where each member of the same family contributed to a stake on the pools, the intention is that the prize shall be shared out irrespective of whose name is on the coupon, and not that the one who sends the coupon in shall be entitled to keep the whole of any prize that is won. It is reasonable therefore to infer that the intention also was that a remedy by way of action should be given if sharing out was not done.

This question of contractual intention is independent of the provision of any consideration for the promises but it is obviously related to it and was so held to be in *Parker v Clark*. The judge did not accept that Clark could really believe that the law allowed him if he chose, 'to tell the Parkers when they arrived that he had changed his mind, that they could take their furniture away, and that he was indifferent whether they found anywhere to live or not'. It is somewhat surprising therefore that *Jones v Padavatton*, [1969] 2 All E.R. 616 was decided as it was by the Court of Appeal. The plaintiff was the daughter of the defendant and in reliance on the mother's promise to make her an allowance of $200 a month and pay her fees while she was reading for the Bar in London, gave up highly paid and pensionable diplomatic employment in Washington D.C. and moved to London. This promise was confirmed in writing by the mother's attorney in Trinidad. The majority of the Appeal judges held there was no contractual obligation intended, but one can only endorse the observation of Lord Justice Salmon, dissenting, 'I cannot think that either intended that if, after the daughter had been in London, say, for six months, the mother dishonoured her promise and left her daughter destitute, the daughter would have no legal redress. And, surely, there can be no stronger indication of contractual intention than having a letter sent by a lawyer.'

The position regarding families can be summarised in four propositions:

1. Normally, the members of the same family do not intend to contract and the presumption is that any arrangements, even financial, that they make amongst themselves is not a contract.
2. This presumption can be rebutted by evidence to the contrary.
3. The test is not what the parties themselves in fact intended or what their own views were or are, as to their legal liabilities, but what a reasonable man would conclude was their intention. 'The reasonable man' being in reality the view of the Court as to what the mythical reasonable man might believe.
4. Where husband and wife are about to separate, or have done so, any agreement about the disposal of property will be presumed to have been intended as a contractual obligation to be enforced by action if necessary.

Social Arrangements

There is an even stronger presumption that social arrangements, such as taking friends out to dinner, promising to take a girl to the cinema, or away on holiday, are not intended as contractual obligations. That is so even if money may pass from one to another. A man named Coward regularly travelled to work on the pillion of a friend's motor cycle and paid him for the privilege. 'In the absence of evidence that the parties intended to be bound contractually, we should be reluctant to conclude that the daily carriage by one of another to work upon payment of some weekly sum involved them in a legal contractual relationship,' held the Court of Appeal: *Coward v Motor Insurers Bureau*, [1962] 1 All E.R. 531. A similar arrangement in *Buckpitt v Oates*, [1968] 1 All E.R. 1145 was described by the judge as 'a friendly arrangement . . . which gave rise to no legal obligation or rights except those which the general law of the land imposed'.

But in some circumstances even social arrangements might be

found by a court to be intended as contractual, especially if one party has wholly performed his obligations and the other has not—even though that factor is not really relevant to the imputed intention of the parties at the time when the agreement was made. It is possible that an agreement between two friends that on a journey across Europe one will pay for the petrol and the other the hotels might well be construed by the Courts, along the lines of *Parker v Clark* and *Simpkin v Pays*, as a contract. In all these matters of intent, it is essentially an issue of fact to be decided upon the evidence.

Parol Promises without Consideration

Even if a promise be intended to amount to a contractual obliga- tion it will not be enforced unless there is consideration for it. But this only applies to what are termed 'parol' or simple promises— those not contained in a deed under seal; that is to say, those made orally, in writing, or by conduct. English law has a superstitious reverence for deeds, even though nowadays the act of executing a deed consists of nothing more than signing it and putting a finger on a circle while proclaiming, 'I deliver this as my act and deed.'

But if a man promises another £10 at Christmas in writing, that cannot be sued upon successfully; if he does so by deed, it can be. And it can be too if, in return for the promise of £10, he requires a peppercorn, or, apparently, a couple of used chocolate wrappers.

In the 19th century lawyers were given to defining **consideration** in terms of profit or loss. The classic, oft-repeated definition is that given by the Court in *Currie v Misa* 1875, [1874–80] All E.R. Rep. 686:

> 'some right, interest, profit or benefit accruing to one party, or some forbearance, detriment, loss or responsibility given, suffered or undertaken by the other'.

In other words, consideration is a benefit to the promisor or a detriment to the promisee.

But this definition is defective in that:

(i) it does not make it clear that a promise given in exchange for a promise is adequate consideration. This has been the law ever since, in *Strangborough v Warner* (1589), the reporter noted 'a promise against a promise will maintain an action on an *assumpsit*'. (Probably what he really meant, however, was that the plaintiff need show no loss other than the fact that he had bound himself by promise in return for the defendant's.)

(ii) a detriment to the promisee incurred at the request of the promisor is sufficient consideration even though no benefit is conferred on the promisor, and

(iii) there is consideration if the promisor does benefit (or some third party at his request) even though it costs the promisee nothing.

Another well-known definition is that of *Dunlop v Selfridges*, 1915 [1914–15] All E.R. Rep. 333, a case which, as Lord Dunedin said in the course of it, 'is apt to nip any budding affection one might have for the doctrine of consideration'.

'An act or forbearance of one party, or the promise thereof, is the price for which the promise of the other is bought and the promise thus given for value is enforceable.'

How this extraordinary doctrine originated is a matter of some controversy amongst legal historians, but about its purpose there can be no dispute. It was thought originally to provide a test of which promises the law should enforce. If a man got something for his promise it could be presumed that he had intended his promise to be enforceable at law and therefore had undertaken contractual obligations; i.e. it was purely of evidential value in determining contractual intent. But, as is abundantly apparent from *Jones v Padavatton* (see page 79), this function has entirely disappeared.

It should also be remembered that right up to the middle of the last century there were two sorts of consideration sufficient to support a promise. As J. T. Powell put it in his *Essay on Law of Contract and Agreement*, the first legal monograph on the subject, which went through successive editions both here and in the United States after the first in 1788:

'A contract may be supported either by a valuable consideration: as marriage, work done etc. or by a good consideration: as that of blood or natural affection between near relations.'

Today, 'good consideration' is bad consideration. An antecedent moral obligation, family reasons or affection is not sufficient to make a promise binding. The facts of the case which was largely responsible for this change in law as it had been understood and established for two hundred and fifty years is, in itself, sufficient condemnation of the present doctrine. Sarah Sutcliffe had been left an orphan and Eastwood, her guardian, spent his own (borrowed) money on her education and the preservation of her small estate. When she came of age she promised to reimburse him; later she married a Mr. Kenyon, bringing to him of course by the laws of those days all her estate, and he also promised in writing the same. When they were sued, however, it was held that there was not sufficient consideration to support these promises: *Eastwood v Kenyon* 1840, [1835–42] All E.R. Rep. 133.

How long we shall have to live with this legal coelacanth is difficult to say. The Law Revision Committee in 1937 recommended the abolition of the rule in its present form, but no action has been taken on that report.

One result is that today there is neither logic nor juridical justification for many of the decisions on consideration. If the judges want to uphold a promise they find consideration, or discreetly ignore the absence of it; if they don't want to, they find there is no consideration. The Court of Appeal have even found a *contractual* licence where a woman was allowed to live in a house rent free for the rest of her life: *Binions v Evans, The Times* 28th January 1972. The reader will find more of the real reason for the decision in *Combe v Combe,* [1951] 1 All E.R. 767 in Denning L.J.'s comment: 'I do not think it right for this wife, who is better off than her husband, to take no action for six or seven years, and then demand from him the whole £600', than in the legal ones advanced in the judgment. The reader must not therefore expect to find in the decisions that follow any connection at all with logic and little with justice.

Consideration may be executed or executory but it must not be past

By **executed consideration** is meant performance by one party contemporaneous with the promise of the other. If a man gives another a pot of paint in return for the promise, express or implied, of the other to pay for it, the consideration on the seller's side is executed.

Executory consideration is consideration which lies in the future—something still to be performed. The consideration on the part of the man who has yet to pay for his pot of paint is executory. So it is, of course, on both sides in all contracts where a promise is exchanged for a promise.

Past consideration is something that has happened before the promise is made. A man rescues a boy from drowning in a canal and the grateful father promises him £10 when he gets his pay packet on Friday. The promise is unenforceable—the act was completed before the promise was given. Mr. Eastwood in the case cited earlier spends his own money to educate Sarah and prevent her cottages falling down. Too bad, says the law. Her promise and that of her husband, who is now enjoying the fruits of Mr. Eastwood's expenditure, do not create a contractual obligation to reimburse him. For by the time when the promises were given, it had all been done.

A doctor called to an unconscious man gives expensive injections and when the patient recovers he promises to pay the doctor a reasonable fee. The doctor cannot sue—the consideration was past.

This is 'The law of the ingrates', as a European writer, reared in the Roman law tradition, has called it, as will be seen from *Re McArdle,* [1951] 1 All E.R. 905. When Mr. McArdle died he left a will under which his widow was entitled to live in the house for her lifetime and after her death their five children were to be entitled to it in equal shares. One daughter-in-law expended money on repairs and improvements to the house in question and later the five children all signed a document promising to repay her when the house was eventually sold. It was held that since this agreement came into existence after the money had been expended, it was not binding. The five children were entitled to take the house with the benefit of the improvements and not pay the daughter-in-law a penny.

There is one situation, however, where the common law still retains some of its original virtue. If the plaintiff does something *at the request of the defendant* and if the thing is of such a nature that a promise to pay can reasonably be implied at the time, a subsequent promise will be binding.

Brathwait had killed a man and asked Lampleigh to obtain a pardon from the King for him. This Lampleigh succeeded in doing, and the other then promised him £100 for his services. The Court held that 'The previous request and subsequent promise were to be treated as part of the same transaction': *Lampleigh v Brathwait* (1615).

Two inventors assigned a third of their joint patents to a Mr. Casey 'on consideration of your services as the practical manager in working both our patents'. It was argued that the assignment was not valid because all that Casey had done took place before the assignment and therefore the consideration was past. Bowen L.J. in rejecting this argument said:

'The fact of a past service raises an implication that at the time it was rendered it was to be paid for, and if so . . . when you get a subsequent promise to pay, the promise may be treated either as an admission which evidences, or as a positive bargain which fixes the amount of that reasonable remuneration, on the faith of which the service was originally rendered.' *Re Casey's Patents* (1892).

Consideration need not be adequate but must be of value in the eyes of the law

Provided a promisor got *something* for his promise, the common law always refused to inquire into whether it was an adequate recompense. That was up to the parties. If one chose to sell a Rolls-Royce in return for a packet of cigarettes, well—that was his contract and he had to stick to it.

The Court of Chancery, however, would formerly grant relief for what it termed 'unconscionable bargains', as in the case of the 'commodity loans' of Elizabethan times, where young men with expectations were induced to give their bond under seal for a consignment of goods which were then sold for a fraction of the price they had undertaken to pay for them; a moneylending device at extortionate rates of interest. Equity would also grant relief where a man sold his reversion in an estate for a trifle or, like the Earl of Aylesford of 1873 who, at the age of 22, borrowed money, at 60% interest per annum against his large expectations. Much of this equity jurisdiction has now been replaced by either *Moneylender Acts* or by the *Infants' Relief Act*, and although it would perhaps be premature to describe the equity doctrine as completely obsolete, there are no recorded cases since the Eighties of the last century. (Although, there was, apparently, an unreported case in 1968.) But even as early as 1676, it was being said 'The Chancery mends no man's bargain.'

The present legal position seems therefore to be that the Courts will not interfere with 'unfair' contracts. Miss Frances Day, the then well-known comedienne, made a contract with Gaumont-British which, her counsel complained, showed 'a want of mutuality' —in other words, the contract she had made was unfair. But she was held to it: *Gaumont-British v Alexander*, [1936] 2 All E.R. 1686.

Nestlé, the chocolate manufacturers, offered gramophone records for 1s 6d, plus three used chocolate wrappers. A question having arisen under the Copyrights Acts whether the 1s 6d was the sole consideration, the Court decided that the used chocolate wrappers comprised further consideration: *Chappell and Co. Ltd. v Nestlé's*, [1959] 2 All E.R. 701. Logically, therefore, even three used chocolate wrappers can constitute the sole consideration for a contract—even if they are thrown away immediately they are received. Provided a man gets that for which he stipulated, and it is of some value, the Courts will not enter into whether a consideration was adequate or not. As Lord Somervell said in the Nestlé's case: 'A peppercorn does not cease to be good consideration even if it is established that the promisee does not like pepper and will throw away the corn.'

The second half of the proposition above, that the 'consideration must be of some value in the eyes of the law', is much more difficult to justify or explain.

In the first place, it means in these days that *'good consideration'*— that is to say moral obligation, affection or family duty—is not valuable consideration sufficient to support a promise. It means, too, that the consideration must not be entirely illusionary—so that, at present, the promise of a fortnight's holiday on the moon is hardly likely to rank as valuable consideration. What is more, *unlawful or illegal consideration*—whether it be a promise to pay a girl £20 per week while she cohabits with the promisor, or to divide in equal

D

shares the proceeds of a bank robbery—is not valuable consideration in the eyes of the law.

In the last century, one could have said with some confidence that valuable consideration meant something of some value—however trifling—in a commercial or economic sense. But our mercenary ancestors of the 19th century have given way to more humane theories and, as we shall see, the Court of Appeal apparently is prepared to hold that a promise to keep a child 'well and happy' afforded valuable consideration (see page 87).

It is also somewhat difficult to see what valuable consideration exists in other cases. *Godfrey Davis v Culling*, (1962) arose out of the collapse of an insurance company called Fire, Auto. A motorist took his car in for repairs under his policy of insurance with this company, and the company specifically authorised the garage to effect the repairs at its expense. When the company became insolvent after the work was done, and the garage knew they were unable to recover their expenses from the insurance company, the garage sued the motorist. The Court held there was no obligation on the motorist, on the impeccable grounds that (a) he had never promised, expressly or implied, to pay for the repairs and (b) there was no consideration to support a contract between the garage and the motorist.

A somewhat different situation arose in *Charnock v Liverpool Corporation*, [1968] 3 All E.R. 473. Here the motorist had taken his car into a garage for repairs at the charge of his insurance company but the garage negligently delayed executing the work, and the motorist sued for the hire of a substitute vehicle. The Court of Appeal this time held there *was* a contract between the motorist and the garage. What constituted valuable consideration moving from the promisee was glossed over, and it is difficult to see how the mere act of leaving a car with a garage for them to effect repairs to it could possibly constitute valuable consideration. It was nothing more than a condition precedent to his receiving a benefit.

Forbearance to sue is Valuable Consideration

After a good deal of hesitation, and numerous conflicting decisions, it was eventually decided that a promise to refrain from instituting legal proceedings amounts to valuable consideration, as does the compromise of the action which has already begun. So that if Tom offers Harry that if Harry will promise not to sue Bert for an outstanding debt, he—Tom—will pay the debt, the promises are binding.

Even the surrender of a possible but somewhat nebulous right to bring an action for the rectification of a document has been held to provide valuable consideration. When Mr. and Mrs. Horton separated, the husband executed a separation agreement whereby he promised to pay his wife 'the monthly sum of £30'. A later, supplemental, agreement was signed by the husband whereby the monetary consideration was made '£30 a month *free of tax*'. The only consideration the Court of Appeal could discover to make this second promise binding was a forbearance by the wife from suing to correct the first agreement: *Horton v Horton No. 2*, [1960] 3 All E.R. 649.

But this principle does not apply where the forbearance is entirely illusionary—as where a bookmaker agrees to refrain from suing an undergraduate on a gaming debt in return for a promise from the youth's father to pay. For the bookmaker knows full well that he cannot possibly succeed at law (see page 133) and therefore he is not in fact giving anything up at all. There is no detriment to him in a promise to give up a right which he knows he does not possess.

Nor does it apply if what the promisee surrenders is merely a moral and not a legal claim against the promisor: *Scott v Ricketts*, [1967] 2 All E.R. 1009.

If, however, an intending litigant believes in all good faith that he has a claim at law, even though in reality he has not, and such a one promises to renounce his right to sue in return for some consideration from the other party, then this is sufficient to make the contract binding. The test, therefore, appears to be whether the renunciation is of a legal right which is believed to be a valid and *bona fide* cause of action.

The compromise of a disputed claim is therefore always good consideration, provided there is in fact a genuine dispute: *Callisher v Bischoffsheim* (1870).

Consideration and the Performance of Existing Duties

An area of considerable controversy amongst lawyers is whether there is valuable consideration in a promise to perform a duty which in one way or another, already rests on the promisor; and whether the actual performance of that duty can be valuable consideration. Lord Denning has said, more than once, 'I have always thought that a promise to perform an existing duty or the performance of it, should be regarded as good consideration because it is a benefit to the person to whom it is given.' *Williams v Williams*, [1957] 1 All E.R. 305. But every promise is a benefit to the person to whom it is given—the promisee—and that certainly does not amount to consideration unless the promisee is required to do something for it in exchange. 'Whenever a person promises without benefit arising to the promisor or loss to the promisee, it is considered as a void promise' is the classic definition.

The whole subject however, is involved with two other problems. The first one is **public policy.** By that is meant the doctrine that there are some otherwise valid contractual obligations which are not enforced because the judges think it is not in the public interest that they should be. That is a doctrine which has to be examined later in some detail (see page 121). But there are cases which appear in the current textbooks where promises were held not to be enforceable for want of consideration, where the real reason was that it was not regarded as being in the public interest that they should be enforced.

The other problem is that of the **unilateral contract** (see page 145). If the promise is unilateral, as opposed to synallagmatic, and the promisee does the very thing for which he is to be rewarded, is there any reason why he should not receive the promised remuneration —even though he may already be under an existing duty to do the very thing? A police constable has a duty to arrest criminals. If he arrests one for whose arrest a reward has been offered, is there any reason why he should not claim the reward? Our ancestors thought not, as early as *England v Davidson* (1840). Now, however, Statute has intervened regarding police officers and rewards.

The manager of a supermarket is under a duty to promote sales to the full extent of his ability. But, is there any reason, if the proprietor offers him £500 bonus if he doubles the sales during the next month, why he should not be entitled to claim it? Can the proprietor shrug it off by saying, when the manager has achieved the specified target, 'There was no consideration for my promise of an extra £500 —you were only doing what it was your duty already to do'?

These are two of the problems which have confused discussion of whether there is consideration present when there is an existing duty.

It is useful to discuss this topic under four headings:

(i) Where the existing duty is a moral one, even though it does also constitute an obligation imposed by the general law.
(ii) Where the existing duty is purely a legal one.
(iii) Where the existing duty is a contractual obligation to a third party, i.e. neither the promisor nor the promisee.
(iv) Where the existing duty is a contractual obligation to the other contracting party.

Consideration and Existing Moral Duty

The father of an illegitimate child promised the mother of the child one pound a week provided the child was 'well looked after and happy'; and for some considerable time paid the money. Later the mother married another man, and the father then discontinued the payments. When sued, he raised the defence that there was no consideration for his promise because, in law and morality, the mother of an illegitimate child is bound to maintain and support it. The Court of Appeal held the promise was binding. Denning L.J. regarded it as a unilateral promise, 'a promise in return for an act, a promise by the father to pay £1 a week in return for the mother's looking after the child. Once the mother embarked on the task of looking after the child there was a binding contract.' In other words, the only necessary consideration was doing what the promisor required—even though it was already her duty. What the two other judges held is far from clear, but they appear to have decided that in promising to keep the child 'well and happy' she was doing more than her duty and there was therefore fresh consideration: *Ward v Byham*, [1956] 2 All E.R. 318.

In another case around the same period, a wife had deserted her husband and thereby, of course, forfeited all right to maintenance from him so long as she remained in desertion. Notwithstanding that, the husband entered into an agreement with her to pay her thirty shillings a week 'so long as the wife shall lead a chaste life', and provided she maintained herself. Later the husband disputed the agreement for want of consideration and once again the Court of Appeal was called on to decide this point. Undoubtedly she, by promising to lead a chaste life and to maintain herself, was only doing what she was already under both a legal and moral duty to do. Once again, Denning L.J. grasped the nettle: 'A promise to perform an existing duty is, I think, sufficient consideration to support a promise, so long as there is nothing in the transaction which is contrary to the public interest.' Again, what the other judges decided is obscure, but they appear to be saying that there was some fresh consideration in that the wife might change her mind and offer to return to the husband, in which case his liability to maintain her might revive: *Williams v Williams*, [1957] 1 All E.R. 305.

The only conclusion one can draw from these decisions is that the Courts will not be over zealous in finding want of consideration where the promise was made and the existing duty was a moral one.

Incidentally, the law was altered about maintenance agreements between husband and wife shortly after *Williams v Williams* by the *Maintenance Agreements Act, 1957* (now the 1965 Act). One view of the wording of the Statute is that maintenance agreements do not require consideration at all.

Consideration and Existing Legal Duties

In *Collins v Godefroy* (1831) the plaintiff was served with a subpoena to attend a trial in the King's Bench at Westminster Hall and was promised by the party requiring his attendance one guinea a day for his loss of time. It was held by Lord Tenderden C.J. that this was a promise without consideration, for the duty on the plaintiff to attend was one imposed by law. Although expressly based on that ground by the judge, earlier decisions to similar effect seem to have been based on the more rational idea that it was in those days contrary to public policy that witnesses called to give evidence should be paid. Nowadays, of course, we accept that as a commonplace and reasonable requirement.

That decision has bedevilled English law for nearly a century and a half. For it has been taken to mean that if there is a legal obligation on a person to do something and he undertakes to another to do the same thing, in return for a promise of remuneration, then the promisor is not obliged to fulfil his promise because there is no consideration for it.

In 1921 the Glamorgan Police Force were asked to provide 100 police officers to be billeted on the premises of Glasbrook's Colliery near Swansea for fear that striking miners were going to get the safety men 'out', and the mine would therefore be flooded. The proprietors of the mine signed a document that they would not only pay for the services of the officers but also their travelling expenses and provide them with food and sleeping accommodation.

In due course the bill for these services, amounting to £2,200 11s 10d was rendered by the police authority, the Glamorgan County Council; and the colliery owners, Glasbrook Bros. Ltd., refused to pay the bill, raising the defence that the police were doing no more than was their duty and therefore there was no consideration for their, Glasbrook's, written promise to pay for the protection they had enjoyed. The case was fought all the way up to the House of Lords, where a bare majority of the Law Lords—three to two—decided that the colliery owners' promise was binding, on the ground that the number of constables provided was in excess of what the local police superintendent thought was necessary and therefore provided consideration over and above the obligation resting on the police to take all steps necessary for protecting property from criminal injury: *Glasbrook Bros. Ltd. v Glamorgan County Council*, [1924] All E.R. 579.

The case has been a leading authority ever since; so that if you request constables to police a pop festival or guard your wedding presents from light-fingered gentry who may be masquerading as guests, your promise to pay for their services will amount to a contractual obligation.

Had it occurred to their Lordships, it would have been a more satisfactory and logical justification for their decision, to hold that the obligation to provide the constables was, on a true construction of the contract, a unilateral obligation. In other words, that the obligation was not in reality mutual; for it can scarcely have been held that if the Chief Constable had withdrawn every single officer from Glasbrook's pit because they were needed to cope with a massive riot in some adjacent town, and the mine had been flooded by the withdrawal of the safety men, that the Police Authority would have been liable for the enormous damages which might well have resulted.

However, as the law stands at the moment the position appears to be that if nothing more is done in return for the promise than is already an existing duty in law, there is no consideration for a promise to pay, and the promise is not binding; whereas if something more is done, then the promise is binding.

Consideration and Contractual Obligations to Third Parties

Happily, here the law is both simple and clear (though the Law Revision Commission of 1937 thought it wasn't). If Tom is under a contractual obligation to Harry to do a certain thing, and Bill chooses to promise Tom further remuneration for doing exactly the same thing, there is consideration for both contracts. As Baron Wilde said as long ago as 1861: 'There is no authority for the proposition that where there has been a promise to one person to do a certain thing, it is not possible to make a valid promise to another to do the same thing.'

In *Scotson v Pegg* (1861), the plaintiff was the owner of a ship which contained a part cargo of coal consigned to the defendants. It was therefore, in any event, the plaintiff's contractual duty to the shipper to deliver the coal to the defendant. The defendant promised the plaintiffs to discharge the cargo of coal at the rate of 49 tons a working day, but failed to do so and when sued for damages set up the defence that since the plaintiff was already under a contractual duty to the shipper to deliver the coal to him, there was no consideration for *his* promise. The promise was held binding.

In the course of argument Baron Martin put the case: 'Suppose a man promised to marry on a certain day and before that day arrived he refused, on the grounds that his income was not sufficient, whereupon the father of the intended wife said to him, "If you will marry my daughter, I will allow you a £1,000 a year." Could not that promise be enforced?'

Somewhat similar circumstances arose in a case called *Shadwell v Shadwell* (1860). An uncle wrote to his nephew, a young barrister, 'I am glad to hear of your intended marriage with Ellen Nicholl and as I promised to assist you at starting, I am happy to tell you that I will pay to you one hundred and fifty pounds yearly during my lifetime.' The promise was held to be a contractually binding obligation. There was much discussion about detriment and benefit and whether there was any consideration, since clearly on the facts the young man was not marrying at his uncle's request. The case has been bitterly fought over by academic lawyers ever since, and disapproved of by Salmon L.J. Is it in reality any different than if I were to promise you a wedding present and failed to deliver it?

Perhaps the only satisfactory explanation is to construe the letter as a simple unilateral promise to the effect 'if you marry Ellen Nicholl I will pay you £150 a year' and forget all about benefit to the promisor or detriment to the promisee; though one cannot help wondering whether if the recipient of the promise had been a young doctor instead of a young barrister, the conclusion would have been the same.

Consideration and Contractual Obligations to the Promisor

When a promisee is already under a contractual duty to a promisor, the general rule is that there can be no consideration for a further promise by the promisor, unless the promisee has to do something more than he had originally undertaken.

The cases originally relied upon for this doctrine are those of sailors who have been promised higher wages for doing what they had already contracted to do—working a ship to a port. But, once again, the question whether there was or was not consideration has become confused with the issues of public policy, as to whether such promises should be enforced. In *Harris v Watson* 1791, [1775–1882] All E.R. Rep. 493, a seaman was promised an extra five guineas by the captain when the ship was in danger; for that he had extra work in navigation to do apart from his normal duties. Chief Justice Lord Kenyon in dismissing the sailor's claim said: 'If this action was to be supported, it would materially affect the navigation of the Kingdom. . . . If in times of danger, (sailors) were entitled to insist upon an extra charge on such a promise as this, they would in many cases suffer a ship to sink unless the captain would pay an extravagant demand.'

But that remarkable reasoning was provided with a rather more rational basis by Lord Ellenborough in a case of which there are two conflicting reports. The plaintiff in *Stilk v Myrick* (1809) was a seaman engaged for a voyage from London to the Baltic and back for £5 a month. When two members of the crew deserted in Cronstadt, the captain promised to divide the wages of the deserters amongst the rest of the crew. 'Those who remain,' Lord Ellenborough held (according to one report), 'are bound by the terms of their original contract to exert themselves to the utmost to bring the ship in safety to her destined port. Therefore . . . (the promise) is void for want of consideration.'

A somewhat similar case, *Hartley v Ponsonby* (1857), where the sailors were held able to recover, is distinguishable because in that case there was an express finding by a jury that because the full complement of thirty-six sailors had been reduced by desertion to a mere nineteen—of whom only four or five of them were Able Seamen—the sailors remaining were discharged from their original contract. The result was that they were free if they chose to make a new contract with their employers, and it was on this new contract that they succeeded.

A modern application of the principle is to be found in *Swain v West (Butchers) Ltd.*, [1936] 3 All E.R. 261. A manager of a butchering business had been caught out removing marks of origin from the carcasses of beasts—an infringement of the law which entitled the company which employed him to dismiss him. The Chairman promised not to dismiss him if he disclosed irregularities which had taken place by the Managing Director. He did so, but even so was dismissed. It was held that there was no consideration for the promise, because the manager was already under a contractual duty to make a full disclosure to the company of all matters concerning their interests.

Presumably therefore, if the management of a company offer a fortnight's holiday in Bermuda to any salesman who doubles his sales within six months, that promise will not be contractually binding since the salesman is already under an existing duty to use his utmost efforts to promote his employers' interests; but one cannot believe that is what a court would really hold. In that case they would probably say, 'This is a unilateral promise and if the salesman performs the act required, that is all the consideration that is necessary.'

Consideration and the Release of Debts

If a creditor is owed £100 and promises to accept from the debtor the sum of £80 in full satisfaction, that promise is not binding because there is no consideration for it. He can, therefore, collect the £80 and sue for the balance in spite of his promise.

This grossly immoral rule of the common law is attributed to what is known as *Pinnel's Case*, [1602] All E.R. Rep. 612. This was an action on a bond under seal by which £8 10s was to be paid on the 11th November, 1600. The defendant debtor at the plaintiff's request on 1st October, 1600—that is earlier than the due date—paid £5 2s 2d which the creditor accepted in full satisfaction of the whole sum. In so far as the case itself is concerned, it made no law; the plaintiff, the creditor, won on a technical knockout because of insufficient particularity of pleading by the defendant. The law was made by Coke's observation in his *Institutes* later, that all the judges of the Court of Common Pleas had agreed 'that payment of a lesser sum on the day in satisfaction of a greater cannot be satisfaction for the whole . . . but the gift of a horse, a hawk or a robe etc. in satisfaction is good'. This observation, which of course formed no part of the *ratio decidendi* of *Pinnel's Case*, first saw the light of day in print more than a quarter of a century after the case that is reputed to have given rise to it, and there are reported cases in the interval that refute it. However that may be, it passed into law and in the 19th century received the accolade of the House of Lords in another case of dubious logic and even worse law.

In 1875 a Mrs. Julie Beer obtained judgment in the High Court against Dr. John Foakes for the sum of £2,000 19s. Since Dr. Foakes could not pay at once, a document in writing was drawn up between the parties whereby Mrs. Beer promised 'not to take any proceedings whatever on the said judgment' provided Dr. Foakes paid the money by instalments, This the Doctor did; every penny of it. Mrs. Beer then broke her promise by proceeding to enforce the judgment by asking for leave to levy execution for the interest accrued since the judgment—£350. The case wended its way from the High Court to the Queen's Bench Divisional Court to the Court of Appeal until it finally appeared in the year 1884 in the House of Lords. In spite of the fact that Dr. Foakes was not seeking to set up a contract, the House of Lords held that the rule in *Pinnel's Case* applied and Mrs. Beer was entitled to her £350—plus costs, of course: *Foakes v Beer* 1884, [1881–5] All E.R. Rep. 106.

The same principle has been applied within recent times in *D. & C. Builders Ltd. v Rees*, [1965] 3 All E.R. 837, where the plaintiffs were owed £482 13s 1d for work done as jobbing builders; being under financial pressure, they accepted £300 in full satisfaction and gave a receipt which read, 'Received the sum of £300 from Mr. Rees in completion of the account: Paid.' Then they successfully sued for the balance.

Had the receipt been delivered in a deed under seal, of course the release would have been binding; for such instruments, of course, require no consideration. And, of course, it would have been binding if the plaintiffs had accepted the £300 and a cigarette in discharge of the £482; for then there would have been fresh consideration which would have made the promise binding.

But the doctrine is law to date, notwithstanding (as Lord Denning has said) that it was ridiculed by Jessel M.R., held to be mistaken by Lord Blackburn and condemned by the Law Revision Committee.

Common Law Exceptions to the Rule in *Pinnel's Case*

Happily, this distasteful doctrine has been mitigated by certain common law exceptions:

Fresh consideration. As has been suggested already, if there is some fresh consideration—however trifling, since the law will not enter into the adequacy of consideration—the promise to release the rest of the debt will be binding. If the receipt in *D. & C. Builders v Rees* had read '£300 and a cabbage', the plaintiffs would have failed. Once the mere receipt of payment by cheque—which is, of course, a negotiable instrument—instead of cash was held to be fresh consideration; but in the *D. & C. Builders* case, the Court of Appeal held that it was not, reversing a decision which had stood unchallenged for more than 60 years.

Alteration in time or place of payment at the request of the creditor. Fresh consideration is also provided if the lesser sum *is at the request of the creditor* paid at an earlier date than due or in some other place than that nominated by the original agreement. But if this is done at the request of the debtor, this is not fresh consideration as an unfortunate Mr. Vanbergh discovered. He owed St. Edmunds Properties Ltd. a sum of £208 under a Court judgment. The solicitor for the company agreed that if Mr. Vanbergh paid that sum in cash into a bank at Eastbourne, no bankruptcy notice would be issued against him. Mr. Vanbergh did so—and was then served with a bankruptcy notice. The Court of Appeal held that there was no consideration for the promise not to issue the bankruptcy notice and therefore it was not binding. *Vanbergh v St. Edmunds Properties Ltd.*, [1933] All E.R. Rep. 488.

Payment of lesser sum by third party. In 1817 a creditor sued a son after having accepted in full and final satisfaction from his father half the money owed by the son. It was held that the creditor could not succeed. *Welby v Drake.* This principle was extended in *Hirachand v Temple* (1911), where Sir Richard Temple sent a draft for a lesser sum than that owed by his son in full settlement of the debt. Without comment, the draft was cashed and the plaintiff then sued the son for the balance. 'This draft having been sent to the plaintiffs and retained and cashed by them, we ought to draw the conclusion that the plaintiffs . . . agreed to accept it on the terms on which it was sent,' *held* Vaughan Williams L.J.

A quite astonishing variety of reasons have been advanced for this principle and it is better not to try to submit them to logical analysis, but to accept as a rule of law, as Fletcher Moulton L.J. put it: 'If a third person steps in and gives a consideration for the discharge of the debtor, it does not matter whether he does it in meal or malt, or what proportion the amount given bears to the amount of the debt . . . the debt (is) absolutely extinguished.'

Composition with creditors. If all the creditors of a debtor agree to abate their respective claims or even to forgo them entirely (*West Yorkshire Darracq Agency v Coleridge*, 1911) all these creditors are bound by their promise one to another. Again, it is profitless to seek for the consideration for these promises or the legal principle behind this rule. As the Law Revision Committee itself said, 'the problem (is) still unsolved, of discovering the consideration for a debtor's composition with his creditors'.

It would, of course, be presumptuous to suggest what, apparently, no judge has yet done, that the real explanation of both the last two circumstances described is the common law principle of estoppel.

Compromise of dispute as to amount. If in fact there is a genuine dispute as to the amount of the debt, a compromise of the acceptance of a lesser sum than that claimed will amount to fresh consideration.

Promissory or Equitable Estoppel

There is now a further restraint upon the doctrine that promises without consideration which are relied upon by the promisee as a release of existing contractual obligations to the promisor may be binding.

And just as the law in *Pinnel's Case* was made by an *obiter dictum*, so, too, this new doctrine emerged from observations made that were certainly no part of the *ratio decidendi* of the case in which they were expressed.

In 1947, Denning J., as he then was, was trying at first instance a case called *Central London Property Trust Ltd. v High Trees House*, [1956] 1 All E.R. 256, a case of so little legal importance, apparently, that the All England Law Reports did not then consider it worthy of inclusion in their series. The plaintiffs had granted to the defendants by deed the tenancy of a block of flats at a ground rent of £2,500 p.a. two years before the Second World War. When the war started the flats became virtually impossible to let, and by a simple agreement the plaintiffs and the defendants agreed to reduce the ground rent to half the sum specified in the lease. At the end of the war, the plaintiffs' successors in title then sought to return the ground rent to its original figure. In the course of argument, it was pointed out that not only were the plaintiffs not bound by the agreement at the outbreak of the war, but they could have, had they so chosen, on the basis of *Pinnel's Case*, have sued for the whole of the arrears, then amounting to £7,916.

To that proposition—which was not in issue before the Court— Denning J. came up with an answer which was to earn immortality for the *High Trees Case*. Where a promise is made 'which was intended to create legal relations and which, to the knowledge of the person making the promise, was going to be acted upon by the person to whom it was made, and which in fact was so acted upon . . . the promise must be honoured'. Even if there was no consideration.

'The logical consequence', the judge went on to say, 'is that a promise to accept a smaller sum in discharge of a larger sum, if acted upon, is binding notwithstanding the absence of consideration; and if the fusion of law and equity leads to the result, so much the better.'

The principle upon which he was proceeding—and extending—

was that set out by Lord Cairns in *Hughes v Metropolitan Rly.* 1877, [1874–80] All E.R. Rep. 187: 'It is the first principle upon which all courts of equity proceed that if parties who have entered into definite and distinct terms involving certain legal results . . . afterwards . . . enter upon a course of negotiation which has the effect of leading one of the parties to suppose that the strict rights arising under the contract will not be enforced . . . the person who might otherwise have enforced those rights will not be allowed to enforce them where it would be inequitable . . .' It was a principle that seven years later the same Court, the House of Lords, appears to have overlooked in *Foakes v Beer*.

This principle has now come to be described as *promissory estoppel* or *equitable estoppel*, although that is a contradiction in terms. Estoppel, as we have seen on page 33, only applies where there is a statement of existing fact, never where there is a promise as to future conduct. But whatever it may be called, it is now well-established law, making a promise without consideration binding in the following circumstances:

(i) Equitable estoppel 'affords a defence against the enforcement of otherwise enforceable rights but it cannot create a cause of action'. In other words, 'it is a shield but not a sword'. It applies only to the modification or discharge of existing contractual rights. 'The doctrine of consideration is too firmly fixed to be overthrown by a side wind,' said Denning L.J. in *Combe v Combe*, [1951] 1 All E.R. 767.

(ii) Except in the case of debt, it applies only to the suspension of existing contractual rights—not to their extinction.

(iii) It is still far from clear whether it is a prerequisite of the application of this equitable doctrine that the promisee must have relied upon the promise to his detriment, in the sense at least that he must have changed his position in consequence of it. Lord Denning in an article in the *Modern Law Review* has denied this necessity (1952 15 M.L.R. 1) but several cases seem to suggest the opposite.

(iv) It is essentially equitable relief to be denied to those who have not themselves behaved equitably; as in *D. & C. Builders Ltd. v Rees*, [1965] 3 All E.R. 837, where the plaintiffs were intimidated into signing the release [accepting £300 in satisfaction of the debt of £482 by the words, 'That is all you will get', and with the implied threat that if they didn't accept that they would get nothing at all.

Consideration Must Move From the Promisee

As has already been pointed out, the basic premise on which the doctrine of consideration rests is that the person to whom the promise

is made has to do something for it. It is not enough that consideration
has been given. It must be given by the very person to whom the
promise is made. So that if Tom promises Harry fifty pence if Bert
washes Tom's car, that promise is not binding. It is not binding
even if Bert is also a party to the contract. The consideration must
move from the promisee. As the Law Revision Committee acidly
remarked: 'We can see no reason, either of logic or public policy,
why *A* who has got what he wanted from *B* in exchange for his
promise should not be compelled by *C* to carry out that promise,
merely because *C*, a party to the contract, did not furnish the consideration.' But it is still the law. William owed John Price £13.
Easton promised William that if he would do some work for him,
he would pay John the £13. William did the work but Easton failed
to keep his promise to pay John Price. John Price sued Easton—and
lost. *He*, it was held, had given no consideration for the promise.
Price v Easton (1833). The doctrine appears to have originated with
the case of *Bourne v Mason* (1670), where the plaintiff failed because
'he did nothing of trouble to himself or benefit to the defendant but
was a mere stranger to the consideration'.

Dunlop sold tyres to a wholesaler called Dew and Co., and as a
term of the contract the latter undertook that the tyres should not
be sold to the public at less than the manufacturers' retail prices
and that this condition would be imposed on any person to whom
they resold the tyres. Selfridges bought them from Dew and Co. and
specifically covenanted in writing: 'We will not sell any Dunlop
tyres to any private customers at prices below those mentioned in
the said price list current at the time of sale.' Selfridges then sold the
tyres at cut prices, as they had already intended to do at the time when
they signed the undertaking not to. Dunlop sued Selfridges and
failed. There were two separate contracts; but, more important, the
House of Lords held that there was no consideration moving from
Selfridges to Dunlop. 'What then did Dunlop do or forbear to do,
in a question with Selfridges? The answer must be: "Nothing",'
said Lord Dunedin. 'To my mind, this ends the case.' *Dunlop v
Selfridges* 1915, [1914–15] All E.R. Rep. 333.

The 'Privity of Contract'

Closely related to the doctrine that consideration must move from
the promisee is another principle—if indeed it can be distinguished
at all—called **'privity of contract'**. Only a person who is a party to
a contract can sue on it. 'Our law knows nothing of a *jus quaesitum
tertio* arising by way of contract', to use Lord Haldane's famous
expression, which means that even if a contract is expressly made for
the benefit of somebody who is not a party to it, that person cannot
sue to enforce it.

Lord Haldane may have been categorical, but he was not accurate. For something like two hundred years the rule was 'if one person made a promise to another for the benefit of a third, that third person may maintain an action upon it'; provided, of course, that there was good consideration in the old sense of family duty or moral obligation (see page 82) for the promise.

It is, however, unquestionably the law today and has been ever since what Lord Denning, not without justification, termed 'the unfortunate' case of *Tweddle v Atkinson* 1861, [1861–73] All E.R. Rep. 369. There Crompton J., because, as he expressly said, of the change in the law about the nature of consideration, was prepared 'to overrule the old decisions'.

In 1855 William Guy promised in writing to pay £200 to William Tweddle his son-in-law and John Tweddle also promised by the same document to pay £100 to William Tweddle, his son. The instrument ended up by declaring 'the said William Tweddle has full power to sue the said parties in any court of law or equity for the aforesaid sum'.

Father-in-law died without having paid William Tweddle the promised £200, so William sued his executors—and lost.

Since then the House of Lords has expressly approved this principle on at least three occasions, in spite of a gallant attempt by Lord Denning in *Beswick v Beswick*, [1967] 2 All E.R. 1197 to find in s. 56 (1) of the *Law of Property Act, 1925* grounds for claiming that the rule had been set aside by that Statute.

No person can have obligations imposed on him by a contract to which he is not a party

It follows, of course, that strangers to a contract cannot have obligations imposed on them by contracts to which they are not parties. In 1904 the manufacturer of goods issued them in a box on the lid of which was printed the words 'acceptance of the goods by any purchaser will be deemed to be an acknowledgement that they are sold to him on condition' that they were not to be on sale to the public below a specified price. An action brought by the manufacturers against a retailer who sold them at less than the specified price failed, because there was no contract between the parties: *McGruther v Pitcher* (1904). At one time it was thought that this rule did not apply to merchant ships if they were acquired with the knowledge that it was a breach of a charterparty or some other contractual obligation, but the general view now is that Diplock J. in *Port Line Ltd. v Ben Steamers Ltd.*, [1958] 1 All E.R. 787 was right to reject this suggestion. So a person who acquires goods with knowledge that his possession of them is a breach of a contract between two other persons is not liable in contract, though he may be in tort. At a time when motor cars were in short supply, one was bought with a promise by the buyer that he would not re-sell it for one year. Within that period, he re-sold it to a man who had knowledge of that promise and who was held liable in tort for wrongfully inducing a breach of contract.

Now by the *Restrictive Trade Practices Act, 1956*, s. 25, price maintenance agreements which have not been declared void under the *Resale Prices Act, 1964* can be enforced against third parties who buy with notice. Books are practically the only commodity now covered by this provision.

It follows from this that exemption clauses in contracts that purport to protect not only one of the contracting parties, but also all their servants are probably ineffective, in spite of dicta to the contrary: In *Alder v Dickson*, [1954] 3 All E.R. 397, a passenger on a P & O liner who was injured by the negligence of crew members and who was travelling under a ticket which excluded all liability by the *company*, succeeded in an action against the crew members concerned, who were not parties to the contract. And in *Scruttons v Midland Silicones Ltd.*, [1962] 1 All E.R. 1, the House of Lords held that stevedores discharging a ship were not protected by a clause limiting liability to $500 in the bill of lading—the contract between the shippers and the shipowners.

But in neither of these cases were the crew or the stevedores specifically mentioned in the original contracts and attempts have since been made to draft exclusion of liability clauses that, most improbably, make the shipping line the agents for all their crew in the contract with the passenger; and attempts have been made to restrain actions against servants not parties to a contract but named therein, by injunctions; but this is a complex matter best dealt with when exemption clauses are considered in detail later (see page 168).

Exceptions to the 'Privity of Contract' Doctrine

As usual, having enunciated principles, it is necessary to deal with the exceptions. With the privity of contract rule they are rather numerous. They may be divided into various classes:

Trusts: As was explained earlier (page 45) the beneficiaries of trusts can always sue.

Covenants Running with Land: Under the doctrine of *Tulk v Moxhay*, 1848 [1843–60] All E.R. Rep. 9, restrictive covenants as to the use of land are binding on subsequent purchasers. So you can do with land, what you cannot do with chattels.

Assignments: Third parties can have contractual rights assigned to them (see page 246).

Agency: The right of an undisclosed principal to adopt a contract has been discussed on page 22.

Bankers' Confirmed Credits: A banker who has notified to a foreign seller that he has opened an irrevocable credit in his favour against presentation of shipping documents is liable even though there is no contract between the seller and the banker, and no consideration. See *Hamzeh Malas v British Imex*, [1958] 1 All E.R. 262. This probably is on the ground that it is part of the Law Merchant and is what Lord Mansfield was talking about in 1765 in *Pillan v Van Mierop* when he said 'a *nudum pactum* does not exist in the Law Merchant' and 'in commercial cases amongst merchants, the want of consideration is not an objection'. But there has been considerable discussion about the legal basis in English law of this obligation (see 52 L.Q.R. 225–40).

Statutory:

1. By s. 11 of the *Married Women's Property Act, 1882*, where a man insures his life expressly for the benefit of his wife and children, they, although not parties to the contract, become the beneficiaries of a trust in their favour and can therefore sue.
2. By the *Road Traffic Act, 1960*, any person driving with the consent of the owner can be protected in the manner laid down by the Act even though he is not, of course, a party to the contract of insurance.
3. Third parties injured may in the circumstances set out in the *Third Parties (Rights Against Insurers) Act, 1930* and the *Road Traffic Act, 1960* sue the insurance company directly.
4. The *Fire Prevention (Metropolis) Act, 1774*—which in spite of its title applies to the whole country—enables a tenant of a house to claim toward the rebuilding of it under his landlord's policies, and a landlord can claim under a tenant's.
5. Contracts of marine insurance can benefit others besides the contracting parties: *Marine Insurance Act, 1906*, s. 14 (2).

Does the Law need the Doctrine of Consideration?

It will be apparent from these paragraphs that there have been dozens of cases where promises were given which were intended to be contractual obligations but where the promisors have escaped legal liability through the technicalities of the doctrine of consideration.

The Law Revision Committee in its 6th Interim Report 1937 made criticisms of it, which may be summarised as follows:

(i) Although the main purpose of consideration is to provide evidence that the parties intended legal obligations, it fails to do so.
(ii) It enables a party to snap his fingers at a promise he has given and which should have been enforced.

(iii) The rule that the Court won't inquire into the adequacy
of consideration has reduced the doctrine to farce. That clearly
was the view of Jessel M.R., as long ago as 1881, when he said
in reference to compositions with creditors: 'Not every debtor
has a stock of canary birds or tom-tits or rubbish of that kind
to add to his dividend.'

(iv) If past consideration is sufficient for a cheque, why not for a
contract?

The relevance of these criticisms has not diminished with the years
that have passed but nothing has been done to reform the law. In
part this is due to the idea that the whole English law of contract
would fall apart if the necessity of consideration were abolished. As
Professor C. J. Hamson put it: 'Consideration, offer and acceptance
are an indivisible trinity, facets of one identical notion which is that
of bargain' [1938] 54 L.Q.R. 234. But the law since those days has
moved far from the concept of 'bargain' and in fact when that word
appeared recently in a judgment it was used in contradistinction to
contract; as meaning a non-enforceable arrangement whereby a
local authority appointed somebody to enter into a contract as sub-
contractor to their contractor. We are now really in a position when
all the learning about consideration could be quietly ditched and
still leave a viable and more just law of contractual obligations.

CHAPTER SEVEN

PROMISES THE LAW WILL NOT ENFORCE: FOR WANT OF CAPACITY

Corporations and their Contracts

As has been noted on page 3 of this book, in addition to ordinary human beings the law recognises as persons corporations, such as limited liability companies created under the *Companies Acts 1948* and *1967*. Until 1948 companies could only make contracts under seal, and the same applied to other corporations until the *Corporate Bodies' Contracts Act, 1960*. Now all corporations can make contracts in exactly the same way as real persons.

There are, however, some important qualifications upon the contractual ability of companies. These are:

1. A company cannot make a contract until it comes into existence, which is the moment when it is registered. This may appear self evident, like saying that an unborn child cannot contract, but every day, business men make arrangements for companies not yet registered; they are not binding.
2. Even after a company has come into existence it cannot ratify or adopt contracts made on its behalf before incorporation. There must always be a completely new contract after incorporation for it to be enforceable. This applies even to the costs of the formation and it is necessary for there to be a contract after incorporation before the promoter of the company can be reimbursed.
3. A company incorporated under the *Companies Acts* can only make contracts binding on it provided they are within the scope of the objects clause of its Memorandum of Association. Any contracts which are outside the objects clause are not binding on the company.

Introductions Ltd. was a company formed for the purpose of providing facilities for overseas visitors to the Festival of Britain 1951, and its objects were framed accordingly. After many vicissitudes, it ended up pig breeding and a bank which had lent the company £29,000 on debentures for that purpose was unable to claim on the liquidation of the company: *Introductions Ltd. v National Provincial Bank Ltd.*, [1969] 1 All E.R. 887.

Another company was by its objects clause entitled to carry on business as costumiers; it diversified into veneer panelling, and the builder of a factory, and suppliers of veneers and coke were held not entitled to receive any portion of the company's assets on its liquidation: *Re Jon Beauforte Ltd.*, [1953] 1 All E.R. 634.

The leading case on this *ultra vires* ('outside the powers') doctrine, as it is called, is the House of Lords decision in *Ashbury Railway Carriage v Riche* (1871), where the objects clause read: 'to make and sell, or lend or hire railway carriages or waggons . . . and to carry on the business of mechanical engineers and general contractors'. The company obtained a concession to run a railway in Belgium and entered into a contract with Riche to build it for them. It was held that Riche could not recover damages for breach of contract because the apparently binding contract was outside the powers of the company to conclude.

Money borrowed for a purpose outside a company's powers cannot be recovered as a debt, although if the money can be identified or traced, equity will assist in its recovery on a quasi-contractual basis (see page 46).

To enter into contracts with Limited Companies therefore can be a hazardous operation since everybody is presumed to know what is contained in their Memorandum of Association. All the company documents are available for inspection for a small fee at Companies House, City Road, London EC14 1BB, and a prudent man would no doubt read these carefully before he made a contract with any company; whether he would find time for any other business is, of course, debatable.

The company can rely as a defence upon its own wrong in making a contract which is *ultra vires*; but can the other contracting party also set this up as a defence? Can a defendant sued by a company on a contract that is *ultra vires* that company escape liability for damages for breach of contract? Can a defendant do this, even when the company has performed the whole of its own obligations? If the *Jon Beauforte Ltd.*, mentioned above, had delivered a load of veneer panels to a customer, could he have refused to pay for them?

Anglo-Overseas Agencies Ltd. v Green [1960], 3 All E.R. 442 proceeded on the basis that the *ultra vires* defence was available to the other contracting party, and in 1965 Mocatta J. expressly so held in *Bell Houses Ltd. v City Wall Properties Ltd.*, [1965] 3 All E.R. 427; but that case was reversed on other grounds by the Court of Appeal [1966] 2 All E.R. 674. However, Salmon L.J., in passing, observed: 'It seems strange that third parties could take advantage of a doctrine, manifestly for the protection of shareholders, in order to deprive the company of money which in justice should be paid to it by the third party'; and with that view most academic authors seem to agree.

But perhaps we shall never know the answer to the conundrum, for the Court of Appeal held in that particular case that if the objects clause included power 'to carry on any business which, in the opinion of the board of directors can be advantageously carried on with, in connection with, or as ancillary to, its authorised business', there was nothing that was *ultra vires* the company. The *European Communities Act, 1972* will also make this irrelevant, and, in effect, abolish the *ultra vires* rule.

The Contractual Capacity of Drunks, the Insane and Married Women

At one time the law classed drunks, lunatics and married women in the same category. But by the *Law Reform (Married Women and Tortfeasers) Act, 1935* 'a married woman shall . . . be capable of suing and being sued, either in tort or contract or otherwise . . . in all respects as if she were a *femme sole*'—a single woman, that is. And another section enables husband and wife to sue and be sued . . . 'in like manner as if they were not married'. A married woman has full capacity therefore to contract with anyone, including her own husband—but, of course, as has been noted (see page 78), many agreements between husband and wife lack contractual intent.

The present position regarding drunks is as follows:

The contract can be set aside on proof that:

(i) they were incapable of understanding what they were doing at the time when they made the contract.
(ii) this condition was known to the other party at the time.

But for necessaries sold and delivered they are, by virtue of s. 2 of the *Sale of Goods Act, 1893*, liable to pay a reasonable price. And if the contract is ratified later, when sober, it is binding.

The same principles apply to the insane, except where one is under the control of the Court under the *Mental Health Act, 1959*, in which case he is deprived of all contractual capacity.

Contracts on which Minors are Liable

Until the *Family Law Reform Act, 1970*, 'an infant' was a person under the age of 21; since the 1st January 1971, 'a minor' is any person who has not yet reached his eighteenth birthday.

These changes were effected as a result of the Report of the Committee on the Age of Majority 1967 ('the Latey Committee').

'The only matter on which all our witnesses agreed was that the present law governing the contracts of persons below the age of majority is unsatisfactory,' said the Committee. Perhaps for that reason the subject remains the examiners' happy hunting ground and must therefore be dealt with in greater detail than its importance in real life.

Necessaries. 'An infant may bind himself to pay for his necessary meat, drink, apparel, necessary physic and such other necessaries and likewise for his good teaching or instructions whereby he may profit himself afterwards' was how Sir Edward Coke decided the obligation on those who were then described as 'infants'.

The word is not necessities but *necessaries*. It obviously includes the things mentioned by Coke. But, to quote Alderson B., in *Chapple v Cooper* (1844), where an infant widow was held liable to pay for her husband's funeral as a 'necessary': 'As man lives in society, the assistance and attendance of others may be a necessary to his well-being . . . hence attendance may be the subject of an infant's contract . . . the nature and extent of the attendance will depend on his position in life . . . articles of mere luxury are always excluded, though luxurious articles of utility are in some cases included.'

Necessaries therefore are not confined to such articles as are the necessities of life 'but extend to articles fit to maintain the particular person in the state, station, and degree in life in which he is'. Class is therefore an important feature in this aspect of the law. The millionaire's son may be liable to pay for necessaries which the butcher's boy, if he can con the tradesman to letting him have them on credit, will not have to.

In *Elkington and Co. v Amery*, [1936] 2 All E.R. 86, the Court of Appeal held that the infant son of a former Cabinet Minister was liable to pay for a diamond ring (which he said was an engagement ring) and a diamond and platinum 'eternity ring'; but not for a ladies' gold vanity bag; and in 1898 a racing bicycle costing £12 10s was held to be a necessary for an apprentice earning 30 shillings a week. In 1866 tobacco for an infant army officer was not held to be a necessary; but, it might well be today.

By a later development of the doctrine, it was held in *Barnes v Toye* (1884) that articles which might otherwise be necessaries ceased to be so if the infant was already adequately supplied with them. The youth who only has one other suit at home has to pay his tailor; but the one who can prove that, unknown to the unfortunate tailor, he has fifty already in his wardrobe does not have to pay; nor can the suit be recovered from him. This incredible doctrine is now part of the *Sale of Goods Act, 1893*, s. 2, and was approved by the Court of Appeal in 1905 in a case where a Savile Row tailor sued the infant defendant for £145 of goods supplied while he was an undergraduate at Trinity College, Cambridge. The crucial point in the case was that the infant defendant's father gave evidence that his son was amply supplied with clothes 'suitable and necessary and proper for his condition in life'. The one fact of the case that inevitably attracts the attention of all law students is the charming irrelevancy that the clothes supplied included eleven fancy waistcoats; but the decision would have been no different if the goods supplied had been a couple of sober suits: *Nash v Inman* 1908, [1908–10] All E.R. Rep. 317.

The Common Law position has been replaced by s. 2 of the *Sale of Goods Act, 1893*, the relevant part of which reads:

'Provided that where necessaries are sold and delivered to an infant (or a minor) . . . he must pay a reasonable price therefor.'

' "Necessaries" in this section means goods suitable to the conditions of life of such infant (or minor) . . . and to his actual requirements at the time of sale and delivery.'

Points worthy of note in this connection are as follows:

(i) The obligation is not to pay the contractual price but a reasonable price. The obligation therefore is clearly not contractual but quasi-contractual. If the minor promises to pay £50 for his suit, this does not help the tailor. All he can recover is 'a reasonable price', a *quantum valebant* in other words, which may or may not be the agreed price.

(ii) The goods must be necessaries both at the time of sale and the delivery. If when the minor bought an off-the-peg suit it was a necessary, but he left it in the shop to have the sleeves altered and in the period before delivery he was given twenty suits, he is not liable to pay for the one delivered to him.

(iii) The goods must have been delivered to the minor. If, therefore, the minor orders a made-to-measure suit from a tailor and fails to take delivery he is not liable to pay for it. In spite of *dicta* to the contrary, there is no reported case in which a minor has ever been held liable on an executory contract for necessary goods; nor in view of the words of the Act can he be. The position is different for necessary services which are not subject to the *Sale of Goods Act, 1893*.

(iv) The necessaries must be for the personal use of himself or his family and not for any trading concern he may be engaged in (see page 4).

Necessary services. Obviously, services such as legal and medical ones are necessaries as well as education, and it would appear here that the old Common Law Rule applies and that the minor is liable both to pay the contractual price and to pay damages if he fails to perform the contract, irrespective of whether or not he has received any benefit. That certainly is the basis of the decision in *Roberts v Gray*, [1913] All E.R. 870, where an infant defendant was held liable in damages for breach of a contract with the plaintiff to join him on a billiard-playing tour of the world. This accords with Coke's view that for necessaries 'an infant may bind himself'. As Hamilton L.J. said: 'If the contract is binding at all, it must be binding for all such remedies as are appropriate to the breach of it.' 'A contract which is in itself binding . . . (does not) cease to be binding merely because it is executory.'

Contracts of service, such as apprenticeship and employment and those of a similar nature, provided they are for an infant's benefit, are also binding on him. And when Charlie Chaplin's son entered into a contract with publishers whereby he was to provide the information for two literary 'ghosts' to write a book, later described as 'a muck raking search for profits', and entitled *I Couldn't Eat The Grass on My Father's Lawn*, the Court of Appeal held it to be for his benefit and therefore binding: *Chaplin v Leslie Frewin*, [1965] 3 All E.R. 764.

But if the contract of services is not for the infant's benefit as a whole, it will not be binding, as appeared from *De Francesco v Barnum*, [1890] All E.R. Rep. 414, where infants entered into contract to learn stage dancing on terms that the Court of Appeal held gave such 'inordinate power' over the infants' lives that they were not for the infants' benefit. If there is a contract for an infant's benefit, such as an apprenticeship contract, but one term is onerous and can be deleted while still leaving a valid contract, the onerous term will be severed and will not be enforced against the infant; as where the infant entered into an apprenticeship but one term of the contract denied him the right to sue his employers if he was injured by their negligence: *Olsen v Corry and Gravesend Aviation*, [1936] 3 All E.R. 241.

But where the contract as a whole is for his benefit and there is no possibility of severance, he cannot elect which terms he will adopt and which he will reject.

An infant professional boxer was held to the term of his contract with the British Boxing Board of Control, whereby he forfeited the whole of his fee of £3,000 for a fight, because he was disqualified: *Doyle v White City Stadium*, [1934] All E.R. Rep. 252.

If a minor goes into business his trading contracts are not binding on him even though, as was ingeniously argued in *Cowern v Nield* (1912), it is analogous to a service contract and for the infant's benefit that he should learn how to carry on a trade. The youth in that particular case carried on business as a hay and straw merchant. The plaintiff ordered clover and hay from him and paid him in advance £35 19s. The clover sent was bad and was rejected and hay was never sent at all. But the plaintiff failed. So if a minor receives money for goods which he fails to deliver or receives goods (not necessaries) for which he fails to pay, neither goods nor money can be recovered.

Contracts not Binding on Minors

Hitherto it has been found possible to avoid referring to some rather imprecise terms that are sometimes applied to contracts.

A **void contract** is a contradiction in terms. A void contract is one which does not and never has ever existed, even though the parties themselves may think there was one. The result of this is that:

(i) there are no contractual obligations whatsoever on either party;

(ii) if the void contract is for the sale of goods, the apparent 'buyer' does not become the owner and therefore anybody he sells to cannot become the owner. In lawyers' language, a void contract cannot pass the title in goods;

(iii) if money or goods have passed as the result of the void contract they are recoverable under the quasi-contractual doctrine of restitution (see page 46).

Unhappily, these principles do not apply *in toto* to contracts which are said to be void for illegality (see page 121). Nor, it would appear, do they bear the same meaning, when applied to the interpretation of the words of section 1 of the *Infants' Relief Act, 1874*. So that the term 'void contract' is a semantic monstrosity.

The Infants' Relief Act, 1874 (which was described by the Latey Committee as 'short, sententious and badly drafted') was introduced into the House of Lords. It applies to the contract of minors for:

(i) the repayment of money lent or to be lent.

(ii) goods supplied or to be supplied other than necessaries; and the Act says that such contracts 'shall be absolutely void'.

One would have thought that the use of the adverb *'absolutely'* was to emphasise that they were to have no legal effect whatever. In some cases it has indeed been given that meaning.

In *Coutts v Browne-Lecky*, [1946] 2 All E.R. 207 the adult guarantors of an infant's overdraft with a bank were held not liable because he was, as a result of the *Infants' Relief Act, 1874*, under no liability. (The Banks and Hire Purchase Companies, of course, immediately after that case altered the terms so that the guarantee became an indemnity (see page 117) and therefore the adult became primarily liable.)

And in *R v Wilson* (1879), the conviction of an infant for the offence of leaving England after a bankruptcy petition had been served on him was quashed on the grounds that the transactions which gave rise to the alleged debts were 'absolutely void'.

But in other cases:

(i) The other, adult, contracting party has been held to be under a contractual obligation. In *Thornalley v Gostelow* (1947) an infant plaintiff succeeded in an action for breach of warranty on the sale of a ship.

(ii) The property in non-necessary goods passes to the minor, as in *Stocks v Wilson* (1913), where an action for conversion failed because the infant had become the owner. But the strongest authority is to be found in *Watts v Seymour*, [1967] 1 All E.R. 1044, which was a case of a sale of a rifle to a youth under 17, where the acid test, to quote Winn L.J., was: 'after the transaction in question could (the minor) have validly sold, so as to transfer the property in the rifle to somebody else?' A unanimous Court of Appeal held that he could.

(iii) In *Valentini v Canali*, [1889] All E.R. Rep. 883 it was contended that an infant was entitled to the return of moneys paid under a contract which had been held to be 'absolutely void' under the *Infants' Relief Act.* Lord Coleridge C.J. said: 'No doubt the words of section one of the *Infants' Relief Act, 1874* are strong and general, but a reasonable construction ought to be put upon them ... when an infant has paid for something and has consumed or used it, it is contrary to natural justice that he should recover back the money which he has paid.'

'Absolutely void' therefore, in the *Infants' Relief Act, 1874*, certainly does not mean absolutely void; what the words mean remains a matter of speculation.

S. 2 of the *Infants' Relief Act, 1874* further provides: 'No action shall be brought whereby to charge any person upon any promise made after full age to pay any debt contracted during infancy, or upon any ratification made after full age of any promise or contract made during infancy whether there shall be or shall not be any new consideration of such promise.'

Exactly what that section means, if anything, most certainly cannot be made simple, and as the Latey Committee observed, with justice, 'The distinction between a ratification for a new consideration and a fresh contract is one that has defeated better minds than ours.'

A voidable contract is one that is a perfectly good contractual obligation except that it is liable to be set aside either (i) at the option of one of the parties or (ii) by the Courts.

It follows, therefore, that the obligations are binding until some step has been taken to set them aside and therefore the ownership of goods sold under a voidable contract will pass provided the transaction takes place before the contract has been avoided.

Generally speaking, all contracts of minors other than those specifically dealt with already under Necessaries and the *Infants' Relief Act* are voidable at his option. But he has to meet obligations already incurred before he has avoided the contract. If he rents premises and disclaims the lease, he will be liable for the rent during his period of occupation; and if, for example, he has paid money, he cannot recover it unless there is a total and not merely a partial failure of consideration. An infant bought shares, that were not fully paid up in a company. She then avoided the contract, and claimed:

(i) to be removed from the company register.
(ii) to be relieved from her obligation to pay future calls on the shares.
(iii) to be repaid the money she had paid to subscribe for the shares.

The Court of Appeal held she was entitled to (i) and (ii) but could not recover the money she had paid because she had received consideration for it, i.e. the shares: *Steinberg v Scala Ltd.*, [1923] All E.R. Rep. 239.

A minor cannot be held liable on a contract by bringing an action against him in tort

An infant persuaded moneylenders to lend him £400 by the fraudulent misrepresentation that he was of full age.

Aware that they could not sue for recovery of the sum lent because of the *Infants' Relief Act*, the moneylenders sued (a) for damages for the tort of deceit and (b) in quasi-contract for the restitution of money had and received to the plaintiff's use. The Court of Appeal disallowed both claims. 'This would be nothing but enforcing a void contract', said Lord Sumner: *R. Leslie Ltd. v Sheill*, [1914] All E.R. Rep. 511.

So, too, where an infant hired a mare and injured her by riding her too hard, he was held not liable (*Jennings v Rundall*, 1799); likewise where an infant hired a car to go six miles and drove twelve and the car caught fire: *Fawcett v Smethurst* (1914).

But if the tort is quite outside the contract, the minor may be liable; and where one hired an amplifier on weekly hire and parted with possession of it, he was held liable in detinue (*Ballett v Mingay*, [1943] 1 All E.R. 143); and an infant who hired a mare which he was told was not to be used for jumping and he lent her to a friend who used her for that purpose and injured her was held liable: *Burnard v Haggis* (1863).

Equitable Remedies against Minors

But where there has been fraud on the part of the infant by a false representation as to his age, and he is still in possession of the goods or money so obtained, Equity may order **restitution**—that is the return of the very thing obtained. 'But restitution stops where repayment begins.'

If money is borrowed in spite of the *Infants' Relief Act*, it is recoverable if actually expended on necessaries. So that if a minor says to a friend: 'Lend me a fiver to pay my bookmaker' and he obtains the money and spends it on groceries, his friend can recover it under the equitable doctrine of **subrogation**—that is he is allowed to stand in the shoes, so to speak, of the tradesman whose enforceable claim has been satisfied. But if the minor says: 'Lend me a fiver to buy food' and he actually uses it to back a horse, the loan is not recoverable. A loan for necessaries is void, but the expenditure of borrowed money on necessaries gives a cause of action.

'Subrogation' therefore means no more than the substitution of one person for another—the creditor of a minor who has actually spent the borrowed money on paying for necessaries for the tradesman who would have been entitled to sue the minor for necessary goods sold and delivered.

CHAPTER EIGHT

PROMISES THE LAW WILL NOT ENFORCE: FOR WANT OF FORM

Contracts that Must be Evidenced in Writing

From the time when the action of *assumpsit* (see page 28) made its appearance on the English legal scene, no special requirements were necessary to make a promise enforceable by the action. A promise made orally was as effective as one made in writing. As time has passed, however, Parliament has enacted that an increasing number of contracts have had to be made in special form, usually for the protection of one of the parties.

The first enactment of this nature was the Statute of Frauds 1677 which originally required six classes of contracts to be put in writing before they were enforceable. All but one part of that enactment—that relating to contracts of guarantee—has since been repealed or re-enacted in other legislation.

What was the position if a contract was not in writing when the Statute of Frauds required it to be? For many years judges took the view that the contracts were void and as late as 1837, for example, Lord Abinger was saying in *Carrington v Roots*: 'The meaning of the Statute is not that the contract shall stand for all purposes except being enforced by action but it means that the contract is altogether void.' But by 1852 in *Leroux v Brown*, the judges were holding that the meaning of the Statute was the exact opposite of that attributed to it by Lord Abinger, namely that the contracts were not void but unenforceable. So besides void, and voidable contracts, there is another class called, equally unhappily, **unenforceable contracts.** In other words: 'The contract shall stand for all purposes except being enforced by an action at law.'

The effect can be seen by reference to one of the Statutes which replaced part of the Statute of Frauds.

S. 40 of the *Law of Property Act, 1925*

For convenience of commentary later it is set out in separate lines.

'No action may be brought upon any contract
for the sale or other disposition

113

of land
or any interest in land
unless the agreement upon which such action is brought
or some note or memorandum thereof
is in writing
signed
by the party to be charged
or by some other person thereunder by him
lawfully authorised'

To deal with it in detail:

1. no action may be brought upon any contract. This means that:

(a) the contract is perfectly good for every other purpose except being sued upon. For example, if a deposit is paid on an oral contract, the deposit can be retained. Fry gave Low a cheque for £450 as a deposit on a contract relating to land which was not in writing. Fry repudiated the contract and stopped the cheque. Low was able to sue successfully on the cheque: *Low v Fry*, [1935] All E.R. Rep. 506.

(b) if this defence provided by s. 40 of the *Law of Property Act* is relied upon, it must be specifically pleaded and set up by the defendant. If not, the Court will ignore the absence of writing.

(c) it is not necessary for the written evidence to be in existence when the contract is made; if it comes into existence before the case is heard, the Statute is complied with.

(d) any writing with sufficient details, even in separate documents which can be connected, will provide sufficient evidence to support an action.

2. for the sale or other disposition. Mortgages, leases—even leave to enter and take a cutting of grass (but apparently not cultivated crops)—have been held within these words.

3. land. In English law land includes not only the soil and the buildings on it but the air above and the minerals beneath—'up to heaven and down to hell' as the ancients put it.

4. or any interest in land includes shooting rights, partnership in a colliery, and a building which has been purchased for the purpose of demolition. (Incidentally, apparently some things can be 'land' for the purpose of this section and 'goods' for the purposes of the *Sale of Goods Act, 1893*.)

5. unless the agreement upon which such action is brought. The distinction between an agreement and a memorandum is that an agreement contains *all* the terms of the contract.

6. or some note or memorandum thereof. This has not been defined by Statute but the Courts have held that the necessary details must include:

(a) the identity of the parties.
(b) the subject matter of the contract.
(c) the consideration.
(d) any special term, e.g. as to the date of possession. But there is a doctrine that if a material term has been omitted from the writing and it is exclusively for the benefit of the plaintiff, he can waive it and still enforce the contract.

The note or memorandum does not have to have been in the same documents and in *Stokes v Whicher*, [1920] All E.R. Rep. 771, the vendor's agent signed a carbon copy of a contract which contained no purchaser's name, a receipt for a cheque was given on the carbon copy, the cheque existed and there was a top copy of the contract signed by the purchaser. The Courts held there was sufficient memoranda.

But a different situation existed in *Timmins v Moreland St. Property Co. Ltd.*, [1957] 3 All E.R. 265. At a meeting between the parties, the defendant company agreed to buy property for £39,000. They gave the plaintiff, who was the sole surviving trustee of an estate, a cheque for £3,900 drawn in favour of his employers, Messrs. Holt, Beever and Kinsley, Solicitors. Timmins gave a receipt: 'Received of Moreland Street Property Co. Ltd., the sum of £3,900 as a deposit for purchase of Nos. 6, 8 and 41 Boundary Street, Shoreditch, which I agree to sell for £39,000.'

Because the only document signed 'by the party to be charged', i.e. the defendants, was the cheque and that could not be connected with the plaintiff's receipt, it was held there was insufficient evidence to satisfy the Statute. Had the cheque been drawn in favour of Timmins instead of his employers, there would have been internal evidence sufficient to link all the documents.

It will be noted that even a letter of repudiation can amount to sufficient evidence for the purpose of s. 40 of the *Law of Property Act, 1925*. So if you make an oral agreement to sell your house and you write to the proposed buyer: 'Dear Mr. Buggins, I know I promised to sell you my house for £5,000 but I've changed my mind and as there is no contract in writing there is nothing you can do about it' and you sign the letter and address the envelope to him—you have provided all the memoranda necessary for an enforceable agreement.

7. **signed.** The signature does not need to be at the end of the memoranda, it does not have to be in full—initials alone are sufficient—and even a printed name may amount to a signature.

8. **by the party to be charged.** This is always the one sought to be

held liable on the contract. In other words, the defendant. So that a plaintiff who has signed nothing can hold a defendant who has signed sufficient memoranda liable. Timmins would have been liable in the case mentioned above, though the contract was unenforceable against the Company.

9. **or by some other person thereto by him lawfully authorised.** The person authorised as agent does not have to be authorised in writing, and auctioneers, for example, are authorised by law to sign memoranda for the purchaser (as well as the vendor). So if you go to an auction and bid for property which is knocked down to you, it is no good thinking you can escape by refusing to sign the agreement. The auctioneer is empowered by law to sign on your behalf, so long as he does it in the auction room or elsewhere within a reasonable time afterwards.

The Equitable Doctrine of Part Performance

The Statute of Frauds which first imposed this obligation was passed in 1677, in the reign of Charles II; within eight weeks of the Act coming into force, the Court of Chancery had specifically enforced an unsigned contract for the sale of land.

'Equity', it was said, 'would not allow a Statute to become an instrument of fraud' and so came into existence the remarkable doctrine that, in spite of the Statute, even when there is no memorandum in writing as required, the contract was still enforced by the Courts if there is an act of **part performance**. The *Law of Property Act, 1925*, s. 40 (2) and 55, has expressly preserved this equitable doctrine.

It is applicable under the following conditions:

(i) If the contract is of such a nature that it would have been enforceable by the Court of Chancery, i.e. where the conditions for specific performance apply (see page 65).

(ii) Where the circumstances are such that it would be a fraud on the part of the defendant to take advantage of the contract not being in writing.

(iii) The act of part performance must be of such a nature that it proves the existence of *some* contract between the parties. Earlier law suggested that it had to prove the specific contract alleged and none other. The modern law was set forth in *Kingswood Estate Ltd. v Anderson*, [1962] 3 All E.R. 593, where the defendant was the rent controlled tenant of a house owned by the plaintiffs. To get her out of the premises, the plaintiffs orally promised that if she would move into one of their flats elsewhere, she should have it for her lifetime. They thereby got her to surrender her protected tenancy. She moved into the new flat and they then gave her notice to quit. She didn't go, so the plaintiffs sued her for possession. The Court of Appeal held that 'the acts of part performance must themselves suggest the existence of a contract ... although they need not establish the exact terms of that contract'.

A widow gave up her council house to go and look after an elderly man in reliance on his oral promise that he would leave her his house when he died. The Court held that was sufficient act of part performance to establish that there had been some contract between the parties and, that being so, they could then receive oral evidence as to the terms of the contract: *Wakeham v McKenzie*, [1968] 2 All E.R. 783. Other things which have been held to be part performance have been alterations to a flat to meet the wishes of the defendant, *Rawlinson v Ames* (1925), and giving notice to an existing tenant, *Daniels v Trefusis* (1914). The receipt of money can never be an act of part performance because there may be a thousand explanations other than a contract for that; but where one party is found in possession of property belonging to another with the other's consent, the implication that there is a contract between the two is very strong.

But if the alleged act of part performance is explicable on grounds other than the existence of a contract between the parties—as where a housekeeper stayed on without pay after the expiration of her contract, *Maddison v Alderson*, [1883] All E.R. Rep. 742, or a daughter went to live with an aged father: *N.P. Bank Ltd. v Moore* (unreported)—then there is no part performance.

Equity may also enforce a contract which should be evidenced by writing if the defendant has promised to put it in writing but fraudulently has not done so. 'If there was an agreement for reducing the same into writing and that is prevented by the fraud and practice of the other party'—as where instructions were given for the preparation of a marriage settlement but before it was executed the woman was induced to marry the man—then Equity could be prepared to enforce the agreement even if there were no document in writing: *Maxwell v Lady Mountacute* (1720).

Contracts of Guarantee and Contracts of Indemnity

The one extant part of the Statute of Frauds 1677 is s. 4 which now reads:

'No action shall be brought whereby to charge the defendant upon any promise to answer for the debt, default or miscarriage of another person unless in writing and signed by the parties to be charged.'

Cases have decided that 'default or miscarriage' means promises to be responsible for the torts of others; and that this only applies

E

to contracts of guarantee and not contracts of indemnity. The difference between the two was aptly described by Harman L.J. as 'a most barren controversy', 'which has raised many hair-splitting distinctions of exactly the kind which brings the law into hatred, ridicule and contempt with the public' (*Yeoman Credit v Latter*, [1961] 2 All E.R. 294); the case that decided that contracts of indemnity for infants' hire purchase contracts were enforceable.

The difference between a guarantee and an indemnity was described in the leading case of *Birkmyr v Darnell* (1704): 'If two came to a shop and one buys and the other, to gain him credit, promises the seller "if he does not pay you, I will" . . . that is a guarantee and unenforceable without being in writing. But if he says: "Let him have the goods, I will see you are paid" . . . that is an indemnity and enforceable without writing.'

It is a guarantee, therefore, where:

(i) the principal debtor is primarily liable and the guarantor only if he doesn't pay;
(ii) the principal debtor always remains liable;
(iii) the promise is given direct by the guarantor to persons giving credit.

Other Contracts that Need to be in Writing

1. It has been held in *E.T.U. v Tarlo*, [1964] 2 All E.R. 1, that agreements between **solicitors and their clients** relating to remuneration for non-contentious business must be in writing to be enforceable; but that agreements relating to contentious business—such as litigation—do not have to be.

2. By the *Apprentices Act, 1814*, all **contracts of apprenticeship** are required to be in writing; normally in practice they are often made by deed.

3. By the *Moneylenders Act, 1927*, s. 6, all **moneylending contracts** must be in writing and contain the details specified by that Act.

4. By the *Marine Insurance Act, 1960*, all insurances of losses resulting from **marine adventure** have to be in writing and contain the details required by that Act.

5. By the *Bills of Sale Act, 1878 Amendment Act, 1882*, all **bills of sale** whether absolute or by way of security have to be registered at the Central Office of the High Court within seven days of execution and have to be in writing containing the details required by the Act.

6. **Bills of exchange** and **promissory notes** must be in writing.

CHAPTER NINE

PROMISES THE LAW WILL NOT ENFORCE: ILLEGALITY

In the law of contract, the word 'illegality' is used with a considerable lack of precision. ,The word is used to cover at least six different situations:

1. Where the agreement itself and or the acts it contemplates are perfectly lawful in themselves but it is against the policy of the law to enforce such obligations on the ground that it is contrary to public policy. There is nothing wrong in a garage proprietor entering into an agreement with a petrol company to sell only their brand of petrol for 30 years but, in certain circumstances, it may be against the policy of the law to enforce such obligations (see page 127).
2. Where the contract is perfectly lawful but the intention of the parties is to use it to break the law; as in the old case of *Ewing v Osbaldiston* (1836), where the two parties were partners for the management of a London theatre licensed for music and dancing but not licensed for the production of plays— for which purpose they proposed to use it.
3. Where the agreement itself is specifically caught by Common Law or Statute; the *Gaming Act, 1845*, for example, declares 'all contracts or agreements . . . by way of gaming or wagering, shall be null and void'.
4. Where the agreement between the parties has as its object the furtherance of a *criminal offence*. Nobody would expect the Courts to enforce as a contractual obligation an agreement between bank robbers but difficulties arise where the 'crime' is of a technical nature such as infringing the provisions of S.R. & O. 1940, No. 1784 restricting the sale of new machine tools. As Napoleon once said: 'There are now so many laws that it's a wonder we're not all hanged.'
5. Where the agreement has as its object the furtherance of an act which is not criminal but is unlawful. Fornication, whether for money or pleasure, has always been unlawful in England, though no longer punishable by the Ecclesiastical Courts as a crime. As a result, when a prostitute was sued on a contract

119

to supply her with a brougham on hire purchase which a jury found the plaintiffs knew would be used for the purpose of her profession, a Victorian Court held that no action would lie on it: *Pearce v Brookes*, [1866] 1 Ex. 213; and a landlord in 1911 was held unable to recover two quarters' rent for a flat let to a man's mistress, after one of the judges in the King's Bench Divisional Court had received guidance from the Book of Common Prayer. 'The law will not allow a contract which is tainted with immorality to be enforced. It was urged that prostitution is one thing and living as one man's mistress is quite a different thing. They may differ in degree but they both stand upon the same plane,' he said. If that indeed be the law, then every lease must be void where the landlord knows the premises are going to be occupied by a couple who will cohabit although unmarried or a couple of homosexuals living together. If so, there must be many thousands of void leases in London alone: *Upfill v Wright*, [1911] 1 K.B. 506.

6. Where to enforce a contract would be to enable a person or his estate to profit by a crime. A wife who murdered her husband was not allowed to receive his insurance money; nor was the estate of Dr. Crippen allowed to benefit from the murder of his wife. 'It is clear that no person can obtain or enforce any rights resulting to him from his own crime; neither can his representative, claiming under him, obtain or enforce such rights. The human mind revolts at the very idea that any other doctrine could be possible in our system of jurisprudence': *In the Estate of Crippen* 1911, [1911–13] All E.R. Rep. 207. Until 1961, suicide was a crime, and therefore money due under insurance policies on the life of the deceased was not payable; unless, that is, he was insane at the time, in which case he was not guilty of a crime. (This is the reason why so many coroners' juries used to find suicides to be insane.) The present position seems to be that death being a condition precedent to the payment of the money on a life policy, there is an implied term of the contract that the insured will not himself bring about that event; but that implied term will not apply where there is an express term making the policy payable even in the event of suicide.

With so many different concepts tucked away in the portmanteau word 'illegality' it is not surprising that the law to be applied is confused.

Mr. Justice Devlin (as he then was) made some attempt to sort the practice out in *Elder v Averback*, [1949] 2 All E.R. 692, 'by laying down some propositions as to how the Courts should approach the whole problem':

(i) Where the contract on the face of it is illegal, the Courts will not enforce it, whether illegality is pleaded by the defendant or not.

(ii) where the contract is not on the face of it illegal, evidence of extraneous circumstances tending to show illegality ought not to be admitted unless specifically pleaded by the defendant.

(iii) Where unpleaded facts emerge in the course of hearing a case which suggest that the contract was illegal, the Court should not act on this information unless it is satisfied that all relevant facts are before it.

(iv) Where the unpleaded facts emerge in the course of the hearing and the Court is satisfied that all the relevant facts are before it and can clearly see that the contract had an illegal object ... the Court is bound to take notice of the fact and refuse to enforce the contract.

But since that date, it has been held that if Counsel has reason to suspect that a contract may be illegal, he is under a duty to draw the attention of the Court to all the relevant facts in order that the Court may not enforce illegal transactions; and the Court of Appeal in *Small v Unity Finance Co.*, [1963] 3 All E.R. 50 felt itself bound to take the point of illegality of a contract even though the matter had not been pleaded or raised in the County Court.

In view of the confusion and absence of principles about this subject, in this book it is thought best to simplify the subject by dealing with different situations which may arise in commerce.

The Effect of Illegality on Contracts

In most cases the effect of illegality on the contracts is to make them **void** (see page 109).

The unfortunate first printer of the book called *The Memoirs of Harriet Wilson* was held not able to recover his remuneration from the publishers because the Court held that the book, being the autobiography of a harlot, amounted to a criminal libel (*Poplett v Stocklade*, 1825); possibly this was because of the entertaining account she gives of how the Duke of Wellington, straight from the battlefield of Waterloo, was kept waiting outside her door while she was engaged with another client. Printers of porno are therefore well advised to get their remuneration in advance. In *Napier v National Business Agency Ltd.*, [1951] 2 All E.R. 264, the plaintiff was engaged to act as secretary of the defendant company for £13 per week plus £6 a week expenses. Both parties knew that his expenses would not amount to £6 per week and that it was a device to avoid income tax on that part of his salary. The Court held that no part of his re-muneration was recoverable.

But in other cases, where the 'illegal' part can be severed from the rest of the contract, and the judges regard it as proper to do so, that alone will be void. This normally is the case in contracts where a particular covenant only is in restraint of trade and the rest of the contract is unobjectionable.

But such contracts which offend public policy seem to come into a special class. As Lord Denning said in a part of his judgment in *Bennett v Bennett*, [1952] 1 All E.R.: 'They are not "illegal" in the sense that a contract to do a prohibited or immoral act is illegal. They are not "unenforceable" in the sense that a contract within the Statute of Frauds is unenforceable for want of writing. These coven-ants lie somewhere in between. They are invalid and unenforceable. The law does not punish them. They are void, not illegal.'

Normally, if the whole of a contract is void, as we have seen on page 109, money or goods which have passed as the result of the void contract are recoverable.

But where the contract is void for illegality, money or goods which have passed under it are (subject to the exceptions noted below) not recoverable.

Ex turpi causa non oritur actio is said to be the maxim that applies: 'no action will lie in an evil cause'. 'The principle is well settled that if the plaintiff requires any aid from an illegal transaction to establish his cause of action, then he shall not have any aid from the Court.' In one case the plaintiff sued for the recovery of a half bank note which he had deposited with the defendant as security for money due; it was undoubtedly his property but he was unable to recover it when evidence was accepted that the 'money due' was for wine and food supplied in a brothel: *Taylor v Chester* 1869, [1861–73] All E.R. Rep. 154. A plaintiff who was on the 'stop list' of a trade association got somebody else to order cigarettes for him, for which he paid money over. He did not get the goods, nor could he recover the money, since, to do so, he would have to set up his own fraudu-lent scheme: *Berg v Sadler and Moore*, [1937] 1 All E.R. 637.

But this rule does NOT apply:

1. If a right of property quite apart from the contract can be estab-lished

Bowmakers Ltd. were therefore able to recover from Barnett Instruments Ltd. certain machine tools which were leased to the latter company, notwithstanding that the contract of leasing was illegal by S.R. & O. 1940, No. 1784, etc. 'Why should not the plaintiffs have back what is their own?' asked Lord Justice Du

Parc. '*Prima facie* a man is entitled to his own property and it is not a general principle of our law ... that where one man's goods have got into another's possession in consequence of some unlawful dealing between them, the true owner can never be allowed to recover those goods by action.' *Bowmakers Ltd. v Barnett Instruments Ltd.*, [1944] 2 All E.R. 579.

It is even said that a right of property can pass under a void illegal contract. In other words, the contract is void while performance is executory, but once it has been performed the property has passed. In *Feret v Hill* (1854) a lease of a house was taken and the premises converted into a brothel, which had been the intention of the lessee all the time, unknown to the lessor. It was held that the lease was good. And where goods were delivered as the result of an illegal and therefore void contract, the property in them was held to pass to the purchaser (*Kingsley v Sterling Industrial Securities Ltd.*, [1966] 2 All E.R. 414); so that the buyer could maintain an action for damages against anybody—even the seller—who took the goods from him.

Ali knew that he could not obtain a haulier's licence required by government regulations; so he got Singh to buy a lorry on hire purchase and register it in his name. Ali then bought the lorry from Singh, who had obtained the necessary licence, but Singh took it from him. It was held that Ali could recover it since his case rested not upon an illegal contract even though the whole purpose of the transaction was to evade the regulations, but on a property right which had passed: *Sajan Singh v Sardara Ali*, [1960] 1 All E.R. 269.

So when the word 'void' is used in connection with illegal contracts, it does not in two respects have the same meaning as usual (see page 109). By this time, the reader will be no doubt wishing that semantics were required study for lawyers.

2. If the parties are not *in pari delicto*
This means that goods or money which have passed under the void contract may be recovered if the plaintiff is not a willing party to infringing the law. Therefore if a man parts with money or property under an illegal contract as the result of fraud or pressure by the other party, he is able to recover it. 'It can never be predicated as *par delictum* where one holds the rod and the other bows to it' was said in *Smith v Cuff* (1817).

The same principle applies where the Statute which makes the contract illegal has been passed for the purpose of protecting one party to the contract. A tenant is able to recover illegal premiums exacted by a landlord, even though he knew that they were illegal when he paid them: *Craig v Southouse*, [1949] 1 All E.R. 1019.

3. If one of the parties has withdrawn before the illegal transaction is carried out

There is, it is said, a place of repentance for all parties to an illegal contract. If, therefore, a man has paid money out under an illegal contract before 'substantial performance' has taken place, he may be allowed to recover it. In order to defraud his creditors, Taylor assigned all his goods to another; this man then assigned and delivered the goods under a bill of sale to Bowers who was aware of the fraud. It was held that Taylor could recover them back from him because the fraudulent purpose of the transaction had not been carried out, and no creditor had been defrauded: *Taylor v Bowers* 1876, [1874–80] All E.R. Rep. 405.

But if the only reason why the illegal transaction is not carried out, is that one party refuses to perform it, the other party cannot claim that he has repented: In *Bigos v Bousted*, [1951] 1 All E.R. 92.

Contracts in Restraint of Trade

Until the early 17th century, the common law allowed and vigorously supported all sorts of restrictions on trade. Men could not practise a trade unless they had been apprenticed and served their time and unless they were members of the local guild; monopolies could be created and sold, and under the Tudors they frequently were; Sir Walter Raleigh, for example, held the monopoly of sweet wines. The modern law as we know it is largely the invention of Coke and his friends and was a political measure directed at the Royal Prerogative and the right to create monopolies (though there is one earlier case in the last year of Elizabeth's reign).

The tailors of Ipswich tried to stop a man who was not a member of their guild from plying his craft in the town. Coke, then Chief Justice of the King's Bench, held that 'At common law no man could be prohibited from working at any lawful trade, for the law abhors idleness, the mother of all evil . . . And therefore, the common law abhors monopolies which prohibit any from working in any lawful trade': *The Tailors of Ipswich 1615*. It was not a doctrine that commended itself to his royal master; for this and many other matters, the following year Coke was sacked by the King. But what he had invented in this respect, as in much else, passed into the common law.

Prima facie **all contracts in restraint of trade are unenforceable.** A contract in restraint of trade is one that limits competition or prevents one of the parties from exercising his trade or profession however and wherever he may wish. 'Any contract which interferes with the free exercise of a trade or business by restricting (a man) in the work he may do, or the arrangements which he may make with others, is a contract in restraint of trade.' Denning M.R. in *Petrofina v Martin*, [1966] 1 All E.R. 176.

But a contract in restraint of trade will be enforced, provided:

(i) that it is reasonable as between the parties.

(ii) it is not contrary to the public interest.

How the law applies these principles is best studied in three contexts:

1. Contract of employment where the employee ('the servant'—as the law still slightingly calls him) promises that *after leaving his master's employment* he will not engage in that particular occupation within a certain area.

2. Contracts of sale of, *inter alia*, the goodwill of a business when the vendor promises that for a certain period he will not compete with the business in a specified area.

3. Other agreements between traders, particularly what are termed 'solus' agreements whereby a trader undertakes to sell only the product of one particular manufacturer.

1. Restrictive covenants in contracts of employment

The law scrutinises these with care, conscious that there is no equality of bargaining power between a man seeking employment and an employer selecting, perhaps from numerous applicants, an employee. The employee, in his eagerness to get a job, will readily undertake almost any restriction on his activities after he has left the employment. The employee has very little choice in the matter. Therefore, such conditions are only enforceable provided three conditions are fulfilled:

(a) *The master must have a proprietary interest to protect*

That is, the object of the clause of restraint must be to protect his trade connections or his trade secrets. It must not be merely to prevent competition from his former employee. Mr. Saxelby was employed as an engineer by Morris Ltd. and a term of his contract was that for seven years after leaving that employment he would not work in the sale or manufacture of various kinds of machinery. The House of Lords held this term to be invalid because it merely sought to restrain competition with the employer's business and not to protect his trade connection or his secrets: *Morris v Saxelby* (1916) 1 A.C. 688. A prohibition of practice as a 'medical practitioner' was too wide—because it would exclude consultancy—to protect the proprietary interest of a firm of general practitioners: *Lyne-Perkis v Jones*, [1969] 3 All E.R. 738.

But in *Home Counties Dairies v Skilton* [1970] 1 All E.R. 1227 a milk roundsman promised that he would 'not at any time during the period of one year after the determination of his employment under this agreement . . . either on his own account, or as representative or agent of any person or company, serve or sell milk or dairy produce to any person or company who at any time during the last six months of his employment shall have been a customer of the employer and served by the employee in the course of his employment'. This the Court of Appeal held to be enforceable as 'precisely the area the employer was allowed to protect', i.e. his trade connection.

(b) *The restraint must be limited in area to that reasonably necessary for the protection of that proprietary interest*

There are a host of decisions that show that an excessively wide area makes the whole clause void. 'Twenty-five miles from London' was too wide for a canvasser who had been employed in one particular area of London: *Mason v Provident Clothing* 1913, [1911–13] All E.R. Rep. 400; 'twenty miles from Sheffield' for a reporter: *Leng v Andrews* (1909); five miles from a butcher's shop for a manager: *Empire Meat v Patrick*, [1939] 2 All E.R. 35; and ten miles from a tailor's shop for a tailor's assistant: *Attwood v Lamont* (1920). But seven miles from Tamworth Town Hall was reasonable for a solicitor's managing clerk: *Fitch v Dewes*, [1921] All E.R. Rep. 13; and ten miles from a doctor's surgery was held good: *Lyne-Perkis v Jones*, [1969] 3 All E.R. 738.

The test is entirely one of what is reasonable for the protection of the legitimate proprietary interests of the employer. A world-wide prohibition could in certain circumstances be valid though none appears to have been recorded in the Courts, in the case of employees as distinct from vendors of a business.

(c) *The restraint must be limited in time to that reasonably necessary for the protection of that proprietary interest*

A credit drapery salesman covenanted that he would not for five years, following the termination of his employment, canvas or solicit orders from any of his employer's customers. It was held that this period was longer than was necessary for the protection of employers' legitimate interests and was therefore void: *M. & S. Drapers v Reynolds*, [1956] 3 All E.R. 814.

2. Vendors of business

Different considerations apply in cases where a man sells his business and the goodwill of it and promises that he will not compete with it. Here the principle is that a vendor should 'not derogate from his grant'. Obviously, if he sells a business and then opens up again in close proximity the purchaser of the business is likely to lose his customers to the former owner.

Notwithstanding the above:

(*a*) *There must be a proprietary interest to protect*

So, when a company which had a licence to brew beer, but did not in fact brew any, sold the goodwill of its business and promised that for a period of fifteen years it would not compete in beer brewing, this clause was invalid. It amounted to no more than a restriction of competition; no part of the goodwill that the purchasers had bought was due to beer brewing: *Vancouver Malt v Vancouver Breweries*, [1934] All E.R. Rep. 38.

(*b*) *The protection afforded by such clauses will be strictly limited to protection of the actual business interest sold*

In *British Reinforced Concrete v Schelff*, [1921] All E.R. Rep. 202 the vendor had sold a business based in Leicester and engaged in the manufacture of 'hoop' road reinforcements. He covenanted not to engage in the manufacture of road reinforcements of any kind anywhere in Britain. It was held that this was too wide and was aimed at restriction of competition rather than the legitimate protection of the business goodwill acquired.

(*c*) *General restraints, although unlimited in area or time, may well be reasonable*

Nordenfelt, the patentee and manufacturer of weapons of war sold throughout the world, sold his business interests to a Limited Company and covenanted that he would not for 25 years anywhere in the world engage in the business of a manufacturer of arms or ammunition. It was held that the business he had sold being world-wide (unhappily!), the restriction was binding as reasonable: *Nordenfelt v Maxim Nordenfelt Co.*, [1891–94] All E.R. Rep. 1.

And a restriction for the whole of the Dominion of Canada and unlimited in time was held reasonable in *Connors Bros. Ltd. v Connors* (1940).

Once again, it is a question of fact: what is reasonably necessary for the protection of the business sold?

3. Solus agreements

Formerly, the law was little interested in what arrangements business men made amongst themselves; liberty to make what contract they wished and to restrict themselves in any way was not regarded as contrary to the public interest. Solus agreements have been a feature of the licensed liquor trade for many years and often tie publicans to taking only one brand of beer and to taking all their wines and spirits from the brewers—even though they can often obtain them cheaper elsewhere. Such agreements have been enforced certainly since 1792 and probably earlier.

But changes in political and economic ideas have influenced the

Courts, particularly in relation to the distribution and sale of petrol. For what was satisfactory for the sale of beer was not considered satisfactory for the sale of petrol.

Garages distributing petrol in this country have often entered into solus agreements which formerly contained four basic provisions:

(a) 'The tying covenant'—to purchase all their requirements of petrol from one supplier.
(b) 'The continuity covenant'—a clause that if they sold their business to a third party they would insert a similar clause in the contract with him.
(c) 'The compulsory trading' covenant—an undertaking to keep the petrol station open, sometimes during minimum hours.
(d) 'The fixed retail price covenant'—an undertaking not to sell the petrol below the manufacturers' fixed retail price. Such covenants are now illegal and unenforceable as a result of the *Resale Prices Act, 1964.*

The Monopolies Commission report on the Supply of Petrol to Retailers of 1965 led to a voluntary undertaking by the petrol companies to the then Board of Trade, which radically changed the position and, in effect, was changed by something that was not law but belonged to the shadowy hinterland where Government pressure is exerted and the industries submit rather than endure legislation.

One result of the Commission's Report was that the Courts the following year, in *Petrofina (G.B.) Ltd. v Martin*, [1966] 1 All E.R. 126, held that the doctrine of restraint of trade was applicable to solus agreements. There, the tying covenant was for 12 years. The continuity covenant was also criticised as an unnecessary restraint and both were held to be void. This case was followed by *Esso Petroleum v Harper's Garage*, [1967] 1 All E.R. 699, where a tying covenant of 21 years was held void as too long a period, but one which was effective for four years and five months was regarded as valid. The House of Lords in so holding paid regard to the recommendations of the Monopolies Commission that there should be a five-year limit to solus agreements. But this was limited by the decision in *Cleveland Petroleum v Dartstone*, [1969] 1 All E.R. 20, where it was held that if the solus agreement was accepted by the buyer of the garage as a term on which he obtained possession, it was enforceable against him. In 1968 the defendant bought an underlease of a garage from X and accepted solus covenants originally framed in 1960 for 25 years. 'Where a man takes possession of premises under a lease, not having been in possession previously and on taking possession he enters into a restrictive covenant tying himself to take all his supplies from the lessor, *prima facie*, the tie is valid,' said Lord Denning.

It would appear therefore that the doctrine does not apply to clauses in *leases*.

The present legal position therefore seems to be: that if the owner or existing tenant of a petrol station, in return for a mortgage at a low rate of interest, improvements to his garage, or an increased discount rate, or any of the other inducements commonly given by the petrol companies for such covenants, freely covenants to buy nothing but Mogul's petrol for 21 years, together with a continuity covenant, he is not bound by either promise. The next day, if he so wishes, he can sell somebody else's petrol. But if the only terms upon which he can obtain possession at all are by having to accept a lease containing the self-same unreasonable covenants, he is bound by them.

Neither the logic nor the justice of this situation will be immediately apparent to everybody.

If the clause in restraint of trade is unreasonable it is wholly void. So if a man sells his butcher's business and covenants that he will not for the rest of his life engage in the same trade anywhere in the world and this clause is held unreasonable, he may safely set up business next door to his former shop. The Courts are not there to re-write the parties' contracts for them. But even so he may be precluded by equity from canvassing his old customers or holding out that he is carrying on the same business: *Trego v Hunt*, [1896] All E.R. Rep. 804.

This is subject to what has been termed '*the blue pencil rule*', if it still exists. A London dealer in artificial jewellery sold his business and covenanted not to compete with the buyer 'as a dealer in real or imitation jewellery in . . . any part of the United Kingdom . . . the United States of America, Rome or Spain'. This was obviously too wide for the protection of the proprietary interests in the business sold and therefore *prima facie* void. But the Court held that the covenant was severable and they would uphold a covenant which excluded the words 'real' and all places outside the United Kingdom: *Goldsoll v Goldman*, [1914] All E.R. Rep. 257.

As Pearson L.J. commented in *Commercial Plastics Ltd. v Vincent*, [1964] 3 All E.R. 546: 'A good deal of legal "know how" is required for the successful drafting of a restrictive covenant.'

Agreements between Traders: the *Restrictive Trade Practices Act, 1956* and the *Resale Prices Act, 1964*

The sort of agreements which have been discussed in the previous paragraph are sometimes termed 'vertical agreements' because the agreements are between a supplier of goods and those he supplies. Equally important are those termed 'horizontal agreements', namely those between members engaged in a similar trade, whereby they all participated in what has come to be termed 'restrictive agreements'. This refers to the sort of agreement or 'undertakings' whereby all or most of the members of a particular business agreed to restrict:

(i) prices to be charged for goods.
(ii) terms on which goods are to be supplied.
(iii) amounts of goods to be produced.
(iv) process of manufacture.
(v) persons to whom the goods are to be supplied.

British Industry had become burdened with an overlaid criss-cross network of restrictive practices between traders. In 1956 the *Restrictive Practices Act* was passed, and this established the Restrictive Practices Court to deal with what the economist would no doubt describe as 'cartel agreements'.

The common law gave no relief against this sort of conspiracy towards consumers. Indeed, if a group of traders combined to force a competitor out of business, no action in tort would lie unless he could prove that what they had done was not in furtherance of their business interests, but out of malice; an impossible task. The leading case is the *Mogul S.S. Co. Ltd. v McGregor, Gow and Co.*, [1892] All E.R. Rep. 263, where a newcomer attempted to break into the closely organised China–England carrying trade. The fact that all those already engaged in the business ganged up against him and refused to accept any goods for shipment from those who dealt with the newcomer did not confer a right of action on him, although calculated, and indeed intended, to damage him.

The law remains unaltered so far as transactions outside the United Kingdom are concerned. All the ferry services that take passengers and vehicles from the United Kingdom to Europe are at liberty to, and in fact do, agree to fix and maintain minimum prices.

But, so far as these practices within the United Kingdom are concerned, they are now unlawful.

They were struck at by legislation in the United States and Canada as early as 1890; but it was not until 1948 that Britain was willing to recognise that the problem existed. In the slovenly way in which legislation is enacted in Britain, the *Monopolies and Restrictive Practices (Inquiry and Control) Act* was passed in 1948; to be amended by the *Restrictive Practices Act, 1956*. After that by the *Resale Prices Act, 1964*, resale price maintenance was made illegal except as expressly approved by the Restrictive Practices Court.

The 1956 Act requires all parties operating a 'Restrictive Trading' agreement, as there defined, to register it with a new officer termed the Registrar of Restrictive Trading Agreements. It is his duty to bring all such agreements before the Restrictive Practices Court, which is concerned only whether such practices are in the public interest or not. An agreement includes any agreement or arrangement whether or not it is intended to be enforceable by legal action. So that all sorts of bargains between parties are caught by the Act besides formal contracts. As Lord Justice Dankwert commented in 1963, 'Heaven help the lawyer who has to advise a client.' Heaven has helped the lawyers, not least of all in the multiplicity and dura- tion fees for such cases. A test of 'an arrangement' is whether the party would consider himself under a moral obligation to do what he has undertaken to do. It will be seen therefore that agreements which are far removed from the normal concept of contractual obligations may be caught by this Act. 'A wink is as good as a nod.' Even an arrangement whereby manufacturers notified one another of the prices they were charging may be held to be caught by the Act. Section 6 (1) specifically applies to situations where the parties have by some such 'arrangement' limited their freedom to contract with others.

If the agreements between the parties are contractual, failure to register them does not apparently make them unenforceable in the Courts.

The *Resale Prices Act, 1964* made minimum price agreements void except in so far as they are approved by the Restrictive Practices Court, but where they are so approved—as in the case of books, for example, by the *Net Book Agreement, 1957*, [1962] 3 All E.R. 751— these minimum prices are binding on retailers irrespective of whether there is any privity of contract between them and the manufacturers or publishers and regardless of any absence of consideration (see page 81).

Other Contracts which it is Contrary to Public Policy to Enforce

In the same category as contracts in restraint of trade may be classed other types of agreement or clauses in agreements which the law will not enforce.

1. Agreements to oust the jurisdiction of the Courts

While it is always open to the parties to make an agreement ex- pressly excluding contractual intent (see page 74), it is not open to them to exclude the jurisdiction of the Courts. The historical back- ground to this is the long (and losing) battle that the Courts fought to prevent the parties substituting arbitration for litigation. An arbitra- tion results from an agreement between the parties to submit any dis- pute to a tribunal of their own choice and to abide by its decision. So fond are business men of arbitration, that clauses to this effect are to be found in every building contract, every commodity contract and every shipping contract. The advantages are apparent to business men. The tribunal sits in private at a time and place convenient to the parties; the arbitrators are the servants of the parties and therefore much more courteous and considerate than the High Court Judges who still regard themselves 'as lions under the throne' and not as servants of the public; there is a minimum of formality and no recourse to the thousand pages of 'The White Book'—the *Practice of the Supreme Court*; anybody can appear as advocate for the parties; and the dispute is settled more speedily, and at less cost usually than in any Court. The partiality of business men for arbitration is well founded, and in spite of all the efforts of the Courts to prevent it, it has become the most favoured method of settling commercial disputes; so much so that the lawyers have decided that if you 'can't beat 'em—'join 'em!'. High Court Judges are now empowered to sit as arbitrators.

The long battle of the lawyers against arbitration eventually ended in 1855 when the House of Lords—by a majority of one—held that a clause which made arbitration a condition precedent to an action did not infringe the principle that it is unlawful to agree to supplant or oust the jurisdiction of the English Courts: *Scott v Avery*, [1855] All E.R. Rep. Later, it was held in the *Atlantique Shipping* case, [1922] All E.R. Rep., that there was no objection to a clause which deprived a party of an action if he did not go to arbitration within a certain period, e.g. within six weeks after goods have been landed from a ship. The *Arbitration Act, 1950* recognised the reality of the situation and retains some measure of control by the Courts over arbitration.

But the same principle has been applied in recent times to cases where clubs or associations have purported to deprive their members of access to the Courts; see *Lee v Showmen's Guild*, [1952] 1 All E.R. 1175 and *Baker v Jones*, [1954] 2 All E.R. 553.

2. Agreements to the detriment of the institution of marriage

Included in these are promises never to marry at all and marriage brokerage contracts, i.e. the sort of business carried on by marriage bureaux where they undertake to provide a spouse for payment of a fee. But, by a quirk of the law, it would appear that money paid under such a contract is recoverable even though the contract has been substantially performed: *Hermann v Charlesworth* (1905).

3. Agreements contrary to the interests of justice

Formerly, agreements not to prosecute for a criminal offence—such as embezzlement—if the money was restored, were not binding because they were in themselves the criminal offence of 'compounding a felony'. But the *Criminal Justice Act, 1967* abolished this crime, and although it made the acceptance of any consideration for nondisclosure of an arrestable offence a crime, there is an express exception in favour of a consideration which is 'the making good of loss or injury occasioned by the offence'. It would appear therefore that such promises may now be binding.

But any other contract which tends to interfere with the course of justice is not binding; and a contract, for example, whereby one person who has stood bail for another should be indemnified against loss is not merely void but an indictable offence in itself.

4. Agreement for cohabitation

If you promise to pay a girl £20 a week so long as she lives with you, it is contrary to public policy to enforce this promise, whether it be a simple contract or in a deed. Mr. Perkins promised by deed to pay Miss Walker a certain sum while she cohabited with him and after his death £60 per year: *Walker v Perkins* (1764). It was held void. And a promise in writing to pay an allowance to a past mistress is unenforceable because there is no consideration (*Beaumont v Reeve*, 1846); but apparently there is no objection to it, if it be by deed.

This is the law as it stands at the moment on the basis of these old cases; but whether a modern court would hold unenforceable an instrument whereby a man attempted to make provision for the woman he loved during his lifetime and after his death, merely on the ground that he was not married to her, is difficult to say. It is to be hoped that they would not be so heartless, but the history of the common law gives no cause for optimism.

5. Agreements for trading with an enemy

Quite apart from any Statute passed relating to this subject, on the outbreak of war all contracts with enemy nationals are dissolved and any contract make with them is void. An enemy for this purpose is anybody who resides in enemy country, or any territory under the control of an enemy. But if there is 'an accrued right', this may, in some circumstances, be merely suspended and not discharged—as where a husband was held liable for instalments under a separation agreement to a wife who was in enemy-occupied territory: *Bevan v Bevan*, [1955] 2 All E.R. 206.

6. Agreements for procurement of royal honours or otherwise injurious to the public service

A Col. Parkinson was promised by the secretary of the College of Ambulance that if he made a large donation to that body, he would receive a knighthood. The Colonel paid up but did not receive his knighthood and sued for the return of his money: *Parkinson v The College of Ambulance Ltd.*, [1924] All E.R. Rep. 325.

Gaming and Wagering Contracts

The common law had no objection to enforcing promises to pay money lost at gaming or on a bet by the action of *assumpsit*, except that the judges occasionally protested when they were called upon to decide which of two flies had reached the top of a window first, and matters of that nature.

But the aristocracy were very much concerned with relieving their offspring from the consequences of their own folly, with the result that Parliament began to intervene to protect those who had wagered and lost. An Act of 1710 made all securities (such as cheques) given for money lost on gaming absolutely void, but this was in due course replaced by the Act of 1835 to which reference is made later. Gaming is now defined by s. 52 (1) of the *Gaming Act, 1968*, as:

'The playing of any game of chance for winnings in money or money's worth, whether any person playing the game is at risk of losing money or money's worth or not.'

It is therefore presumably not gaming if you stake your wife or fiancée at roulette, since the money element is essential. The same section also provides that 'a game of chance' includes a game of chance and skill combined, or a pretend game of chance; but it excludes 'an athletic sport or game'.

For the purpose of the other Acts, a more extensive definition has been adopted, wide enough to include playing any game for winning money or money's worth and it includes horse-racing.

A wager is simply a bet and wagering was defined by Hawkins J. in *Carlill v The Carbolic Smoke Ball Co.* (1892) as:

'one by which two persons, professing to hold opposite views touching the issue of a future uncertain event, mutually agree that, dependent upon the determination of that event, one shall win from the other, and that other shall pay or hand over to him, a sum of money or other stake; neither of the contracting parties having any other interest in that contract than the sum or stake he will so win or lose, there being no other real consideration for making of such contract by either of the parties. It is essential to a wagering contract that each party may under it either win or lose, whether he will win or lose being dependent on the issue of the event, and therefore remaining uncertain until that issue is known. If either of the parties may win but cannot lose, or may lose but cannot win, it is not a wagering contract.'

It is generally held that the use of the words 'future uncertain event' is too narrow, and that there can be a wager on *past* events, e.g. which footballer scored most goals last year, or any *present* fact, e.g. whether Jupiter is inhabited or even *certain* future events, e.g. what time the sun rises tomorrow; provided that the parties hold different views.

But one thing has been decided beyond peradventure—there can only be *two parties* to a wager. 'You cannot have a multipartite agreement for a bet.'

Stock Exchange and Commodity Market transactions are excluded from wagering, even though there may never be an intention to take up the shares or the commodity, and all the transactions are done on margins. The Court will scrutinise them to see whether they are really commercial transactions or bets.

A bet between two people on the result of a game is a **gaming wager.**

The Statutes and Gaming and Wagering

The *Gaming Act, 1835*: by this Act all securities for money lost on *gaming* or in repayment of money lent for gaming are deemed to be given for an illegal consideration.

They are not void, but if the drawer of a cheque, for example, stops payment the drawee cannot successfully sue on the cheque.

Cases on the Act have held that a third party who takes the cheque and gives value for it can sue the drawer on the cheque if it be dishonoured, provided he does not know that it was received in payment of money won on *gaming*. But even if he does know it is the proceed of money won on a *wager*, (that is, not a gaming wager) he can recover, for this Act deals only with gaming and not wagering. So if you give your grocer a bookmaker's cheque for a case of champagne and tell him you have won it by a bet on the results of the Cup Final, he can sue on it; but not if you tell him you have won it on the Grand National.

Since the *Gaming Act, 1968,* cheques given in licensed gaming houses for play are valid, provided they are not post-dated, they are exchanged for cash or tokens, and they are presented to a bank within two days.

The *Gaming Act, 1845*: This Act provides:

All contracts or agreements whether by parol or in writing, by way of gaming or wagering shall be null and void and no suit shall be brought or maintained in any court of law and equity for recovering any sum of money or valuable thing alleged to be won upon any wager; or which shall have been deposited in the hands of any person to abide the event on which any wager shall have been made. . . .

There are three limbs of the section. The first makes contracts for gaming or wagering null and void; but that does not mean that the contract is illegal, therefore collateral transactions are valid.

The effect, of course, is that you cannot sue your bookmaker if he fails to pay you your winnings; nor can he sue you if he allows you to bet on credit and you lose.

For a long time it was thought that subsequent promises to pay some or all the money lost on bets were enforceable provided that there was fresh consideration, such as a forbearance to report the defaulter to Tattersalls, but this was held, in *Hill v William Hill (Park Lane) Ltd.*, [1949] 2 All E.R. 432, not to be the case. Subsequent contracts are as much caught by the second limb of the 1845 Act as the original bargain. The money is still money 'alleged to have been won on a wager'.

The effect of the Act on stakeholders has been held to be: if both parties hand their stakes to the stakeholder, if he pays over both stakes to the winner, he cannot be sued by the loser. But if, before he does this, the loser (or the winner for that matter) sues to recover his stake he can do so, as money 'had and received' to his benefit. But the winner cannot sue both for his stake and the loser's stake, i.e. his winnings.

The *Gaming Act, 1892* does two things:

(i) It prevents an action being brought for money paid in settlement of bets or gaming debts by somebody other than the principal. If out of charity, you pay off your friend's debt to the bookmaker, you cannot recover it from your friend.

(ii) It prevents a betting agent suing his principal for remuneration.

Loans for gaming or bets. Money lent for this purpose may fall into three classes:

(i) Where the loan consists of paying betting losses direct to the winner, e.g. settling a bookmaker's account. This is clearly caught by the 1892 Act and is irrecoverable.

(ii) Where *A* lends *B* money to pay *B*'s losses. Here the law appears to be that even if *A* knows the purpose for which the loan is required, it is recoverable provided that *A* has not imposed a stipulation that it shall be used only for that purpose and none other: *McDonald v Green*, [1950] 2 All E.R. 1240.

(iii) Money lent for the purpose of laying a bet or playing a game. It is sometimes said on the basis of the decision in *Carlton Hall Club v Laurence* (1929) that this money is irrecoverable. But that is a highly doubtful decision, because there was in fact no loan of money. A cheque was accepted for chips in an illegal gaming house and the action was framed as 'a loan' since obviously the cheque, which was stopped, could not be sued upon by reason of the 1835 Act. The better view is that a loan is recoverable even though the lender may know that the borrower intends to use it for backing a horse or playing roulette. But this does not apply if the loan is made within a licensed gaming house—that is an illegal act by virtue of s. 16 (b) of the 1968 Act.

CHAPTER TEN

MISREPRESENTATION, DURESS AND UNDUE INFLUENCE

The Nature of a Misrepresentation

A false statement which induces a person to undertake contractual obligations is termed a misrepresentation. At one time the term was restricted to statements which had caused a party to enter a contract but which were not a part of the contract itself. Some of the earliest cases deal with the sale of inns. A statement as to the amount of beer sold might induce a man to purchase an inn but would not form any part of the contract of sale, which after 1677 would have to be in writing. This corresponds to the Roman *error in causa*—mistake as to the reason or motive for entering into the contract.

This terminology has become less exact, and the expression is now used for a statement made in the course of negotiations leading up to the acceptance of contractual obligations, whether or not it is incorporated as a term of the contract. The expression 'a mere misrepresentation' is sometimes used now to distinguish those statements which form no part of the contract itself.

If the misrepresentation forms a term of the contract an action for damages will always lie, and it matters not how or why the misrepresentation came to be made.

It is often extremely hard to know whether a misrepresentation has become a term of the contract or not. The test is said to be: 'Is there evidence of an intention by one or more parties that there should be contractual liability in respect of the statement?' In *Oscar Chess Ltd. v Williams*, [1957] 1 All E.R. 325, a statement that a car was a '1948 model' was held to be a mere misrepresentation, and not a term of the contract; while in *Dick Bentley Productions Ltd. v Harold Smith (Motors) Ltd.*, [1965] 2 All E.R. 65, the Court of Appeal decided that a statement that a car had done '20,000 miles' was a term of the contract as well as a misrepresentation. The modern tendency, before the passing of the *Misrepresentation Act, 1967*, was to incorporate a misrepresentation as a contractual obligation wherever possible. The reason was that before that Act, no damages could be given for a mere representation unless it could be proved to be fraudulent, whereas damages could always be given for breach of a term of the contract.

137

To have any effect on a contract a misrepresentation must be a statement of existing fact and not a mere expression of opinion, 'a trade puff' or a promise as to future conduct.

If you are induced to buy a certain soap by the statement that you will 'become lovelier every day', you are unlikely to have a remedy in law if you become uglier. Estate agents' hyperbole, therefore, such as describing land as 'fertile and improvable' or 'valuable', is no more than a trade puff and not meant to be taken seriously.

In *Bassett v Wilkinson*, [1926] All E.R. Rep. 343, the statement by a vendor of land in New Zealand, who had never run sheep on the land himself, that it could carry 2,000 sheep was held to be no more than an expression of an opinion.

But 'it is often fallaciously assumed that a statement of opinion cannot involve the statement of a fact'. It can when:

(i) the opinion is not genuinely held, for 'the state of a man's mind is as much a fact as the state of his digestion'.

(ii) the person expressing the opinion has no reasonable grounds for holding it, as where it was stated that an annuitant was 'believed to have no aggregatable estate' and in fact no inquiries of any kind had been made: *Brown v Raphael*, [1958] 2 All E.R. 79.

(iii) the facts are not known equally by both parties. A statement of opinion by one who is in a position to know the facts very often involves a statement of material fact, for he impliedly states that he knows facts which justify his opinion. In *South v Land and House Property Corporation* the plaintiffs put up for sale a hotel which was described as 'let to Mr. Frederick Fleck (a most desirable tenant)'. Between contract and conveyance, the most desirable tenant went bankrupt. On the facts it was held that this amounted to a misrepresentation, since it was known to the seller that Fleck had paid his last quarter's rent late, by instalments and under pressure.

Silence can also amount to a misrepresentation. Normally, there is no obligation on a person entering a contract to disclose material facts but silence can amount to a misrepresentation where:

(i) what is not said, makes what is said untrue. If a man sells a block of flats asserting that all are let and produce a certain income, what he says may be falsified by knowledge that all the tenants had given notice.

(ii) the contracts are of the class termed '*uberrimae fidei*' ('of utmost good faith'). Most of these are contracts of insurance, where the insured is required to make full disclosure of:

(a) anything that would influence the mind of a prudent underwriter as to whether or not he would accept the risk.

(b) anything that would influence the mind of a prudent underwriter in fixing the premium.

This applies to cases such as those where a parent insures a car in his own name, knowing perfectly well that the only, or principal user, will be his son or daughter under the age of 23. It also applies, of course, to contracts of life insurance where the insured fails to disclose every material fact.

(iii) the relationship between the contractual parties is one of the sort termed **fiduciary.** The principle applies to family settlements, as in the case where a younger son entered into a division of property on the assumption that his older brother was illegitimate. Whereas in fact, he well knew that there had been a secret marriage between his parents before his elder brother was born.

(iv) there has been a change of circumstances which has made the statement that was true before now untrue. Dr. O'Flanagan in January 1934 told a prospective purchaser that his medical practice brought in £2,000 a year. In May the contract for its purchase was signed, but in the meantime Dr. O'Flanagan had become seriously ill, with the result that the income of the practice had declined to not more than £5 per week. Failure to disclose this change in circumstances was a misrepresentation: *With v O'Flanagan*, [1936] 1 All E.R. 727.

The misrepresentation only affects the contract where the party deceived has relied upon the false statement and not where he has entered into the contract in reliance on his own judgment or after investigation by appropriate agents. But if a material representation is made which is calculated to induce a man to enter a contract, it is an inference of law that he has been induced by that.

The Effect of a Misrepresentation

Up to 1883 a misrepresentation had no effect on a contract at common law unless it were fraudulent in the sense that the maker could be shown to have known that the statement was false at the time he made it.

The common law judges even then had no power to rescind it or set aside the contract and all they could do was to award damages in a tort action for deceit. The action was exactly the same as that in *Wilkinson v Downton* (1897), where a wife was held entitled to recover damages when a joker told her falsely that her husband was lying at Leytonstone with a broken leg.

The Court of Chancery in its equitable discretion would refuse a decree of specific performance, in the limited cases where that remedy might lie, if the defendant had been induced to enter the contract by an untrue representation—thereby leaving the plaintiff to his remedy for damages at common law. And it would also rescind the contract if there was 'the most clear and decisive proof of fraudulent misrepresentation'. If that did not exist, there was no remedy, as can be seen from the case of *Attwood v Small* (1838), which was up to that date the longest civil trial that had ever been held in England. It occupied various Courts for no less than 67 days, some 40 of them in the House of Lords. The plaintiffs failed to secure a rescission of a contract to purchase an iron mine, in part because they were unable to prove that the false statement made about the quality of the iron ore was false to the knowledge of the seller.

In 1881, however, the case of *Redgrave v Hurd* 1882, [1881–5] All E.R. Rep. 77 fundamentally altered the law. By an ingenious piece of sophistry, Jessel M.R. held that 'even assuming that moral fraud must be shown in order to set aside a contract, you have it where a man, having obtained a beneficial contract by a statement which he now knows to be false, insists upon keeping that contract. To do so is moral delinquency; no man ought to seek to take advantage of his own false statements.'

In that case a solicitor had inserted an advertisement in *The Law Times* for a partner, 'an efficient lawyer and advocate, about forty, who would not object to purchase advertiser's suburban residence' ... The defendant replied to the advertisement and the plaintiff assured him the business was worth £300–£400 p.a. In reliance on that statement the defendant agreed to purchase the house and a share in the practice for £1,600, paying £100 deposit. After contract but before conveyance, the defendant found out that the gross takings of the practice were less than £200 per annum. This was held to be an innocent and not a fraudulent misrepresentation—presumably only because of the Court's tenderness to those of its own ilk—and at first instance the defendant was ordered to specifically perform the contract and refused rescission, the judge holding that he had not relied on the oral representation. However, the Court of Appeal refused the plaintiff's application for specific performance and granted an order for rescission in favour of the defendant.

Henceforth, the Courts would set aside (grant rescission of) contracts for innocent misrepresentation.

However, rescission could only be granted in limited circumstances. The right to rescind for innocent misrepresentation was lost if:

(i) the parties could not be restored to their original position—if what the law termed *restitutio in integrum* could not be granted.

(ii) the contract had been fully performed. If, for example, the application for rescission in *Redgrave v Hurd* had been made after the conveyance had been completed; or in the case of goods, if they had been accepted and the property passed to the buyer.

(iii) possibly, where there was a great interval of time between the contract and the discovery of the falsity of the misrepresentation.

(iv) the misrepresentation was also a term of the contract, but only a subsidiary one. In that case, the injured party had no right to rescind but could only sue for damages.

(v) an innocent third party had acquired rights as the result of the contract.

(vi) the contract had in any way been affirmed after knowledge of the falsity of the misrepresentation.

The *Misrepresentation Act, 1967*

The first thing the 1967 Act did was to remove two of the bars to rescission mentioned above.

Section 1 enacts removal of certain bars to rescission for innocent misrepresentation

'Where a person has entered into a contract after a misrepresentation has been made to him, and

(a) the misrepresentation has become a term of the contract, or
(b) the contract has been performed or both,

then, if otherwise he would be allowed to rescind the contract without alleging fraud, he shall be so entitled, subject to the provisions of this Act, notwithstanding the matter mentioned in paragraphs (a) and (b) of this section.'

The Law Reform Committee recommended that sales of land should be excluded from the proposed Act but, as will be seen, there is no such exemption. Even where the land has been conveyed to the purchaser the conveyance is now liable to be set aside for innocent misrepresentation. But no such case has yet occurred, and it is much more likely that in these circumstances the Court would take advantage of section 2 (2) not to allow rescission, but to award damages in lieu of it.

Section 2 (1) gives a right to damages for innocent misrepresentation

'Where a person has entered into a contract after a misrepresentation has been made to him by another party thereto and as a result thereof he has suffered loss, then if the person making the misrepresentation would be liable to damages in respect thereof had the misrepresentation been made fraudulently, that person shall be so liable notwithstanding that the misrepresentation was not made fraudulently, unless he proves that he had reasonable ground to believe and did believe up to the time the contract was made that the facts represented were true.'

That means, in plain language, that damages will be awarded for innocent misrepresentation except where the defendant satisfies the Court that he believed on reasonable grounds that what he said was true.

Section 2 (2) confers on the Courts a discretion to grant damages in lieu of granting a decree of rescission

'Where a person has entered into a contract after a misrepresentation has been made to him otherwise than fraudulently, and he would be entitled by reason of the misrepresentation, to rescind the contract, then, if it is claimed in any proceedings arising out of the contract that the contract ought to be or has been rescinded, the court or arbitrator may declare the contract subsisting and award damages in lieu of rescission if of opinion that it would be equitable to do so, having regard to the nature of the misrepresentation and the loss that would be caused by it if the contract were upheld, as well as to the loss that rescission would cause to the other party.'

The Act is silent as to what measure damages are to be given—whether the standard should be that for a deliberate tort or as if for breach of contract (see page 53). The general view is that it is the tort standard that is appropriate.

Section 3 limits the right to exclude misrepresentation by an exemption clause (see page 168)

'Avoidance of certain provisions excluding liability for misrepresentation—if any agreement (whether made before or after the commencement of this Act) contains a provision which would exclude or restrict:

(i) any liability to which a party to a contract may be subject by reason of any misrepresentation made by him before the contract was made, or

(ii) any remedy available to another party to the contract by reason of such a misrepresentation, then

that provision shall be of no effect except to the extent (if any) that in any proceedings arising out of the contract, the court or arbitrator may allow reliance on it as being fair and reasonable in the circumstances of the case.'

The present position therefore is that for all *mere* misrepresentations, i.e. those which are **not terms of the contract,** whether fraudulent or innocent, the aggrieved party can:

1. Sue for damages

If fraudulent, damages are for deceit.

If innocent, the damages are:

    (i) under s. 2 (1) of the *Misrepresentation Act, 1967*

    (ii) and/or for the tort of negligent mis-statement

In the case of innocent misrepresentation the defendant has a defence if under s. 2 (1) he can satisfy the Court that he has reasonable grounds for believing and that he did in fact believe what he said, to be true.

2. Refuse to perform his side of the contract

3. Claim rescission of the contract, save that there is now no absolute right to rescind in the case of innocent misrepresentation and the Court has the discretion to order damages in lieu of rescission.

Duress and Undue Influence

At common law the word *duress* means actual or threatened violence or restriction of liberty. In cases where a person had been induced to accept contractual obligations under the threat of violence or imprisonment, the Court on satisfactory proof will set aside the contract.

The reported cases are where people have promised to reimburse money under the threat or implied threat of prosecution for some criminal offence. The threat to liberty need not be directed against the contracting party but somebody near or dear to him, and it need not be explicit. A guarantee was obtained from a family company under a veiled threat to prosecute a member of the family for an alleged forgery. The guarantee was set aside: *Mutual Finance Co. Ltd. v John Wetton and Sons Ltd.*, [1937] 2 All E.R. 657.

Equity would grant relief more liberally for what is termed **undue influence.**

This may take two forms:

    (i) A presumption of undue influence arises where there is what is termed a **fiduciary** relationship (i.e. a relationship of trust) between the parties. Examples of such relationships are those between parent and child, solicitor and client, doctor and patient and, most common of all, between priest and parishioner, or their equivalents in any religion. There is a general power to set aside a transaction where there is undue influence between the parties even if they are unrelated. Anybody who establishes themselves in a position of trust and domination over another can be held to have exercised undue influence. A woman of 70 took a lodger who so commended himself to her that eventually she transferred the title of her house to him. The lodger sold the house to a purchaser who knew nothing of the circumstances save that the widow was actually in possession of the house. The whole transaction was set aside for undue influence: *Hodgson v Marks*, [1970] 2 All E.R. 684.

(ii) Even where there is no fiduciary relationship, a contract may be liable to be set aside, if one party is clearly under the dominion of the other.

In the first type of case, undue influence is presumed and has to be rebutted, whereas in the second type of case it has to be proved.

CHAPTER ELEVEN

UNILATERAL CONTRACTS

The nature of unilateral contracts has been discussed earlier (see page 40). There are various problems about them which now fall for discussion. The solutions to such problems are not helped by the persistent tendency of textbook writers, following the 19th-century judges, to treat the promise in a unilateral contract as the same thing as 'the offer' of a synallagmatic one.

Logically they are quite different. If a man says to a girl: 'I will give you £10 if you dye your hair blonde by Thursday', that means: 'I here and now accept a contractual obligation to pay £10, subject to your doing the thing I require.' There is no obligation on the promisee, of course, to dye her hair.

If, on the other hand, he makes a proposal in the form of an offer of a synallagmatic contract, he is saying: 'I will accept contractual obligation, if you will also accept contractual obligation.' His offer is strictly conditional on an acceptance by the other, and the assumption of contractual obligations lies in the future. In the first case, there is an immediately binding obligation on the promisor, in the second case there is no binding obligation on the offeror unless and until his offer is accepted. A promise and the offer of a promise are two different things.

So that if the man says: 'If you will promise to dye your hair blonde by Thursday I will give you £10', he is making an offer of a synallagmatic contract which only becomes binding if the offeree promises to do the thing asked.

The distinction between the two sorts of contract may be a fine one, but it is fundamental. For one thing **damages can never be awarded against the promisee of a unilateral contract** for the simple reason that since he assumes no contractual obligations, he can never be in breach of them: *United Dominion Trust v Eagle Aviation*, [1968] 1 All E.R. 104.

The application of this distinction is of vital importance in other respects. In the first case, that of the unilateral contract where the only obligation is on the promisor, the promisee does not have to communicate in any way with the promisor to obtain the promised sum. All she has to do is to dye her hair or whatever is asked for.

In the second case, that of the synallagmatic contract, there is no contractual obligation on the offeror until not only has his offer been accepted by the other party but that acceptance has been communicated to the offeror; then, and then only, does his offer of a promise become a promise.

Most of the problems that have arisen about unilateral contracts can be resolved if this distinction is borne in mind.

Must the Promisee Know?

The problems are:

1. Can the promisee recover the sum promised if he did the act required *before* the promise was made?
2. Can the promisee recover the sum promised if he did the act required in ignorance of the promise?

These two problems are closely related. If the promise of a unilateral contract is equated to the offer of a synallagmatic contract, obviously a man cannot accept an offer which has not been communicated to him. And it would appear to be essential that the act must be done at the request of the promisor and therefore *after* the promise has been made.

It is for this reason that the decision in the case of *Gibbons v Proctor* (1891) has been so hotly assailed over the years. The defendant, a parson, had printed a handbill offering a reward for information leading to the criminal prosecution of the person who had committed a crime. The plaintiff, before he had seen this handbill and, apparently, before he knew that a reward was offered, provided information which led to the conviction of the person who had committed the crime. It was argued on behalf of the defendant that the plaintiff was in no way influenced by the offer of the reward as he did not even know of it. In spite of that fact, he succeeded in being awarded the reward. The same principle is also to be found in the earlier case of *Smith v Moore* 1845, and has been followed in several United States cases; so much so, that a leading textbook in that country sees no obstacle to the creation of a principle that 'where an offer has been published, that act empowers others to create contractual relations by doing the act requested even though without knowledge of the request'. *Corbin on Contracts*, Vol. 1, Sec. 59, p. 245.

If you substitute the word 'promise' for the word 'offer', that is an acceptable proposition in the view of the present author. There is nothing in law, morality or justice that requires that a man know of a promise before he can recover for doing the very thing the promisor required. Indeed, the exact opposite is true. If the promisor was prepared to pay for the information, and gets what he wanted, why should he be allowed to escape from his contractual obligation on a technicality?

However, one thing is clear. A unilateral contract must require some act by the promisee. If it is money to be paid on the happening of a certain event only, it is a *conditional gift* and not a unilateral contract. 'I will give you £10 if there is an earthquake tomorrow' is not a contract at all, but a promise without consideration, a conditional gift, because it requires no action from the promisee. So the promisee cannot recover the £10, even if there is an earthquake. But, of course, the same promise in a synallagmatic contract, such as an insurance contract where the promisee has provided consideration for the promise, would be enforceable.

Can the Promisor Withdraw?

A much more difficult problem is whether the promisor can withdraw his promise before the promisee has completed his performance. And related to that is yet another problem: does the promisor impliedly promise that he will do nothing to prevent the promisee performing the act the promisor requests?

I promise you £100 if you walk from London to York. Am I entitled, as you near the walls of York, to dash up to you and say, 'I withdraw my promise'? Am I entitled to have every road to York barricaded to prevent you earning your £100?

If the promise is the same as an offer it is axiomatic that an offer can be withdrawn at any time before it is accepted. But, as we have seen, it is not really that at all. The rational and sensible solution would be to say that in unilateral contracts, there are implied promises by the promisor that he will not withdraw his promise once the promisee has started on the performance of the act required, and that he will do nothing to prevent the promisee performing the act.

For that sensible suggestion there is some authority. As long ago as 1864 Willes J. said in *Inchbold v Weston*: 'I apprehend that wherever money is to be paid by one man to another upon a given event, the party on whom is cast the obligation to pay is liable to the party who is to receive the money if he does any act which prevents or makes it less probable that he should receive it.' And, more recently, Lord Denning said, where a father had promised to pay £1 toward the maintenance of an illegitimate child: 'I regard the father's promise in this case as what is sometimes called a unilateral contract, a promise in return for the mother's looking after the child. Once the mother embarked in the task of looking after the child there was a binding contract.' *Ward v Byham*, [1956] 2 All E.R. 318. Earlier the same judge had said the same thing in *Errington v Errington and Woods*, [1952] 1 All E.R. 149. The plaintiff in that case brought an action for recovery of a house. The father-in-law of the defendant had promised her that a house that he owned would be hers if she and her husband paid the mortgage instalments.

His Lordship said: 'The father's promise was a unilateral contract, a promise of the house in return for their act of paying the instalments. It could not be revoked by him once the couple entered on the performance of the act . . . The father expressly promised the couple that the property should belong to them as soon as the mortgage was paid and impliedly promised that so long as they paid the instalments to the building society they should be allowed to remain in possession. They were not purchasers because they never bound themselves to pay the instalments, but nevertheless they were in a position analogous to purchasers. They have acted on the promise and neither the father, nor his widow, his successor in title, can eject them in disregard of it.'

Unhappily against these sensible observations there is the express authority of the House of Lords. In *Luxor (Eastbourne) Ltd. v Cooper*, [1941] 1 All E.R. 39, two companies each promised an estate agent £5,000 if he should introduce a person who would buy two cinemas they owned. The estate agent found such a person but, instead of buying the cinemas, the transaction was effected by the purchaser buying the shares in the two companies which owned the cinemas. The House of Lords held that the estate agent was not able to recover anything. 'Contracts by which owners of property, desiring to dispose of it, put it in the hands of agents on commission terms, are not (in default of specific provisions) contracts of employment . . . *No obligation is imposed on the agent to do anything.*' In other words, it was purely a unilateral contract.

'Implied terms as we know can only be justified under the compulsion of some necessity. No such compulsion or necessity exists in the case under consideration. The agent is promised a commission if he introduces a purchaser at a specific price . . . The agent takes the risk in the hope of substantial remuneration for comparatively small exertion . . . A sum of £10,000 (the equivalent of the remuneration of a year's work by a Lord Chancellor) for work done within a period of eight or nine days is no mean reward and is one well worth the risk.'

Most estate agents' contracts, however, are not now unilateral contracts but synallagmatic ones, for the agent expressly promises, amongst other things, to use his best endeavours to sell the property.

CHAPTER TWELVE

CONTRACTS OF MUTUAL OBLIGATION
(SYNALLAGMATIC CONTRACTS)

Is Offer and Acceptance Essential?

Older textbooks, and the most elementary and inaccurate ones of today, describe Offer and Acceptance as being essential to a contract. This is just not true. There are many cases where it is impossible to find any Offer or Acceptance, and still more where the so-called Offer is an artificial invention of the Courts.

A fair example of the case where there is no discoverable Offer or Acceptance is *Clarke v Dunraven* (1897). Two yachts were entered in a race run on the Clyde by the Mudhook Yacht Club when one collided with the other as the result of the breach of the rules by one of the yachts, the *Satanita*, but without negligence on the part of the owner or skipper. If there was no contract between the two owners, the damages the owner of the *Satanita* would be liable to pay would be, by the *Merchant Shipping Act Amendment Act, 1862*, limited to the trifling sum of £8 per ton for the small tonnage of the *Satanita*. If, however, there was a contract between the various owners entered in the race, the owner of *Satanita* was liable for 'all damages arising therefrom'.

That there were contracts between the Club and each individual entrant is obvious. But the House of Lords held that there was also 'a contractual relation between the parties to this litigation', i.e. between one entrant and another. Some ingenuity has been expended in discovering an Offer and Acceptance in this case, but the truth of the situation is that there is none. The House of Lords addressed itself to the correct crucial issue: on the facts of the case, did the parties accept contractual obligations one to the other?

The same result followed in *Brogden v Metropolitan Railway* (1877), where the plaintiff sent a signed copy of a proposed contract to the defendants' agent, who altered it in a minor particular and put it in his desk unsigned. The parties behaved as if there was a concluded contract between them, by the plaintiff supplying coals on the terms of the contract to the defendants. The Court held they had assumed contractual obligations to one another in the terms of the unsigned contract.

More recently, a contract for a telephone answering service was found to exist even though the written document had not been signed on the part of the owner as required: *Robophone Facilities Ltd. v Blank*, [1966] 3 All E.R. 128.

In the case of contracts in writing for the sale of land, the contractual obligations are assumed not when the contracts are signed but when the last signed counterpart is received: *Eccles v Bryant and Pollock*, [1947] 2 All E.R. 865.

In many cases, too, the so-called offer is an entirely artificial concept and no more than a matter of business convenience. Who, except the English judges, would have thought of finding that the pushing of a piece of pasteboard towards an intending passenger by a booking clerk is the offer of a contract and that the taking up of the piece of pasteboard is the acceptance of the contract, with a multitude of conditions quite unknown to the acceptor? And who, but English judges, would have held that when a shopkeeper puts goods in his window for sale, he is not offering to sell them?

Invitations to Treat

If there is a particular item displayed in a shopkeeper's window, is a member of the public entitled to walk in and demand it at the price marked?

According to English law (but not Continental law), he is not. For the exhibition of the goods in the window is not an offer to sell the goods, which can be accepted, but is an indication that the shopkeeper is prepared to receive offers for them—at the price stated.

'In the case of an ordinary shop, although goods are displayed and it is intended that customers should go and choose what they want, the contract is not completed until, the customer having indicated the articles which he needs, the shopkeeper or someone on his behalf, accepts that offer. Then the contract is completed.'

It follows that if a fur coat is offered by mistake in the window for £10 instead of £100, the shopkeeper is entitled to refuse to sell it for the marked price (though he may now be liable to criminal proceedings under the *Trade Descriptions Act, 1968*).

In a self-service shop the goods are not offered for sale by being exhibited on the shelves. The offer to buy them is made by the customer who presents them at the cash desk. Boots had in one of their shops a self-service section with goods subject to Part I of the Poisons List, and which therefore could only be sold under the supervision of a qualified pharmacist. It was not disputed that a pharmacist was stationed at the cash desk, but the Pharmaceutical Society contended that the contract was made, and the property passed, when a customer took an article from a shelf and put it in a receptacle, the taking of such an article being an acceptance of the trader's offer. This contention was rejected by the judge of first instance and by the Court of Appeal. As Somervell L.J. said, 'I can see no reason at all . . . from drawing any different implication as a result of the layout' from that prevailing in an ordinary shop. As a result, the goods were dispensed under the supervision of a qualified pharmacist: *Pharmaceutical Society v Boots*, [1953] 1 All E.R. 452.

Advertisements in newspapers and periodicals which offer goods for sale are also not offers but invitations to treat. They are an indication that the would-be seller will receive offers. Partridge advertised in the Classified Advertisements column of the magazine *Cage and Aviary Birds* 'Quality British bramblefinch hens for sale'. It is a criminal offence under the *Protection of Birds Act, 1954* to, *inter alia*, offer for sale certain species of birds, of which this was one. A customer replying to the advertisement was supplied with a bird, and as a result Partridge was prosecuted under the Act. The Court held that he had not made an offer for sale by his advertisement. It was only an invitation to treat: *Partridge v Crittenden*, [1968] 2 All E.R. 421.

A declaration of intent or what is now commonplace in commercial practice, the letter of intent, *prima facie* does not constitute an offer and has no contractual significance. So where a father wrote to the man who was considering marrying his daughter: 'My daughter will have a share of what I leave after the death of her mother'; this was held to be a mere expression of intention and not a promise intended to create contractual obligations: *Farina v Fickins* (1900). But where 'a letter of intent' is of such a nature that serious obligations are incurred as a result of it, or the parties subsequently acted as if it were a binding contractual obligation, it would be open to a Court to find that contractual obligations were intended.

Where offers are made 'subject to contract', 'subject to the preparation of a formal lease', acceptance of them does not create a contractual relationship, for the parties have clearly indicated that they do not intend to assume obligations until a later event (see page 76).

The Relationship of Tenders to Offers

Few words have more meanings than the word 'tender'. In the expression 'legal tender' it means currency that cannot be refused in payment of a debt; in the law regarding performance of a contract, it may mean the offer of coins of the realm in satisfaction of a debt.

But it also has a meaning in the formation of contracts, as where a local authority invites 'tenders' for work.

In this connection, the word is less than precise and examiners who invite students to distinguish 'a tender' from 'an offer' betray their own ignorance. For a tender may simply be an offer in writing. If a body invites tenders for the supply of a new ambulance they are doing no more than inviting offers, and each tender is an offer.

In other senses, however, a tender may be a continuing offer to supply goods at a price 'as and when' required by the buyer. If so, like any other offer it can be withdrawn at any time before acceptance; that is before any particular order is placed, but not after.

Much will depend on the wording of the contract, but in this sort of case there is no obligation on the party inviting the tender to place an order at all. But if the party inviting the tender promises to take *all* his requirements from the party submitting the accepted tender, he will not be entitled to obtain any of them from somebody else. Nor will he be entitled to make use of this contractual arrangement to obtain goods not for his own requirements but for resale.

In all these situations, the meaning to be attached to 'tender' depends on the terms of the documents in question and there is no legal or standardised definition that can be ascribed to the word.

Offers may be made **by conduct** so that if a man who contracted to supply goods of another kind sends those that are not in accordance with the contract, this is considered to be an offer of the goods sent, which can be accepted or rejected at the volition of the other party.

Likewise, acceptance can be made by conduct, as where the auctioneer taps with his gavel to signify the acceptance of the final offer.

But whether the offer of a synallagmatic contract is made by acts or words, it must be communicated to the offeree.

The Lapsing of Offers

The offer remains open until it is brought to an end:

1. **By non-acceptance within a prescribed time.** A man offered another six weeks in which to decide whether he wanted to take a lease. After the expiration of that period, the offeree purported to accept it. He could not do so. The offer had come to an end with the expiration of the period.

   It should be noted that a promise to keep an offer open for a fixed time is not, however, binding on the offeror. If he cares he can withdraw it by notice of revocation a minute later. The reason for this is that there is no consideration for his promise. But if consideration, however trifling, is accepted, whether it be a cigarette or a peppercorn, in return for the promise to keep the offer open, it is termed *an option* and is binding. The promisor will be liable in damages if he withdraws his offer or contracts with some other party.

2. **After the lapse of a reasonable time.** What is a reasonable time is an issue of fact for the Court to decide in the circumstances of any particular case. In June, Mr. Montefiore applied for shares in the Ramsgate Victoria Hotel Company Ltd. Such applications have been held to constitute an offer. In November, a

letter of allotment, which is the acceptance, was sent to him. It was held that the offer had lapsed, and there was therefore no contract: *Ramsgate Victoria Hotel Co. Ltd. v Montefiore* (1866).

3. **Where a state of affairs, in reliance on which an offer was made, ceases to exist.** There is, as yet, little authority for this proposition except observations, which were *obiter*, made by Lord Denning in *Financings Ltd. v Stimson*, [1962] 3 All E.R. 386. 'Suppose an offer is made to buy a Rolls-Royce at a high price on one day and before it is accepted, it suffers the next day severe damage. Can it be accepted and the offeror bound? My answer is: no, because the offer is conditional on the goods at the moment of acceptance remaining in substantially the same condition as at the time of the offer.' This seems an eminently sensible proposition, especially since by virtue of s. 6 of the *Sale of Goods Act*, where specific goods have perished without the knowledge of the seller, the contract is void. In France in the case of partial loss or deterioration, the buyer has the choice of either rescinding the contract or, if he accepts the goods, securing abatement of price on a valuation; but this is not yet English law and unfortunately there seems to be express authority against it, to the effect that rotten potatoes are still potatoes for the purpose of section 7 of the *Sale of Goods Act, 1893*—goods perishing after agreement to sell but before sale. *Horn v Minister of Food*, [1948] 2 All E.R. 1036. But there are so many objections to this decision, that it seems hardly likely that the case will be followed by a superior court; or any other, for that matter.

These three cases are sometimes described as those where the offer *lapses*, as a distinction from those where the offer is revoked by the offeror.

The Revocation of an Offer

In addition to these situations, **an offer may be revoked at any time before acceptance** by the offeror; and that, as we have seen, notwithstanding he has promised to keep it open for a fixed period.

Revocation—the withdrawal of the offer—is not effective unless it has been communicated to the offeree.

In *Byrne v Van Tienhoven* (1880).

On **1st October,** Van Tienhoven and Co. from Cardiff posted a letter to Byrne in New York, offering him 1,000 boxes of tinplate.

8th October. The company posted a letter revoking their offer.

11th October. Byrne received the letter of the 1st October and immediately telegraphed acceptance.

20th October. The letter of revocation was received.

It was held that there was a binding contract made on 11th October.

To this principle there is said to be an exception, based on the case of *Dickinson v Dodds* (1876).

On **Wednesday** Dodds made Dickinson a written offer to sell certain houses, 'this offer to be left open until Friday 9 o'clock'.

On **Thursday** Dodds made a contract for the sale of the same property to Allan. Dickinson was informed that negotiations with Allan were going on and therefore hurried and accepted the offer.

On **Friday** before 9 a.m., his acceptance had been communicated to Dodds.

On those facts, Bacon V.C. made a decree of specific performance against Dodds. In that he was clearly wrong, because the contract with Allan was first in time. But Dickinson should have been entitled to damages against Dodds in that there was a contract between the two for the sale of the property which Dodds had broken by placing it outside his power to perform. On appeal however the Court of Appeal held there was no contract between Dickinson and Dodds. The headnote to the Law Report read: '*semble* the sale of the property to a third party would of itself amount to a withdrawal of the offer, even though the person to whom the offer was first made had no knowledge of the sale'. That is, in fact, what the judges in the Court of Appeal decided. 'To constitute a contract, it must appear that the two minds are one, at the same moment of time that is; that there was an offer continuing up to the time of acceptance,' said James L.J. Mellish L.J. said: 'If it be the law that, in order to make a contract, the two minds must be in agreement at some one time . . . If a man makes an offer to sell a particular horse in his stable, and says "I will give you until the day after tomorrow to accept the offer" and the next day goes and sells the horse to somebody else . . . can the person to whom the offer was originally made, then come and say "I accept" so as to make a binding contract and so as to be entitled to recover damages for the non-delivery of the horse?'

Mellish L.J. did not answer his own rhetorical question and implied that the answer was 'No'. But clearly on principle the correct answer is 'Yes'. There can be two contracts relating to the same subject matter, and even if the vendor cannot perform both contracts, he is liable to damages to one party. But, apparently, the learned judge thought the obvious answer was 'No'—which is in defiance of the well-established principle that an offer remains open until it lapses, is revoked or is rejected.

Ridiculous as the reasoning is in *Dickinson v Dodds*, the case has passed into the body of law in support of the proposition that a man cannot accept an offer that he knows—from any source—to have been withdrawn. The American *Restatement of the Law of Contract* adopts this position in a slightly modified form, limiting it to contracts of sale (why?) and where *reliable* information has been received. But in *Cartwright v Hoogstoel* (1911), a judge followed the earlier case. It may therefore appear to be reasonably well-established law, but there is no ground for believing that a modern court would follow a decision so patently rooted in fallacy, and so contrary to the principle that revocation of an offer must be communicated to the offeree by the offeror.

The Rejection of an Offer

An offer may also come to an end by **rejection** by the offeree. A **counter offer** is **rejection** of the offer.

In *Hyde v Wrench* (1840).

On **6th June** Wrench offered to sell his farm to Hyde for £1,000. Shortly afterwards, Hyde's agent called on him and offered £950, which offer Wrench asked for time to consider.

On **27th June** Wrench wrote and refused the £950.

On **29th June** Hyde wrote purporting to accept the offer of £1,000; but Wrench refused to accept it. Hyde brought an action for specific performance of the contract of sale.

The Court held that there was no contract; 'there exists no obligation of any sort between the parties'.

Therefore unless acceptance corresponds exactly with the offer it is a counter offer.

A company in North Wales sent a telegram to one in Canada: 'Confirming sale to you Grummond Mallard aircraft. Please remit £5,000.'

The Canadian company cabled back: 'Confirm purchase of Grummond Mallard aircraft terms set out your cable . . . £5,000 sterling forwarded your bank to be held in trust for your account pending delivery. Please confirm delivery to be made thirty days within this date.'

The trial judge construed the first telegram as an offer and the second as a counter offer because it introduced two new terms:

(i) the £5,000 asked for was only to be released on delivery;
(ii) there was no reference to delivery within 30 days in the original telegram.

Therefore there was no contract: *Northlands Airliners Ltd. v Dennis Ferranti Ltd.* (1970).

This is an example of the erroneous application of a correct principle to the facts. Clearly, the first telegram was not an offer but the confirmation of a concluded oral contract.

The principle is correctly seen in *Neale v Merritt* (1930). Merritt offered land to Neale at £280. Neale replied accepting and enclosed £80 and a promise to pay the balance by four monthly instalments of £50. This variation of the offer was held to be a counter offer and therefore a rejection.

With more reality, the Uniform Law on the Formation of Contracts for the International Sale of Goods, which has become part of British law by virtue of the *Uniform Laws on International Sales Act, 1967*, but which has still not yet been put into force, says that an acceptance which contains additional or different terms not materially different from the offer constitutes a valid acceptance unless promptly rejected by the offeror.

The Effect of Death on Offers and Acceptances

Where an offeree knows of the death of the offeror, it appears to be established law that he cannot accept the offer. Death acts as a revocation of the offer. In *Coulthart v Clementson* (1879), the death of a guarantor was held to bring to the end a continuing guarantee, which was in law a standing offer revocable by the guarantor, where a bank knew of his death and that he had left a will.

But there is no reason to believe that the death of the promisor in a unilateral contract terminates his obligations where the promisee has actually started on the performance—unless, of course, the thing promised is not just payment of money but some personal service which can only be rendered by the promisor.

'If a man who makes an offer dies, the offer cannot be accepted,' said Mellish L.J.; but it may be doubted whether there is any express authority for that proposition where the offeree does not know of the offeror's death. And it has been suggested that while it may well be correct in so far as the contract is dependent on the personal services of the offeror there is no reason why it should otherwise apply.

There is no specific authority about the death of the offeree. But, in principle, since an offer cannot be accepted by anybody but the person to whom it is addressed, it seems likely that the deceased's executors could not accept the offer. But the objection has been raised that since his executors acquire all rights that the deceased had, there is no reason why they should not be able to accept an offer addressed to him, provided it does not call for his services personally.

Acceptance of an Offer

Acceptance, as we have seen, must correspond exactly with the offer and be unconditional.

Acceptance must also, for there to be a binding contractual obligation, **be communicated to the offeror.** There is, so far as synallagmatic contracts are concerned, only one exception to that rule—contracts made by post. These were discussed earlier on page 42.

These rules only apply where the offeror expressly or by implication makes known to the offeree that he will accept acceptance by post: *Quenerduaine v Cole* (1883). They may be said to apply by implication where the offer is made by post and no other mode of acceptance is specified, but they would equally apply if the offer were by telephone and an acceptance by post requested.

In those cases, the posting of the letter constitutes the acceptance: *Adams v Lindsell* (1818). It is still a binding contract even if the letter does not reach the offeror: *Household Fire Assurance v Grant* (1879).

Compare also *Adams v Lindsell*. On **2nd September,** Lindsell at St. Ives wrote offering wool to Adams. The letter was wrongly addressed to Bromsgrove, Leicestershire, instead of Bromsgrove, Worcestershire, so that it did not reach Adams until the **5th September** at 7 p.m. The same evening a letter of acceptance was posted.

On **8th September** Lindsell, not having received a reply in the time anticipated, sold the wool.

On **9th September** he received the letter of acceptance.

The Court held that there was a binding contract, made when the letter of acceptance was posted.

Interesting questions arise out of these decisions. If the offeror's letter by the date or postmark indicates to the offeree that it had been long delayed in the post, could the offeree still accept it in law by letter? If the acceptance is wrongly addressed, is the contract still binding as soon as it is posted? If a postal strike intervenes between the posting of the acceptance and the receipt of it, does the rule still apply? And what if the offeree rejects the offer by post and then changes his mind and posts an acceptance: is the contract still complete when the letter of acceptance is posted, so long as the letter of rejection has not been received by the offeror? If a letter of acceptance has been posted, can it be withdrawn by a telegram or a telephone call? In the United States it has been held that there was no contract when a subsequent telegram was received before the letter of acceptance, but that might turn on the postal regulations of that country. In England, it would appear that the contract being concluded when the letter is posted, a subsequent telegram which arrives before the letter cannot have any effect on it.

To these, and other intellectual exercises of a similar nature, there is no satisfactory answer, for it is impossible to predict what attitude a modern court would adopt to a rule formulated in 1818 which rejects a fundamental principle of the law of contractual obligations. They might even come to their senses and decide that in these days, when the Post Office is very much less reliable and swift than it used to be, it is wrong to saddle an offeror with contractual obligations without express knowledge of them.

The same rule apparently applies to telegrams. The contract is made when the telegram is handed in: *Cowan v O'Connor* (1880). But it does not apply to telephone or telex communications; there the contract is not concluded until the acceptance has been received by the offeror and the place where it is concluded is at the recipient's end: *Entores v Miles Far East Corporation*, [1955] 2 All E.R. 493.

The Mode of Acceptance

It is open to the offeror to lay down the manner in which his offer may be accepted. If the offer is accepted in some other fashion, is there a contract?

An early American case presents an interesting example. Eliason and Co. sent an offer to purchase 300 barrels of flour at $9.50 a barrel in a letter sent by wagon to Henshaw.

In the letter, they asked for an answer by the return of the wagon which was to Harper's Ferry. Instead, Henshaw sent his acceptance by post to Georgetown, where Eliason also had an office. As it happened, it arrived later than a reply by the wagon would have done, but that was immaterial. The Supreme Court of the United States held that there was no contract since not only had the letter not been sent by the method required, it had not been sent to the place required: *Eliason v Henshaw* (1819).

English cases have never gone as far as that, and in *Tinn v Hoffman* (1873), the Court held that an acceptance 'by return of post' did not mean exclusively by letter by return of post. 'A telegram or verbal message or . . . any means not later than a letter written and sent by return of post' was sufficient.

The present position therefore appears to be that it is only where the offeror expressly makes it clear that he wants an acceptance in a prescribed form, and none other, that there will not be a contract if some other method of acceptance is adopted; provided, of course, that the acceptance arrives not later than it could have by the method asked for.

Mistake and the Effect on Synallagmatic Contracts

What effect does a mistake by one or both of the parties to a synallagmatic contract have on the contract? No subject is more difficult to deal with in the restricted confines of a book like this, not least of all because the law as enunciated by the Courts has changed radically within recent years and there is anything but agreement amongst judges and academic lawyers as to what it is.

The first task is to look at and analyse the different types of mistake which may have some bearing on contractual obligations. One of the most popular of such analyses is that of Cheshire and Fifoot, in their book on Contract, which has had some judicial approval. According to this, mistake may be divided into three classes:

1. **Unilateral mistake:** where one only of the parties is labouring under mistake.
2. **Common mistake:** where both parties to a contract share the same mistake.
3. **Mutual mistake:** where the parties misunderstand one another in the process of making the contract.

Unhappily, there is no general agreement on the use of these words and lawyers are as imprecise as was Dickens when he referred to '*Our mutual friend*', when what he really meant was '*Our common friend.*' Chitty on Contracts uses the term 'mutual' for 'common' and in *Magee v Pennine Insurance Co. Ltd.*, [1969] 2 All E.R. 891, Denning M.R. referred to the mistake in question as being 'common'; Winn L.J. said it was 'mutual'; and nobody suggested that it might have been unilateral. Yet since it is more than possible on the facts that only one of the contracting parties was under a mistake, this seems to be the most apt expression for it.

In fact, whether the mistake is unilateral, common or mutual, whatever this may mean, it is certainly clear that no general principles of English law can be derived from this analysis.

The Romans have been here before us in the same predicament, and it is helpful to look at their analysis of the various kinds of mistakes, so long as we do not assume that their answer should be our answer. Unfortunately, as a result of the influence of Pothier (see page 29) and the *consensus* theory, judges in the 19th century were inclined to do this, and even as recently as 1939 one judge based the whole of his judgment on an extensive quotation from Pothier—and inevitably arrived at the wrong answer, as everybody is now agreed: *Sowler v Potter*, [1939] 4 All E.R. 478.

According to the Romans, the sort of mistakes which might affect a contract were of two classes:

1. *Error in causa:* that is, in the motive or reason for entering the contract. Such contracts were voidable for fraud (*dolus*) and this corresponds with our law about misrepresentation (see page 137).
2. *Error in consensu:* where there appeared to be a mistake in the agreement. This might be due to:
    (a) *error in negotio:* mistake as to the nature of the contract, where the parties are mistaken about the type of the transaction, i.e. *A* thinks it is a contract of sale, *B* thinks it is a contract of hire.

(b) *error in corpore:* mistake as to the subject matter of the contract. *X* sells *Y* Stichius a slave. *X* is thinking of one Stichius, and *Y* of another of the same name.

(c) *error in substantia:* where there is a substantial difference between the thing bargained for and the thing as it is actually—whether the mistake be that of both parties or only of the buyer; and this includes the situation where the subject matter of the contract, unknown to the parties, has ceased to exist at the time when they are making their agreement. In the case of goods, what the Romans termed *res extincta*.

(d) *error in persona:* mistake as to the identity of the other contracting party, where the identity of the other contracting party is material. *X* thinks he is contracting with *Y* but in fact he is contracting with *Z*. There is little authority in Roman law about mistake as to the **quality** of a person, as distinct from his **identity**, e.g. where *A* mistakenly believes *B* to be rich but knows his true identity. A mistake of this nature appeared to have had no effect on a contract.

This is a helpful analysis and therefore we shall look to see how English (i) common law and (ii) equity dealt with these problems.

Error in Negotio

The most material application of this sort of mistake is where a person executes a legal instrument as the result of a fraudulent misrepresentation by another as to what the contract is all about. In *Lewis v Clay* (1898), Lord Richard Neville induced the defendant, who was a friend of his of many years' standing, to put his signature to a document covered by a piece of blotting paper in which four apertures had been cut. Lord Richard falsely represented to his friend that all he was doing was witnessing his signature. In fact the defendant was signing two promissory notes for £11,000 and two letters authorising payment of the proceeds to his lordship.

On these facts, there was no question but that the document was *voidable*—that is, it would be set aside for fraud. But until the defendant knew of the fraud and took steps to avoid the obligation by exercising his right to repudiate it, the obligation was good and if any innocent third party acquired rights in it in the meantime, the obligation could not be avoided.

The defendant therefore fell back on the doctrine of *non est factum* ('it is not my act'), on the analogy of the case given in Coke's Reports as *Thoroughgood's Case* (1584). There an illiterate man had a deed read over to him falsely and to it he then put his seal. He was held not to be bound in any way by it. In other words, the whole transaction was *void* from the very start, with the result that nobody, not even an innocent party, could acquire any rights under it.

Similarly, in *Foster v MacKinnon* (1869), the defendant, who was 'a gentleman advanced in years', was induced to endorse a Bill of Exchange under the misrepresentation that it was a guarantee. The Court of Common Pleas held that 'the defendant never intended to endorse a bill of exchange at all, but intended to sign a contract of an entirely different nature'. That being so, it was as if he had written his name '. . . in a lady's album . . . and there had been, without his knowledge, a bill of exchange or a promissory note . . . inscribed on the other side of the paper'. It was not his act and he was in no way liable on it, unless the jury were to find that he was negligent in putting his signature in this fashion on what turned out to be a negotiable instrument.

The doctrine of *non est factum* has recently been considered by the House of Lords in *Saunders v Anglia Building Society*, [1970] 3 All E.R. 961, which is the same case as that reported in the Court of Appeal as *Gallie v Lee*, [1969] 1 All E.R. 1062, by which name it is more familiarly known to lawyers. In view of that authoritative decision, it is profitless to set out the convolutions and controversies that have existed for a century about this part of the law, save to note that many of the existing cases were expressly overruled and some others are highly suspect as a result.

The law as it now exists may be summarised in three propositions:

(i) 'Whenever a man of full age and understanding, who can read and write, signs a legal document . . . which is put before him for signature then . . . if he signs it . . . relying on the word of another as to its character or contents or effect, he cannot be heard to say it is not his document.'

'By his conduct—in signing it he has represented to all into whose hands it may come, that is his document . . .'

In other words, a man is estopped by his signature (though, according to Lord Pearson, it is wrong to use this word in this connection—one should say 'precluded from denying') unless he is blind or illiterate. We are back to *Thoroughgood's Case*.

(ii) 'If his signature was obtained by fraud . . . he may be able to avoid it up to a point—but not when it has come into the hands of one who has in all innocence advanced money on the faith of its being his document or otherwise has relied on it as being his document'—per Lord Denning in the Court of Appeal. In other words, it is not *void* but *voidable* and the ability to avoid it is lost if an innocent third party acquires rights under it before it has been avoided.

(iii) 'A person who signs a document and parts with it . . . *has a responsibility . . . to take care* what he signs, which, if neglected, prevents him from denying his liability under the document according to its tenor'—per Lord Wilberforce in the House of Lords.

So, apparently, even a blind or illiterate person may lose the right to avoid his signature if he has been careless, and a third party acquired rights. In the case under consideration, the elderly Mrs. Gallie intended to make a deed of gift of her leasehold house to her nephew, on condition that she could live there for the rest of her life. She signed a document which she believed to be to this effect. At the time, she had broken her glasses and could not read it, but was told it was a deed of gift to her nephew. It was, in fact, an assignment of the lease to a man called Lee for £3,000, receipt of which she had acknowledged without receiving a penny of it. On the strength of that assignment the Anglia Building Society advanced £2,000 to Lee.

It was held that Mrs. Gallie could not set up the defence of *non est factum* or recover the title deeds.

Error in Corpore

As we have seen earlier on page 70, if the parties to a contract are apparently agreed but one is referring to one thing and the other to another, there is no contract. This is not because there is no agreement between them, because the law demands not real agreement—a true meeting of minds—but only the outward appearance of it.

Lord Atkin in the leading case on Mistake, *Bell and Lever Bros.* 1932, [1931] All E.R. Rep. 1 said 'if mistake operates at all, it operates so as to negative or in some cases nullify consent'. By *negative*, he meant the situation where the parties have misunderstood one another in the process of negotiation, so that although there is an appearance of agreement, there is in reality none. But this proposition does not apply to all cases where there is apparent agreement. It only applies where there is latent ambiguity in what the parties have agreed and therefore no contract that the Court can find to enforce, as in *Courturier v Hastie* 1852, [1843–60] All E.R. Rep. 280 (see page 70). If there is apparent agreement which the Courts could enforce, one party cannot be heard to say that it does not represent his true intentions.

A man, by telegram, ordered three rifles. In the course of transmission this became altered to 'the' rifles and, from previous negotiations, was assumed by the recipient of the telegram to be fifty.

Fifty rifles were therefore despatched. The Court held that there was no contract between the parties, for the excellent reason that although there appeared to be outward agreement on 'the rifles', no court could possibly say whether it was three or fifty. *Falck v Williams*, 1900.

And where the parties enter into an agreement when it is known that there is no consensus between them, they are bound by the apparent terms as interpreted by the Courts. In *L.C.C. v Henry Boot and Sons Ltd.*, [1959] 3 All E.R. 636, the parties disagreed *before* they signed a written contract, about the meaning of an 'up and down' clause in it but did nothing to clarify the situation. Later, one party set up that there was no contract, because there was no true agreement between them—an indisputable fact—in spite of the apparent agreement. The House of Lords held that the apparent agreement, as interpreted by the Courts, was the only material thing. Subjective intent and the *consensus* theory play no part in the modern law.

To summarise: *error in corpore* only affects the contractual obligation in English law if there is ambiguity in the apparent agreement, and the Courts are unable to decide which contract to enforce; and that only because the promises are too uncertain to enforce.

Error in Substantia

This subject may be sub-divided into four classes:

1. **Res extincta**—an agreement made when, unknown to either party, the subject matter of the contract has ceased to exist.

If a chattel, this is dealt with by the *Sale of Goods Act, 1893*, section 6: 'where there is a contract for the sale of specific goods and the goods without the knowledge of the seller have perished at the time when the contract is made, the contract is void'.

Section 7: 'where there is an agreement to sell specific goods and subsequently the goods, without any fault on the part of the seller or buyer, perish before the risk has passed to the buyer, the agreement is thereby avoided'.

This apparently applies not only to specific goods, but to specifically described goods. In *Howell v Coupland* 1876, [1877–80] All E.R. Rep. 878, where there was a contract to supply 200 tons of potatoes to be grown on a particular farm, the crop failed completely. 'Neither party becomes liable if the performance becomes impossible.' This part of the law really relates to the doctrine of **frustration** (see page 174), rather than mistake, since the impossibility of performance is subsequent to the formation of the contract. Clearly, where the seller is under the mistaken belief that the specific goods are still in existence when he makes the contract, by this section the contract is void.

The same principle does not apply to non-specific goods. If I have a cellar full of wine, and sell 50 dozen cases of Château Quim 1969 in the belief that this quantity is safely in my cellar, but in fact it has all been destroyed by fire, I am not excused performance. I have either to go out on the market to buy 50 dozen cases to fulfil my obligation, or pay damages for non-delivery.

The position is less certain where I sell 50 dozen cases of Château Quim 'now in my cellar'. They are not specific until they have been allocated to the contract out of all the other bottles of Château Quim, but the better opinion is that the contract is void. 'In the case where goods have perished at the time of sale . . . they are really contracts which are not void for mistake but are void by reason of an implied condition precedent, because the contract proceeded on the basic assumption that it was possible of performance,' said Denning L.J. in *Solle v Butcher*, [1949] 2 All E.R. 1107. This observation has not received universal approval, but if it is good law, it means that if the seller expressly warrants the continued existence of the goods at the time of the contract, the contract is not void but he may be liable to damages. No implied term can be written into a contract where there is an express term covering the same situation. In an Australian case, *McRea v Commonwealth Disposal Commission* (1951), the defendant sold to the plaintiffs a wrecked oil tanker said by them to be stranded on a certain reef off New Guinea. After the defendants had, at considerable expense, equipped an expedition to recover the ship, they discovered that there was no tanker stranded on the reef, not least of all because there was no such reef. The contract was not void but the defendants were liable because they had, on the true interpretation of their contract, expressly warranted there was such a ship.

2. *Res sua.* A man cannot buy his own property and therefore it has been suggested that all contracts for the sale and purchase of rights that the purchaser in fact already owns, but doesn't know he does, are void. But *Cooper v Phibbs*, the case usually advanced in support of this contention, was an equity action to set aside a lease and the Court proceeded on the basis that the contract was not void at common law but voidable in equity on such terms as the Court cared to impose.

3. **Commercial impossibility** at the time of formation of the contract. In *Griffiths v Bryner* (1903), a contract for the hire of a room overlooking the Coronation procession of Edward VII was held void because at the time of making the contract, the procession had already been postponed. This is consistent with the position that if the postponement took place *after* the contract, the contract was frustrated (see page 174) by supervening impossibility of performance. So too, where the parties contracted to deliver 50 tons of sisal per month from a particular estate for processing, but the estate was unable to produce 50 tons a month: *Sheikh Bros. v Ochsner* (1957).

If I contract to fly you to the moon, when that is impossible, the contract is void.

4. **Wrong contractual assumption.** Contracts entered into under a mistake about a certain fact fall into this class. Both parties may think that a picture is a Constable whereas in fact it is not; both parties may think that a particular prior contract between them is binding, whereas in fact it is not.

In *Bell v Lever Bros.* 1932, [1931] All E.R. Rep. 1, Bell had entered into a contract with Lever Bros. whereby Bell would be employed for a fixed period. In the belief that it was a binding contract, Lever Bros. entered in a second contract to discharge the first, and paid him a share of £50,000 to be released from their obligations. Later, they discovered that Bell had been guilty of breaches of the contract which entitled them to terminate the first contract.

The situation may be expressed symbolically:

Contract 1. *A* has contract No. 1 with *B*. *A* mistakenly believes the contract to be binding on him; therefore makes:

Contract 2. *A* has contract No. 2 with *B* to relinquish rights under contract No. 1.

In *Magee v Pennine Insurance Company*, [1969] 2 All E.R. 891, Magee made a contract of car insurance with the Pennine Insurance Company whereby they insured his car against third party risk and damage, and under that he paid premiums for a number of years. The car was then involved in an accident, so that it became a total write-off. In the belief that the first contract was binding on them, the insurance company entered into a second contract, one of compromise, whereby they undertook to pay £355. They then discovered that Magee had falsely represented that he held a driving licence, whereas in fact he could not drive and had never had a licence, and therefore they were entitled to repudiate the contract of insurance at any time.

The situation therefore was:

Contract 1. *A* has contract No. 1 with *B*. *A* mistakenly believes the contract to be binding on him; therefore makes:

Contract No 2. *A* has contract No. 2 with *B* to relinquish rights under contract No. 1.

In fact, the two cases are logically indistinguishable. In the first case, in 1932, the House of Lords refused to grant any relief to Lever Bros. Although all the judges in the House of Lords apparently appear to have accepted the proposition of Lever Bros.' Counsel that 'whenever it is to be inferred from the terms of the contract or its surrounding circumstances that the consensus has been reached on the basis of a particular contractual assumption, and that assumption is not true, the contract is avoided', they seem to have decided that this only applied 'where the assumption was fundamental to the continued validity of the contract or a foundation essential to its existence'.

In the circumstances, the mistake was not sufficiently fundamental and to adopt Lord Atkins' words: 'the state of the new facts' did not 'destroy the identity of the subject matter as it was in the original state of facts'.

In *Magee v Pennine Insurance Co. Ltd.*, however, the Court of Appeal, by a majority of 2 to 1, exercised equitable discretion to set aside the contract. Lord Denning said 'a common mistake, even on a most fundamental matter, does not make a contract void, at (common) law; but it makes it voidable in equity'; and he distinguished *Bell and Lever Bros.* on the ground that the House of Lords had only been dealing with the Common Law position and had not considered the law of Equity.

Elucidation on the law on this subject apparently awaits a litigant wealthy enough to carry his case up to the House of Lords. But in the meantime, it would be wise to proceed on the assumption that the Court of Appeal has made new law. Even where the mistake is not sufficiently fundamental for the Common Law to declare the contract void, Equity may declare the contract voidable and set it aside. See *Solle v Butcher*, [1949] 2 All E.R. 1107; *Grist v Bailey*, [1966] 2 All E.R. 870.

Error in Persona

Here too the law has, once again, turned a number of rapid somersaults. In 1873 a gentleman with the name of Alfred Blenkarn hired a third floor room at No. 37, Wood Street, Cheapside, London, in which street, at No. 123, was a well-known and reputable firm called William Blenkiron and Sons. Blenkarn ordered goods from Roberts, Lindsay and Co. in Belfast on notepaper correctly printed with his address, but on which he wrote his name in such a way as to resemble that of Blenkiron. In the belief that they were supplying Blenkiron, Roberts, Lindsay and Co. supplied Blenkarn with 250 dozen cambric handkerchiefs on credit, which he promptly sold to Cundy and Co., who resold them without delay.

The question was: were these goods, originally the property of Roberts, Lindsay and Co. obtained from them by fraud, so that the property passed from them, though under a contract liable to be avoided; or did the property never pass from the plaintiffs because they had made no contract at all? On the answer to that lay the answer to the question as to which of the two innocent parties should suffer the loss.

The House of Lords decided there was no contract. 'Of (Blenkarn) the plaintiffs had never heard and of him they had never thought.

With him they never intended to deal . . . as between him and them there was no consensus of mind which could lead to any agreement or any contract whatever.' The innocent Cundy and Co. were liable to pay damages to Roberts, Lindsay and Co. for conversion of their goods.

In *King's Norton Metal v Edridge Merritt and Co.* (1897), the facts were only slightly different. A rogue called Wallis had notepaper printed with the heading 'Hallam and Co., Soho Hackle Pin and Wire Works, Sheffield' with a picture of a large factory with smoking chimneys. On that notepaper he ordered a quantity of brass rivet wire from the King's Norton Metal Co. Ltd. The goods were supplied on credit and rapidly sold to Edridge Merritt and Co. Ltd. The Court of Appeal decided that there was a contract between the plaintiffs and Wallis, and the mistake only related to the qualities of the latter and not his identity; and therefore the defendant got a good title to his goods.

On that basis apparently there may be no contract if the supplier mistakenly thinks that he is dealing with a real person, who does in fact exist, but he is dealing with another; whereas, if he thinks he is dealing with a real person and that person does not exist, there is a contract. Not surprisingly, this conclusion has not been without criticism. The Law Reform Committee in 1966 recommended that all contracts entered into under a mistake as to the identity of the other party should be voidable rather than void so far as innocent third parties are concerned. Even if Parliament does not get round to enacting this, there is a strong probability that the judges will make this the law in future cases.

Where the parties are actually face to face, the Courts, after a great deal of vacillation, have come down firmly that there is always a contract, even though the supplier may have been led to believe that the person in front of him is somebody other than he is. In *Lewis v Avery*, [1971] 3 All E.R. 907 a rogue obtained possession of a car by posing as Richard Greene, a television actor, and giving a cheque in that name. The innocent purchaser of the car from the rogue got a good title. The Court of Appeal disapproved of its own previous decision, ten years earlier, in *Ingram v Little*, [1960] 3 All E.R. 332. Even if the seller is mistaken as to the identity of the person before him, he means to sell to that person in front of him 'whoever he may be'.

Implied Terms

In addition to the terms expressly agreed between the parties, there may be terms implied in the contract.

Implied terms in the contract may be:

(i) **statutory**—as a result of an Act of Parliament, as in the case of the implied conditions and warranties, contained in every contract for the sale of goods (page 190). By a kind of parasitic analogy, similar terms may be implied in contracts which are not contracts for the sale of goods but similar to them, e.g. for the repair of false teeth, and dyeing a woman's hair.

(ii) by **custom** of a particular part of the country; in which case the custom must be certain, reasonable and notorious, e.g. that in parts of Norfolk a tenant farmer leaving under notice is entitled to a larger compensation than the Common Law gives for seed and labour in his last year.

(iii) by **usage** of a particular trade, as in the publishing business where the preparation of the index of a book is the publisher's responsibility and not the author's, in the absence of an express agreement to the contrary.

(iv) to give **commercial effectiveness** to the contract; often called *The Moorcock* doctrine, after the case of that name in 1889: [1886–90] All E.R. Rep. 530. A jetty owner entered into an agreement with the owners of *The Moorcock* to discharge her at the berth alongside their jetty. Both parties knew that when the tide ebbed the ship would take the ground. When she did so she suffered damage as the result of settling on a hard ridge. The Court of Appeal held that there was an implied term that the berth was safe for the ship.

This doctrine has only restricted application, as MacKinnon L.J. pointed out: '*Prima facie* that which in any contract is left to be implied and need not be expressed is something so obvious that it goes without saying; so that if, while the parties were making their bargain, an *officious bystander* were to suggest some express provision for it in their agreement, they would testily suppress him with a common "Oh, of course".'

But there can never be an implied term when there is an express term in the contract dealing with the matter.

A charterparty provided that the chartering broker's commission should be paid 'on signing this charter (ship lost or not lost)'. This was held to be an express term allowing the broker's commission even though, as happened, the ship was requisitioned by the French Government and never actually sailed under the charterparty. An implied term by custom that the broker should only be entitled to commission if hire was actually earned under the charterparty was therefore rejected as inconsistent with the express term: *Les Affréteurs Réunis v Leopald Walford* (1919).

Exemption and Limitation Clauses

In contracts of adhesion and in common form documents (see

page 35) it is usual to find terms which limit the responsibility of the party who requires the other to sign the contract by:

   (i) excluding all liability for tort, or
  (ii) excluding all terms implied by Statute, if this is possible.
 (iii) limiting liability to a fixed sum. (Where this is a genuine pre-estimate of losses, it is liquidated damages and is not to be regarded as an exemption clause (see page 62).)

Since the parties are rarely in equal bargaining positions, the Courts tend to restrict such clauses wherever possible by one method or another.

1. The exclusion clause **must be contained in a contractual document** to be effective. In *Chapelton v Barry U.D.C.*, [1940] 1 All E.R. 356, the plaintiff hired a deckchair for 2d and received a ticket on the back of which was a notice purporting to exempt the Council from all liability. He sat on the deckchair and it collapsed under him, injuring him. The ticket, it was held, was a mere receipt, its object being to prove that the plaintiff had paid for the chair.

2. The condition **must be imposed before the contract is concluded.** In *Fosbroke-Hobbs v Airwork Ltd.*, [1937] 1 All E.R. 108, passengers on a pleasure flight were actually seated in the 'plane when a notice excluding liability was handed to them. See also *Thornton v Shoe Lane Parking* (page 39).

3. **No person can hold another to the terms of a printed form to which assent has been induced by a misrepresentation, albeit innocent, as to its terms or effect.** In *Jaques v Lloyd D. George and Partners*, [1968] 2 All E.R. 187, a contract was represented as containing 'the usual terms' of estate agents, whereas in fact it made the agent's commission payable under exceptional conditions. In *Curtis v Chemical Cleaning*, [1951] 1 All E.R. 631, a customer who took a dress to be cleaned was asked to sign a document containing the words 'the company is not liable for any damage howsoever arising'. She queried it and was told that it meant that the company could not accept liability for damage to beads or sequins. The dress was returned stained and the company could not rely on the exemption clause. When Mendelssohn left a car in the garage of Normand Ltd. he was told by an attendant who had apparent authority that he must not lock the car. Mendelssohn pointed out there were valuables in the car and the attendant promised to lock it after he had moved it. The valuables were stolen and the company could not rely upon an exemption clause contained on a ticket: *Mendelssohn v Normand Ltd.*, [1969] 2 All E.R. 1215.

4. **Exemption and limitation clauses cannot protect one contracting party against claims by those who are not themselves parties to the contract.** The master and boatswain of a P. & O. liner were not protected by an exemption clause in the ticket against an action against *them* for negligence by a passenger who was injured, since the only contract was between the company and the passenger: *Adler v Dickson*, [1954] 3 All E.R. 397 (see also page 36). British Rail has tried to escape this by drafting the clause: 'the Board enters into contracts of carriage for and on behalf of themselves and contractors employed by them and their respective servants and agents, all of which shall have the benefit of the contract and shall be under no liability to the trader or anyone claiming through him in respect of merchandise'. It is highly doubtful whether it will be upheld in law, but the effect is, of course, to deter possible claims since a claimant will know that British Rail, with the vast public funds behind it, will fight the case all the way up to the Lords if needs be. As Oliver Cromwell remarked: 'The legal system, as at present constituted, exists only to enrich lawyers and enable the rich to oppress the poor'—*plus ça change . . .*

5. Exemption clauses are to be construed *contra proferentem* those who drafted them. That is, the strictest interpretation to be put on them. General words are not to be construed as excluding liability for specific torts. A clause excluding liability 'for any loss or damage to goods which can be covered by insurance' was construed as not to exclude liability for negligence; but 'any loss however arising' has been held to exclude liability for negligence.

   But if there are two possible grounds of liability such as breach of contract, and negligence apart from the contract, a clause reading 'nothing in this agreement shall render the owners liable for any personal injuries to the riders of the machine hired' was held to relate to contractual liability only. White had hired a bike on these terms from John Warwick and Co. and was injured when the saddle suddenly tipped up and he was thrown off: *White v John Warwick and Co. Ltd.*, [1953] 2 All E.R. 1021.

6. **If the exemption clause is repugnant to the main purpose of the contract** it is ineffective.

   A clause in a Bill of Lading provided that the responsibility after the goods had been discharged should cease absolutely. The carriers discharged them from the ship into the hands of their agents in Singapore, who handed the goods over to a person, who to their knowledge, was not entitled to them. Since the purpose of the contract was the proper delivery of the goods 'to order of his or their assigns', the exemption clause was completely repugnant to this, since it would enable the carriers to give away the goods or burn them or throw them into the sea, if so minded, without any liability: *Sze Hai Tong Bank Ltd. v Rambler Cycle Co. Ltd.*, [1959] 3 All E.R. 182.

7. If a party commits **a fundamental breach of contract** he is precluded from relying on a protection clause in the contract.

A fundamental breach is one which has the result of depriving the other party of substantially the whole of the benefit he could expect under the contract. Wayne Tank and Pump Co. Ltd. undertook to design and supply a system for keeping molten wax flowing through a factory making plasticine. The contract contained a term that the maximum damages to which they were to be liable was the value of the contract, namely £2,330. The system they designed and installed consisted of plastic pipes wrapped round with heating cable and when it was switched on without supervision the factory was burned down, at a total loss of £151,420. Because the breach of contract was fundamental they could not rely on the limitation of damages clause and were liable for the whole sum: *Harbutt's Plasticine Ltd. v Wayne Tank Co. Ltd.*, [1970] 1 All E.R. 225.

8. The same is true of **the breach of a fundamental term.** A fundamental term is a term of the contract which the parties have expressly or by implication agreed to regard as going to the root of the contract, so that the breach of it should discharge the other party from any further performance (see also page 177).

Discharge of Contractual Obligations

The obligations assumed may be discharged:

(i) by subsequent agreement between the parties.
(ii) by their full performance.
(iii) by some supervening event which renders performance by one or both parties impossible (so-called 'frustration'), or
(iv) as the result of a breach by the other party.

Discharge by Agreement

'As the parties have been bound, so they may be loosed.' Therefore it is always open to the parties to terminate their contractual obligations by subsequent agreement.

There are, however, some technical points that arise in this connection. If the obligations are released by deed there is no problem, even though there is no consideration. This is what is termed a **release.**

Where something still remains to be done by *both* parties to the contract, a new agreement to abandon the contract is effective. There is consideration for the fresh promises. This agreement may sometimes be implied from the conduct of the parties, such as lapsing into somnolence for a long time with neither party exercising rights or seeking to enforce rights under the contract.

The rescission of a contract by agreement does not have to be in the same form as the original contract. Even where the original contract has by Act of Parliament to be in writing (see page 113) an effective discharge of the obligation so created can be made by a subsequent oral agreement. (But an agreement required to be in writing cannot be *varied* without writing.)

It is only where one party has fully performed his obligations, so that on his side nothing remains to be done beyond receiving the performance of the other, that accord and satisfaction are necessary. In that case if a promise is made to receive *less* than the full performance due in full satisfaction, there is then no consideration for that promise, unless there is some separate and new advantage to the promisor. The full effect of this has been considered in the discussion on *Pinnel's Case* (see page 93).

Accord simply means the agreement. Satisfaction means the fresh consideration necessary to support this. Both are necessary.

But, as has been observed earlier, while this may still be the law that 'a mere accord without satisfaction' does not put an end to contractual obligations, the invention of the doctrine of **promissory estoppel** (see page 96) has mitigated the harshness of this common law rule.

The same doctrine has full application to *waiver* of contractual rights by one party. It is a commonplace and sensible commercial practice for one party not to insist upon the full performance of his contractual rights. He may agree to postpone performance by delaying delivery, or agreeing to receive payment later than due.

If there is fresh consideration for these alterations, then it is in law a *variation* and binding on both parties.

But if there is no fresh consideration, it is a mere waiver of rights. Until 1947, the party who had waived his rights was not bound by his promise not to exercise them in full. But now 'if one party, by his conduct, leads another to believe that the strict rights arising under the contract will not be insisted upon, intending that the other should act on that belief and he does act on it, then the first party will not afterwards be allowed to insist on the strict rights when it would be inequitable for him to do so'.

Discharge by Performance

Only the full, complete and exact performance of his contractual obligations will discharge a party. It is not a discharge if he does something of similar, equal or even greater value for the other contracting party. For the English law of contractual relations is based not on benefit conferred but on promise, expressed or implied. A firm of surveyors agreed with Mrs. Knight to supervise alterations to her house for an inclusive fee of £30. The alterations originally estimated at £600, finally came to £2,283, but there was no subsequent or new agreement to pay any further remuneration to the surveyors. They, however, sent a bill for £135, being the £30 agreed plus 100 guineas for what they reasonably regarded as the extra work. The Court of Appeal held that there had been no fresh agreement, and no circumstances in which a promise to pay a *quantum meruit* (see page 50) could be implied, so Mrs. Knight was liable to pay only the £30 agreed. An observation in the House of Lords by Lord Dunedin in *The Orlanda* (1917) was referred to:

> 'As regards *quantum meruit*, when there are two parties who are under a contract, *quantum meruit* must be a new contract and in order to have a new contract you must get rid of the old contract.' *Gilbert and Partners v Knight*, [1968] 2 All E.R. 248.

Similarly in *The Liddesdale* (1900) a shipyard did repairs to a ship purportedly under a contract for a lump sum. However, they did not comply with the contract specifications but did work which was more expensive and used materials which were more suitable. It was held that the yard could recover nothing. Under the contract nothing was due because they had not performed it all in the manner specified. Nor could they recover on a *quantum meruit*, for that could only exist where a promise to pay could be implied, and to quote Lord Dunedin again, 'in order to have a new contract you must get rid of the old contract'.

The harshness of this rule has been mitigated to some extent in the case of building contracts by:

(i) **regarding the contract as divisible into parts,** where separate sums are named in a lump sum contract as being payable on completion of various parts of the work, e.g. a contract to build a house for £10,000, £2,500 being due when the foundations are complete etc.

(ii) **the doctrine of substantial performance,** where the builder has substantially finished the house but has not done all the work in accordance with the specification, or has left minor tasks undone. The builder can now recover the contract price, less so much as ought to be allowed for items found to be defective: *Dakin and Co. Ltd. v Lee* (1916).

But apart from that, the rule of law is as it was laid down in *Cutter v Powell* in 1795, [1775–1802] All E.R. 159 for lump sum contracts.

Nothing is recoverable unless the whole of the work promised has been done. Powell promised to pay Cutter 30 guineas 'provided he proceeds, continues and does his duty as second mate' on a voyage from Jamaica to Liverpool. Cutter served all the way across the seas, but when the vessel was nearing its destination, he died. It was held that his widow, as administrix, was entitled to recover nothing.

Discharge by Supervening Impossibility

If the law imposed a general obligation on a person to do a certain thing, he was excused, if external circumstances made it impossible for him to do it. But where the obligations were contractual, the basic rule of the common law was that the promisor 'must perform it or pay damages for not doing so'. He was not excused if some unexpected event happened which prevented his fulfilling his obligations. The reason, it was said, was because the obligations were voluntarily assumed it was open to him to stipulate for a release from his obligations, if something happened to prevent his performing them.

Paradine v Jane 1647, [1558–1774] All E.R. Rep. 172, was an action in debt for three years' arrears of rent for land. The defendant pleaded that a certain German prince, Rupert, had invaded the realm with a hostile army and expelled him from the land, so that he was unable to benefit from the lease or receive profit from the land. The slighting reference to Charles II's nephew and his army fighting for that monarch may have commended the defendant to the Court but did nothing to excuse his non-payment of rent. It was held that 'where the law creates a duty . . . and the party is disabled from performing it without any default in him . . . the law will excuse him' but 'when a party by his own conduct creates a duty . . . he is bound to make it good . . . notwithstanding any accident by inevitable necessity'. The reason was 'because he might have provided against it by his contract . . . Though the land be surrounded by wild fire, yet the lessor shall have his whole rent.'

But even in those early days, death was regarded as frustrating a contract of personal service so that, for example, the executors of an author were not liable to pay damages to publishers if the author died before he had completed a commissioned book.

The first real breach of this rigid doctrine of 'perform or pay' came in 1863.

The plaintiff in *Taylor v Caldwell* 1863, [1861–73] All E.R. Rep 24, had hired the Surrey Music Hall for the purpose of giving a series of concerts but, before they could begin, the hall was burnt down. He therefore sued for damages. The Court held that the defendant was excused from performance. 'In contracts in which the performance depends on the continued existence of a given person or thing, a condition is implied that the impossibility of performance arising from the perishing of the person or thing shall excuse the performance.'

This doctrine was extended in *Jackson v Union Marine Insurance* 1874, [1874–80] All E.R. Rep. 312, to include a case where the thing still existed, but was not effective for the purpose of performing the contract. *The Spirit of Dawn* was chartered to sail with all possible despatch to Newport to load a cargo of iron rails for San Francisco. The vessel stranded in Caernarvon Bay and was under repair for several weeks. It was held that the contractual obligations were discharged by supervening impossibility of performance.

The present position may be set forth in the words of Lord Reid: a contract is frustrated 'whenever the law recognises that, without default of either party, a contractual obligation has become incapable of being performed because the circumstances in which performance is called for would render it a thing radically different from that which was undertaken by the contract . . . *Non haec in foedera veni* ('It was not this that I promised to do').'

Lord Reid's summary was: 'Is the contract in its true construction wide enough to apply to the new situation? If not, then it is at an end.'

Examples of frustration are:

1. **Contracts of personal service.** These may be ended by death, incapacity or prolonged illness as in: *Grave v Cohen*, 1930 (the death of racehorse owner frustrated a jockey's contract with him); *Robinson v Davidson* 1871, [1861–73] All E.R. Rep. 699 (the illness of a pianist prevented the fulfilment of a concert engagement); *Horlocks v Beal* 1916, [1916–17] All E.R. Rep. 81 (the internment of British seamen frustrated their contract of employment and therefore their wives were not entitled to wages); *Morgan v Mansen*, [1947] 2 All E.R. 666 (a music hall artist was called up for National Service and was therefore unable to fulfil his contractual obligations).
2. **Supervening illegality.** This arises where a contract is not illegal when made but where performance of it becomes illegal subsequently. A further example is where the government intervened to requisition chattels, the subject matter of the contract. *Bank Line v Capel* 1919, [1918–19] All E.R. Rep. 504 (ship on charterparty requisitioned).
3. **The cancellation of an expected event.** An example of this occurred when the coronation of Edward VII was postponed: *Knell v Henry*, [1900–3] All E.R. Rep. 620. A contract for hire of rooms to watch the procession was frustrated by the cancellation of the

procession. But note: *Herne Bay Steam Boat Co. v Hutton* 1903, [1900–3] All E.R. Rep. 622, a case concerning the hire of a boat 'for the purpose of viewing the naval review and for a day's cruise round the fleet'. The contract here was held not frustrated because although the naval review was cancelled, the boat could still be used for the day's cruise round the fleet.

4. **Physical destruction of subject matter of the contract.** An example of this has been shown by *Taylor v Caldwell*, above.

5. **A fundamental change in circumstances** short of complete destruction of subject matter. See above, *Jackson v Union Marine Insurance*, and note also *Joseph Constantine v Imperial*, [1942] 2 All E.R. 165, where a ship at the start of a charterparty voyage was incapacitated by the explosion of a boiler. But it is important to note what Blackburn J. stressed in *Taylor v Caldwell*: 'It is not enough that the performance of the contract has become unexpectedly burdensome.' The ship in *The Captain George K.*, (1970) found the Suez Canal closed as a result of the Six Days' War when it approached it; as a result the ship had to sail 18,400 miles instead of 9,700 miles. The claim was therefore made by the shipowners that, since it was contemplated by both parties that the ship should use the Suez Canal, the voyage had been frustrated and they were therefore entitled to remuneration on a *quantum meruit* basis for all the extra expense. It was held that although the voyage had become much more expensive than originally contemplated, it was not frustrated.

A contract is not frustrated if the real reason for non-performance is the default of one of the parties. In *Maritime National Fish Ltd. v Ocean Trawlers Ltd.*, [1935] All E.R. Rep. 86 a trawler was let out on charterparty with no 'otter trawl' licence, without which it could not lawfully be used, because the owner had appropriated all available licences to his other vessels. The owner was held liable for breach of contract and his plea of frustration was rejected, since it was his fault the vessel had no licence.

The effect of frustration is now set out in the *Law Reform (Frustrated Contract) Act, 1943*:

(a) Money paid before the discharge by frustration is, subject to the qualifications below, recoverable.

(b) If a person is in possession of the money and has incurred expenses before the discharge by frustration, a Court can allow him to retain as much as may be just.

(c) One contracting party can recover from the other expenses he has laid out in the performance of the contract.

(d) If one party has obtained a benefit as the result of anything done by the other, the Court can make such an order for payment as it considers just.

Certain types of contracts are excluded from the effect of the Act, notably contracts for the sale of specific goods (already covered by the *Sale of Goods Act, 1893*); contracts of insurance; contracts for the carriage of goods by sea (subject now to the *Carriage of Goods by Sea Act, 1971*); and contracts where there is already provision for the event which has resulted in the contract not being performed.

Discharge by Breach

As has already been noted (see page 57), with some exceptions, a repudiation—that is to say an express refusal to perform the contract—is not in general a breach unless it is accepted as such by the innocent party.

Breach may take place by:

(i) an accepted repudiation.
(ii) wrongful performance—as where a pilot flew an advertisement trailer behind an aircraft over a city during the two minutes silence on Armistice Day: *Aerial Advertising v Bachelors Peas*, [1938] 2 All E.R. 788.
(iii) neglect or failure to perform the obligations of the contract.

The effect of a particular breach may:

(i) have been defined in the contract in advance in the form of an exclusion of liability, limitation of damages or liquidated damages clause. Here, if the innocent party elects to affirm the contract, with knowledge of the breach, he is restricted to such remedies as he is given for the breach in the contract; as was the case in *Suisse Atlantique v Rotterdamsche*, [1966] 1 All E.R. 61, where the contract provided for $1,000 a day demurrage for excessive lay days of a ship, and the House of Lords held that no more than this could be recovered, even though the damages were much greater. But if the contract is brought to an end by a fundamental breach in such circumstances and the innocent party chooses to reject the contract, or the breach is of such a nature that he cannot go on with the contract, the guilty party cannot rely on the terms of the contract to protect him: *Harbutts Plasticine v Wayne Tanks*, [1970] 1 All E.R. 234 (see page 171).

(ii) be dealt with by Statute, as for example in s. 50 of the *Sale of Goods Act, 1893* which deals with damages for non-acceptance of goods sold (see page 61).

In other cases, neither the parties nor Parliament may have defined the consequences of the breach. Formerly, in these cases the

Court would construe the contract to decide whether this was a breach of a **condition** or a **warranty.**

A condition has been defined by Fletcher Moulton L.J. as 'an obligation which goes so directly to the substance of a contract or, in other words, is so essential to its very nature, that its non-performance may fairly be considered by the other party as a substantial failure to perform the contract at all'. As a result the innocent party, if so minded, was entitled to refuse to perform his own obligations and regard the contract as being at an end: *Behn v Burness* (1863).

A charterparty of the 19th October 1860 described the ship as 'now in the port of Amsterdam'; in fact on that day she was just outside the port and could not get in owing to strong gales; she got in a day or two later, when the gales abated.

On these facts the Court held that the words quoted were a condition and for breach of it the charterer was discharged from his performance and was not obliged to produce a cargo of coal in Newport to be carried to Hong Kong.

A warranty, on the other hand, was a term of the contract which was subsidiary or collateral to the main purpose of the contract, as in *Bettini v Gye* 1876, [1874–80] All E.R. Rep. 242. The plaintiff was an opera singer who entered a contract to sing for the defendant, the manager of the Italian Opera House in London. A term of the contract was that the plaintiff would arrive six days before his engagement began, for rehearsals. He failed to do so, arriving four days late, and was sacked. The Court held that his breach of contract not being in a substantial matter which went to the root of the contract, the other party was not entitled to end the contract and therefore Bettini was entitled to damages for breach of contract by Gye.

This distinction between conditions and warranties was one that was based on the old form of pleadings and the words themselves appear to have been adopted by one of the first 19th-century writers about contract law, Sir Frederick Pollock. They received statutory approval in the *Sale of Goods Act, 1893*, where they are preserved, like bees in amber, until another Act replaces it. But increasingly for other contracts the Courts have moved away from this concept, as is apparent from the judgment of Lord Mansfield in *Boon v Eyre* (1779), Lord Blackburn in *Mersey Steel and Iron v Naylor* 1884, [1881–5] All E.R. Rep. 365 and Lord Atkin in *Associated Portland Cement Manufacturers v Houlden* (1917), where unlike *Behn v Burness* it was held that a promise that a ship would be ready to load on the 25th May was not of the essence of the contract.

The climax of the rejection of this view came in *Hong Kong Fir v Kawasaki*, [1962] 1 All E.R. 474, where the Court of Appeal held that unseaworthiness on the day a charter was due to start—which had before that date been regarded as a breach of a condition of any charterparty—was not such a breach as would entitle the charterer to treat the contract as being at an end. There was an eloquent, closely reasoned and entirely convincing judgment by Diplock L.J. which came to be accepted as a true exposition of the modern law.

Beginning with the memorable sentence: 'Every synallagmatic contract contains in it the seeds of the problem: in what event will a party be relieved of his undertaking to do that which he agreed to do but has not done.'

He concluded that: 'it was really the *event* resulting from the breach which relieved the other party of further performance of his obligations' and that one party was only discharged by the other's breach, if that breach had consequences which, if they had happened without the default of either party, would have frustrated the contract.

'The question whether an event which is the result of the other party's breach of contract has this consequence cannot be answered by treating all contractual obligations as falling into one of two separate categories: "conditions", the breach of which gives rise to an event which relieves the party not in default of further performance of his obligations, and "warranties", the breach of which does not give rise to such an event.'

'Lawyers tend to speak of these classifications as if it were comprehensive, partly for historical reasons . . . and partly because Parliament itself adopted it in the *Sale of Goods Act, 1893* . . . *But it is by no means true of contractual undertakings in general at common law.*'

Having pointed out in passing the inconsistency and incoherence of 19th-century judges about the use of these words (e.g. Bramwell B.: 'it was an implied *condition* . . . that a particular kind of breach of an express *warranty* should not occur'), Lord Diplock mentioned that 'the common law evolves not merely by breeding new principles but also, when they are fully grown, by burying their ancestors'.

Most lawyers concluded that 'conditions' and 'warranties' were safely buried, especially since Lord Diplock's observations were greeted kindly in various cases in the House of Lords.

In 1970 Mr. Justice Mocatta proceeded to apply them in a highly satisfactory and erudite judgment in *Maredelanto Compania v Bergbau-Handel*, [1970] 1 All E.R. 673. By a charterparty of 25th May 1965, the vessel *Mihalis Angelos*, 'now trading and expected to load under this charter about 1st July 1965', was to proceed to Haiphong and load a cargo of apatite (natural crystallised phosphate of lime). Another clause expressly allowed cancellation of the charter if the vessel was not ready to load by 20th July.

On 17th July, the charterers, who hadn't got a cargo of apatite to ship, purported to cancel the contract on the grounds of *force majeure* because the Americans were bombing the port of Haiphong.

By the time of the trial, it was admitted that this was no justification for cancellation, and another defence was set up, i.e. that because the vessel could not have been, on 25th May, 'expected to load under this charter about 1st July', as at that date she was discharging in Hong Kong, there was a breach of a condition and therefore they were entitled to cancel. This was rejected by Mocatta J., who awarded £4,000 damages to the shipowner.

The decision was reversed by a Court of Appeal led by Lord Denning which, while accepting that the division into 'conditions' and 'warranties' was not exhaustive, proceeded to hold that the clause in question was a breach of a condition, and therefore the charterers were exercising their right. [1970] 3 All E.R. 125. The ancestors have been resurrected.

However, in *Wickman Machine Tools v Schuler* (1972), the Court of Appeal was called upon to construe the words: 'it shall be a condition of this agreement' . . . that the plaintiff should send its representatives to visit six named motor manufacturing firms . . . 'at least once in every week for the purpose of soliciting orders for panel presses'. Lord Denning pointed out that the word 'condition' has three possible meanings and, in the particular case, held that it was used in its common sense as simply 'a term' of the contract and not as carrying the consequences that the other party was quit of his future obligation for a trifling breach of the 'condition'.

Normally, time is not of the essence of a contract unless it is expressly or impliedly made so. So if an author fails to produce for his publishers the manuscript on a due date, this is not grounds for repudiation of the contract, or even for claiming damages, unless the contract expressly confers these rights. But time can be made of the essence by proper notice. A Mr. Oppenhaim ordered a Rolls with a special body for delivery by 20th March. It was not delivered then. Finally he said in June that he would not accept delivery after 25th July. This made time of the essence, and when the car was tendered in October, it was held that he was entitled to refuse it: *Charles Richards Ltd. v Oppenhaim*, [1950] 1 All E.R. 420.

In the case of a contract where goods are to be delivered by instalments and payment made by instalments, failure to pay is not a repudiation of the contract unless, on the facts, it shows an intention no longer to be bound by the contract. The other party is not entitled to discontinue supplies, but payment for one instalment can, of course, be expressly made a condition precedent to the delivery of the next.

Likewise, failure to deliver one or more instalments is not such a breach as would entitle the other party to treat the whole of the contract as at an end. It all depends on the circumstances, including the ratio of the breach quantitatively to the contract as a whole.

The *Uniform Laws on International Sales Act, 1967* was passed by Parliament but at the time of writing has not become operative. It is based on a text adopted by a Hague Conference of 1964. When it becomes operative by Order in Council, it will apply only to international sales unless it is made effective for home sales by a separate Act of Parliament. What is understood is likely to happen, however, is that a new *Sale of Goods Act*, governing home sales, will be prepared and it is obvious that the two will be reconciled in so far as is possible.

The uniform law abandons the English idea of 'conditions' and 'warranties' in the sale of goods and instead classifies all breaches of contract into 'fundamental' and 'non-fundamental' breach, the first of which discharges the innocent party from any further performance, and the second does not.

A fundamental breach is defined as one where:

'the party in breach knew, or ought to have known at the time of the conclusion of the contract that a reasonable person in the same situation as the other party would not have entered into the contract if he had foreseen the breach and its effects.' Sched. 1, Act 10.

This is a new but valuable concept and it may well be in future that the judges will extend this into realms beyond the international sale of goods. Certainly, outmoded concepts such as 'conditions' and 'warranties' ought to be buried again with all possible speed.

G

BOOK THREE: THE SALE OF GOODS

CHAPTER THIRTEEN

THE TRANSFERENCE OF OWNERSHIP

Nemo dat quod non habet

A contract for the sale of goods is one whereby the seller transfers or agrees to transfer the ownership of (called by lawyers 'the property in') goods to the buyer for a consideration in money called 'the price'. For this purpose, goods indicates anything of which physical possession is possible, except coins of the realm; so that it includes such diverse objects as lion cubs and the biggest oil tanker afloat. Contracts which have as their main object the provisions of services, and only incidentally the supply of goods, are not included in this definition. Artists therefore and photographers are not subject to the provisions of the *Sale of Goods Act, 1893*. Nor are contracts of hire of goods, since it is essential that the contract shall contemplate the transfer of ownership. For this reason, hire purchase contracts, where the hirer has an option to purchase the goods at the end of the period of hire, are not subject to the Act. Straight 'swops' of goods are not sales but barters, for it is essential for a sale that it shall be for a **price in money**; but part exchanges, where there is some money consideration, *are* sales of goods.

The fundamental assumption of English law is that nobody who is not himself the owner of goods can make any 'buyer' an owner. This is expressed in the Latin maxim *nemo dat quod non habet*. It means 'a man cannot give what he has not got'—a principle, as the ladies know, which is wider than the law.

Therefore, in English law, if a bicycle or a car is stolen and passes through the hands of many innocent purchasers, twenty years later the original owner of it can take it from the person who then has it.

This is quite different from the rule in most European countries: in France, for example, stolen goods can only be recovered within a period of three years from the date of the theft and then only from an innocent purchaser who has bought them by auction or in the ordinary course of business, by repaying him what he had paid for them. But there are many exceptions to the principle that only the owner can transfer title to a buyer. They include:

1. **Agency.** A person who sells goods under the authority, or with

the consent of the owner, can make the buyer the owner. The same thing applies where the seller is an Agent of Necessity. (See page 20.)

2. **Estoppel.** This principle has already been explained. It forms an express part of the *Sale of Goods Act*, which, in section 21 (1) reads:

> 'where goods are sold by a person who is not the owner thereof . . . the buyer acquires no better title to the goods than the seller had unless the owner of the goods is *by his conduct precluded from denying the seller's authority to sell*.'

So that is a man who wants to obtain a loan on a car which he owns goes to a garage and signs a proposal form for Hire Purchase from a finance house and states falsely on that form that his car is owned by the garage, he is estopped from denying that fact: *Stoneleigh Finance v Phillips*, [1965] 1 All E.R. 513. Anybody who bought the car from the garage would become the owner of it.

3. **Sale by a seller in possession.** If a seller remains in possession of goods after the sale and re-sells them to somebody else, that person becomes the owner. This is the result of section 25 (1) of the *Sale of Goods Act*. The same thing applies if the seller retains documents of title, such as Bills of Lading.

In the circumstances about the car set out in the previous paragraph, this section will apply to any sale by the previous owner and have the effect of defeating any title vested in a finance company: *Worcester Works Finance v Cooden Engineering*, [1971] 3 All E.R. 708. 'The object of the section is to protect an innocent purchaser who is deceived by the vendor's physical possession of goods or documents and who inevitably is unaware of legal rights which fetter the apparent power to dispose.'

This section applies even if the goods are in the possession of the vendor without the consent of the new owner.

4. **Sale by a buyer in possession.** A person may agree to buy goods (for example, by instalments on a conditional sale agreement) and it may be a term of the contract that the property in the goods shall not pass to him until some time in the future. If he is in possession of the goods *with the owner's consent*, and sells them, an innocent purchaser will get a good title by virtue of section 25 (2). The same thing applies to documents of title.

5. **Sales in market overt.** A market overt is: in the **City of London,** a shop open to the public. Goods are said to be sold 'in market overt':

    (a) when the goods are of such a character that they are usually sold in the shop.

(b) when the sale takes place *by* the shopkeeper (not *to* him).
(c) when the sale takes place in a part of the shop to which the general public has admittance.

In the rest of England, it means a market held on the days appointed by custom, royal charter or Act of Parliament.

Therefore an innocent buyer of stolen goods in such a market becomes the owner.

Formerly, this title was defeated if the thief was prosecuted to conviction; but this part of the *Sale of Goods Act* was repealed by the *Theft Act, 1968*; but by that enactment the Court has the power to order the restoration of stolen goods.

6. **Mercantile agents or factors.** A person who in the ordinary course of his trade buys or sells goods for other people is a mercantile agent or factor. By the *Factors Act, 1889*, section 1 (1), if he sells goods in the ordinary course of his business which are in his possession with the consent of the owner, an innocent buyer from him gets a good title to the goods—even if the goods are not in his possession for the purpose of sale or he sells in contravention of instructions given him by the owner.

But qualifying conditions are as follows:

(a) The sale must be in the ordinary course of his business. To sell a motor car without a log book is not in the ordinary course of business, and even a sale with a log book may still not be, if the log book has been obtained by trickery or theft: *Pearson v Rose and Young Ltd.*, [1950] 2 All E.R. 1027.

(b) The goods must be in his possession as a mercantile agent. A motor car subject to hire purchase, even if it comes into the possession of a mercantile agent such as a garage with the consent of the owner is not in the possession of the garage as mercantile agents: *Belvoir Finance v Harold G. Cole Ltd.*, [1969] 2 All E.R. 904.

7. **Goods taken in execution or distress.** At common law a landlord is allowed to seize goods on the premises for arrears in rent and such distraints make a person to whom the goods are sold the owner of them. Likewise, where execution is carried out and goods seized in satisfaction of a court judgment, the subsequent sale makes a purchaser the owner.

8. **Title transferred by operation in law.** Goods left with an innkeeper may be validly sold after a period by virtue of the *Innkeepers Act, 1878*; and a warehouseman has power in law to sell goods deposited with him for non-payment of charges: *Willet v Chaplin and Co.* (1923); so, too, have pawnbrokers.

And anybody with whom goods are deposited for repair and not collected may sell them after due notice in accordance with the *Disposal of Uncollected Goods Act, 1952*.

Another exception falls under the *Hire Purchase Act, 1964* (see page 211).

Transfer of Title and the Consequences

When the property in the goods passes with the conclusion of the contract of sale this is termed by the Act a **sale**; but when the property in the goods is to pass at some time after the contract has been made this is termed an **agreement to sell**.

The time when the property in the goods has passed is often of vital importance. Normally, the risk passes with the property, so that if the ownership has passed to the buyer and the goods, while still in the seller's possession, are destroyed by fire, the loss is the buyer's. 'Unless otherwise agreed, the goods remain at the seller's risk until the property therein is transferred to the buyer, but when the property therein is transferred to the buyer, the goods are at the buyer's risk whether delivery has been made or not': section 20. Similarly, if goods are sold so that the buyer becomes the owner and then he becomes insolvent, the goods become the property of his trustee in bankruptcy and the seller can only claim a dividend on the price in bankruptcy. But if the property has not passed to the buyer, even though the goods may have done, the seller is entitled to recover them.

The Act provides a number of rules for ascertaining the intention of the parties *in the absence of agreement to the contrary*: section 18.

Specific goods in a deliverable state

'Rule 1. Where there is an unconditional contract for the sale of specific goods in a deliverable state, the property in the goods passes to the buyer when the contract is made and it is immaterial whether the time of payment or the time of delivery or both be postponed.'

'Specific goods' means goods identified and agreed upon at the time. 'In a deliverable state' means that the goods are in such a condition that the buyer would be obliged to accept them as a proper performance of the contract.

A haystack was sold on 6th January on terms that it was to be paid for a month later but not to be removed until 1st May. On 20th January the haystack was destroyed by fire. The loss fell on the buyer: *Tarling v Baxter* (1827).

Specific goods not in a deliverable state

'Rule 2. Where there is a contract for the sale of specific goods and the seller is bound to do something to the goods for the purpose of putting them in a deliverable state, the property does not pass until such thing be done and the buyer has notice thereof.'

An engine installed in a cement works was to be delivered free on rail. Before it reached the railway it was damaged. The property had not passed to the buyer because it was not in a deliverable state: *Underwood v Burgh Castle Cement Syndicate*, [1921] All E.R. Rep. 515.

'Rule 3. Where there is a contract for the sale of specific goods in a deliverable state but the seller is bound to weigh, measure, test or do some other act or thing with reference to the goods for the purpose of ascertaining the price, the property does not pass until such act or thing be done and the buyer has notice thereof.'

Goods 'on sale or return'

'Rule 4. Where goods are delivered to the buyer on approval or 'on sale or return' or other similar terms, the property passes to the buyer:

  (a) when he signifies his approval or acceptance to the seller or does any other act adopting the transaction (e.g. by pledging, lending out or re-selling the goods).

  (b) if he does not signify his approval or acceptance to the seller but retains the goods without giving notice of rejection, then, if a time has been fixed for the return of the goods, on the expiration of such time and if no time has been fixed, on the expiration of a reasonable time.'

Unascertained or future goods

'Rule 5 (1). Where there is a contract for the sale of unascertained or future goods by description and goods of that description and in a deliverable state are unconditionally appropriated to the contract, either by the seller with the assent of the buyer or by the buyer with the assent of the seller, the property in the goods thereupon passes to the buyer.'

A firm in England wrote to a company in Basle in Switzerland and asked them to supply a packet of patent dye by post. The Swiss company posted the packet. It was held that the property in the goods passed to the buyer as soon as the packet was posted: *Badische Anilin v Basle Chemical Works* 1898, [1904-7] All E.R. Rep. 234.

Delivery to carrier

Rule 5 (2). This rule provides that a seller is deemed to have unconditionally appropriated goods to a contract of the delivery of them to the buyer or to a carrier for the purpose of transmission to the buyer.

CHAPTER FOURTEEN

THE TERMS OF THE CONTRACT OF SALE

Conditions, Warranties and Fundamental Breaches

The *Sale of Goods Act* divides all terms of a contract of sale or agreement to sell into **conditions** and **warranties.** A condition is a term of the contract which is so much at the root of the contract that a breach of it gives the innocent party the right to treat the contract as repudiated; whereas a warranty is merely a subsidiary term of the contract, a breach of which entitles the innocent party to claim damages but not to treat the contract as repudiated (see page 178). Whether a particular term is a condition or a warranty will depend on the proper construction (in the sense of 'interpretation') of the contract.

This is subject to the qualifications that:

(i) where there has been a breach of a condition, the innocent party can elect whether he treats it as such or whether he will treat it as a breach of warranty. That is in most cases: whether he will reject the goods supplied or whether he will retain them and sue for damages for the difference between the goods as they were promised and the goods as they were delivered;

(ii) once a buyer has accepted the goods he can only treat a breach of condition as a breach of warranty—that is, he cannot reject the goods but can only sue for damages.

What is meant by **acceptance** is defined by section 35 of the Act. A buyer is deemed to have accepted them:

(i) when he intimates to the seller that he has accepted them;

(ii) when the goods have been delivered to him and he does any act in relation to them which is inconsistent with the ownership of the seller. An action which is inconsistent with the ownership of the seller would consist of re-selling the whole or part, using part, fitting the goods as components or such acts as pawning some or all of the goods in question. But this is now, as the result of an amendment to the *Sale of Goods Act* made by the *Misrepresentation Act, 1967*, subject to the provisions of section 34 to the effect that a buyer is not deemed to have accepted goods unless and until he has had a reasonable opportunity of examining them for the purpose of finding out whether they conform to the contract. Until that amendment, section 34 and section 35 were contradictory;

(iii) when, after the lapse of a reasonable time, he retains the goods without intimating to the seller that he has rejected them.

Here again this is subject now to the provisions of section 34. Before that amendment, a buyer took delivery of a cargo of wheat and resold and delivered part to sub-purchasers. It was then discovered that the whole of the wheat was not in conformity with the contract. It was held that by virtue of section 35, the buyer had lost his right to reject the goods because he had done an act inconsistent with the ownership of the seller. But now this is subject to the overriding provisions of section 34, and since he had no reasonable opportunity of examining the goods before resale, he would not now lose his right to reject the goods. The effect of the amendment to the Act is that a buyer is not now deemed to have accepted the goods unless he has had a reasonable chance of examining them.

A term about payment for the goods is not deemed to be of the essence of a contract of sale: section 10. But it is, of course, open to the parties to make it of the essence if they agree accordingly.

This rule has a particular importance to contracts where the goods are to be delivered by instalments. It means in effect that the party delivering is not entitled automatically to treat failure to pay for an instalment as grounds for refusing to deliver further instalments. **'It is a question in each case depending on the terms of the contract and the circumstances of the case, whether the breach of contract is a repudiation of the whole contract or whether it is a severable breach giving rise to a claim for compensation but not a right to treat the whole contract as discharged': section 31.** If it is desired to ensure that no further deliveries of goods are necessary, it is possible to write into the contract a clause that payment is to be made on delivery or within a fixed time thereafter and 'all payments to be made on due date as a condition precedent to future deliveries'. With that clause in the contract the supplier is entitled to withhold further deliveries until payment has been made.

The same principles apply to default in delivery of the goods.

Whether a term of a contract is a condition or a warranty, it is still subject to the doctrine of **fundamental breach** (see page 177). If the breach by one party is of such a nature that it makes the purported performance of the contract totally different from what the contract contemplated, even if it were only a breach of what otherwise would have been construed as a warranty, this is so fundamental that it is an entire failure to perform the contract at all. As Lord Abinger said as early as 1838: 'If a man offers to buy peas off another and he sends him beans, he does not perform his contract; but that is not a warranty; there is no warranty that he should sell him beans; the contract is to sell peas, and if he sends him anything else instead, it is a non-performance of it.' *Chanter v Hopkins* 1838, [1835–42] All E.R. Rep. 346.

Implied Terms as to Title

In addition to the express terms of a contract, the Act writes several implied terms into every contract of sale. That is, there are conditions and warranties which are not expressed, but are taken to be a term of the contract.

Unhappily, these terms can be excluded by agreement between the parties: which in reality means at the volition of the seller, so far as sales to members of the public are concerned. The motor manufacturer, for example, always takes good care that all these terms are excluded by his so-called 'guarantee'. But it is understood that a new *Sale of Goods Act* is on the way and in that these terms will not be subject to exclusion clauses.

The first of the implied terms is as to title and quiet possession. There is an implied condition that:

(i) the seller has a right to sell the goods.
(ii) the buyer shall enjoy quiet possession of them.
(iii) the goods are free from any charge or encumbrance in favour of a third party: section 12 (1).

An auctioneer sells a horse that was not intended by the owner to be offered for sale by auction. The owner cannot, of course, be forced to part with the horse, but the auctioneer is liable in damages to the buyer for breach of the implied condition of section 12 (1).

Moreover, if there is a breach of this implied condition, the buyer who is forced to surrender goods to an owner is entitled to compensation in full, notwithstanding he has used the goods for a period. A man bought and used a car for some months. It then turned out that the car had been stolen, so he gave it back to the true owner. In an action against the man who had sold the car to him, the buyer was entitled, in spite of his use of the car, to the full return of money paid on a consideration which had wholly failed: *Rowland v Divall*, [1923] All E.R. Rep. 270.

This same principle applies to hire purchase contracts where it turns out that the finance company have no title to the vehicle that it has hired out with an option to the hirer to purchase. The result is that a hirer from a finance company which has no title to the goods can recover from them all the instalments he has paid, notwithstanding that he has had the use of the vehicle: *Warman v Southern Counties Car Finance*, [1949] 1 All E.R. 711.

And as early as 1609, the same principle was applied to contracts of hire in *Lee v Atkinson.*

Implied Terms as to Quality

In every contract of sale, unless such terms are expressly excluded, are three implied conditions:

1. **If the sale is by description, that the goods correspond to the description: section 13.**

   Every sale where the buyer has not seen the goods is a sale by description. That is self-evident. A contract was made for 3,000 tins of canned fruit from Australia packed in cases containing 30 tins a case. When the goods were delivered they were 3,000 tins certainly, but most were packed in cases containing 24 tins a case. The buyer rejected the lot. It was held that he was entitled to do so, since failure to correspond to the contractual description is the breach of a condition: In *re Moore and Landauer and Co.* (1921).

   But it may also be a sale by description where the buyer has seen a sample. In which case the goods delivered must correspond with both the sample and the description.

   And it may be a sale by description, even where the seller has seen the goods.

   Mr. Grant went into a shop and asked for a pair of men's underpants and was sold a pair of underpants in a transparent package. He wore them and contracted dermatitis in the most tender part of his anatomy, as the result of corrosive bleach having been left in the garment. It was held this was a breach of the description 'men's woollen underpants' and that he was entitled to damages for his injury: *Grant v Australian Knitting Mills Ltd.* 1936, [1935] All E.R. Rep. 209.

   This is stated by the Act to be 'a condition'; but, once again, that is misleading, for a failure to correspond with the description is a breach of a fundamental term of the contract and the seller cannot therefore rely on an express term of the contract that 'all conditions and warranties, express or implied, are excluded'.

2. There is a further implied condition where goods are bought from somebody who habitually deals in goods of that type, that the goods shall be of **merchantable quality: section 14 (2).** It has taken the Courts nearly eighty years to decide what is meant by 'merchantable' and, even so, there is still no universally accepted definition. One definition that received high

judicial approval was that advanced by the Australian judge, Dixon J., in the *Australian Knitting Mills* case:

'The condition that goods are to be of merchantable quality requires that they should be in such an actual state that a buyer fully acquainted with the facts and therefore knowing what hidden defects exist . . . would buy them *without abatement of price* obtainable for such goods if in reasonable sound order.'

Lord Reid and other judges in the Judicial Committee of the Privy Council expressly approved that definition in the House of Lords in *Kendall v Lillico*, [1968] 3 All E.R. 444. Unfortunately, Lord Reid in a later case put forward another definition which is by no means so lucid: 'It means', he said, 'that the goods in the form in which they were tendered were of no use for any purpose for which goods which complied with the description under which these goods were sold would normally be used, and hence were not saleable under that description.' *Brown Ltd. v Craies Ltd.*, [1970] 1 All E.R. 823. The plaintiffs bought textiles which could be used for different purposes from the defendants. The textiles supplied were suitable for industrial use but not suitable for making dresses, as the plaintiffs intended. The Court held that the material was of merchantable quality. It has also been said that even if the goods are not merchantable, the buyer is only entitled to reject them if such a course is reasonable: *Rapalli v K. L. Take Ltd.* (1958). But it is hard to believe that this is in fact the law, and it certainly seems inconsistent with any possible construction that could be reasonably placed upon the Statute.

3. There is also an implied term that goods should be **reasonably fit for the purpose required**: section 14 (1).

'Where the buyer, expressly or by implication, makes known to the seller the particular purpose for which goods are required, so as to show that he relies on the seller's skill or judgment, and the goods are of a description which it is in the course of the seller's business to supply (whether he be the manufacturer or not), there is an implied condition that the goods shall be reasonably fit for such purpose.'

This does not, however, apply where the goods are supplied under a trade or patent name. But even if they are sold under a trade name, if the buyer makes known his requirements to the seller so as to show that he relies on the seller's skill or judgment, this does not apply. And even if this section 14 (2) is excluded by this proviso, the goods must still be merchantable in accordance with 14 (1).

If the goods are sold for one purpose only, then the buyer has impliedly made known to the seller the purpose for which the goods are required. So when a man bought a hot water bottle and it subsequently burst, he was held to have made known to the seller the purpose for which it was required. People do not buy hot water bottles to keep whisky in, but to keep their feet warm in bed: *Preist v Last* (1903).

So too, where fire extinguishers were sold which subsequently exploded in a fire and increased the damage, it was held that they were unfit for the purpose required: *McAlpine Ltd. v Minimax Ltd.*, [1970] 1 Lloyds Rep. 397. But if the goods are used for a variety of different purposes, the buyer must expressly make known the purpose for which he requires them.

CHAPTER FIFTEEN

THE RIGHTS OF AN UNPAID SELLER

The Unpaid Seller's Lien

As we have seen, in most cases with the contract of sale the property, or ownership, in the goods passes to the buyer.

But that does not mean that the seller has to deliver the goods up to the buyer even if he has become the owner of them before the buyer has paid for them.

The seller has what is termed a lien, which is a right to retain goods belonging to another person.

It exists:

(i) where the goods have been sold without any stipulation as to credit. If the goods have been sold on credit, the buyer has no lien over them.

(ii) where the goods have been sold on credit, but the period has expired.

(iii) where the buyer becomes insolvent. But this does not cancel the contract of sale, and it is open to the buyer's trustee in bankruptcy to affirm the contract and tender the price, in which event the seller is bound to deliver the goods: section 41.

The unpaid seller's lien is lost:

(i) when he delivers the goods to a carrier or other bailee for the purpose of transmission to the seller.

(ii) where the buyer or his agent lawfully obtains possession of the goods.

(iii) if the lien is waived: section 43.

Waiver may take place expressly or it may be done by implication, as where the seller assents to a sub-sale by the buyer or he does some act inconsistent with the buyer's title in them by, for example, re-selling them contrary to law. For a lien is a mere right to retain the goods of another and does not confer on the unpaid seller the right to sell the goods to anybody else.

The Right of Stoppage in Transitu

The unpaid seller who has lost his lien by delivering goods to a carrier for transmission to the buyer does not lose all rights over the goods.

If—but only if—the buyer has become insolvent, the seller is entitled to stop the goods 'while they are still in transit, and retake possession of them': section 44.

For this purpose, a person is deemed to be insolvent if he 'has either ceased to pay his debts in the ordinary course of business or cannot pay his debts as they become due, whether he has committed an act of bankruptcy or not': section 62 (3).

Goods remain in transit from the time they are delivered to the carrier until such a time as they are delivered to the buyer. They do not have to be in motion. They may still be in transit if they are lodged in a warehouse. The essential feature of a stoppage *in transitu* is that the goods should be in the possession of a middleman. But the transit may also end if the buyer obtains delivery of the goods before they reach their destination, or if the carrier acknowledges to the buyer that he holds them on his behalf and if the carrier wrongfully refuses to deliver the goods to the buyer.

The unpaid seller is entitled to retake possession of the goods while they are in transit or give notice to the carrier that he has exercised this right of stoppage.

This may pose difficult questions for the carrier because he often has no knowledge whether the buyer has in fact become insolvent within the meaning of section 62 (3). If he detains them when the seller has a right of stoppage *in transitu*, he may be liable to him for detinue; if he returns them to the seller when the latter has no legal right to them, he may be liable to the buyer for conversion of what is, after all, the buyer's property, even if he has not paid for it. So if both buyer and seller claim the goods, the wisest course for the carrier is to retain possession of them and at once take out **an interpleader summons** asking the Court to determine who is entitled to the goods.

Stoppage *in transitu* can only occur when the goods are the property of the buyer, and it is essentially a right over the goods of another.

If, by the express terms of the contract, ownership has not passed to the buyer—because for example, the seller has reserved a right of disposal if unpaid—the unpaid seller has a right to withhold delivery and this applies even when the goods have left his possession and are in the hands of a carrier. He can go and get them back at any time before they are delivered to the buyer.

The Right to Re-sell

The exercise of the unpaid seller's lien or a stoppage *in transitu* alone does not act as rescission of the contract of sale. But if the seller does in fact re-sell, the new buyer gets a good title by virtue of section 25 (1) and section 48 (2) (see page 186).

But the seller has the right to re-sell if:

(i) the goods are of a perishable nature.

(ii) he gives notice to the buyer of his intention to re-sell, and the buyer does not within a reasonable time pay, or tender, the price.

(iii) he has expressly reserved a right of re-sale in case the buyer should make default in payment. In that event the contract of sale is rescinded, but the seller still may sue the buyer for damages for breach of contract: section 48.

This right of sale apparently only applies to an unpaid seller who has exercised either his lien or his right of stoppage *in transitu*. It would appear not to apply to other unpaid sellers; but in one case where the buyer became insolvent, it was said that a seller might re-sell unless the buyer, or somebody on his behalf, offered the price within a reasonable time. But there is no right to this effect conferred by the Act, which purports to consolidate all the law relating to the sale of goods.

CHAPTER SIXTEEN

INTERNATIONAL TRADE IN GOODS

Making the Contract

In international trade, the order (the **Indent**) constitutes the offer in law (see page 152). Frequently, the British manufacturer or supplier will send back a printed document, occasionally called the **Counterfoil,** which has printed on the reverse the seller's conditions of sale.

The effect of this is to constitute a counter offer—unless there have been previous transactions between the same parties—with the result that there is no contract unless these conditions are specifically accepted by the overseas buyer (see page 155). Without such acceptance the Court may hold, as it did in *Milhem and Sons v Fuerst Brothers* (1954), that there is no contract. And without specific acceptance, the sending of the goods may constitute the offer, which of course the buyer is entitled to reject without giving any reason.

Confirmation slips are a written confirmation of an order received, but where an order is received by telephone or telex they have no specific status in law but may be of evidential value if a court or arbitrator is called upon later to decide whether there is a contract or not. A party who has received a confirmation slip which does not correctly set out the contractual situation may find that if he does not write promptly to repudiate it, he will have great difficulty in convincing a court that it was not a correct statement of the transaction. The most satisfactory form of evidence of a contract is, of course, a signed confirmation slip, but very often these are not possible to obtain. Even though the confirmation slip is not returned, the Court may well be willing to find a contract between the parties. There is now no requirement of English law that a contract for the sale of goods has to be proved by writing. A conversation on the telephone or face to face is just as capable of amounting to a sale as a formal, documented transaction.

When the *Uniform Laws on International Sales Act, 1967* becomes operative in this country by an Order in Council, quite new considerations will arise; for the Schedule II of that Act deals with Formation of Contracts for the International Sale of Goods and it departs radically from the common law position at present prevailing here. In particular under the Act:

(i) an offer cannot be revoked at the wish of the offeror (see page 153).

(ii) an acceptance containing terms not contained in the offer is not a counter offer if the additional terms are not important.

(iii) this qualified acceptance becomes binding on the offeror unless he promptly repudiates the new terms.

Export Trade Terms

In the export trade there are several trade terms in current use which are a convenient shorthand for a bundle of obligations, a definition of the price and also for customs purposes.

These terms represent three things:

(i) a collection of terms and stipulations annexed to the contract of sale by reference.

(ii) a definition of what is included in the figure quoted as the price.

(iii) a definition used by H.M. Customs and Excise for determining the import value of goods liable to *ad valorem* duty and for statistical purposes in the case of goods—such as wines and spirits—which are subject to specific import duties; and likewise for exports.

Unfortunately these terms are by no means standardised, although attempts have been and are being made by the **United Nations Commission on International Trade** (UNCITRAL) to prepare standard contracts. Working parties have prepared a vast variety of general Conditions of Sale and Standard form contracts, both for use in the capitalist world and between capitalist and communist states.

In addition, the **International Chamber of Commerce** publishes a book, *Trade Terms*, with standardised definitions, known in the jargon of the trade as **Incoterms.** If this word or a date follows any of the trade terms discussed below, this means a contract according to the definition contained in the International Chamber of Commerce formulation of that particular year.

The full extent of these variations between one contract and another can be seen in the difference between the export contract for one British port and another. The **Association of British Chambers of Commerce** has prepared a booklet under the title *F.o.b. Vessel* which gives an account of customs in force at the main ports of the United Kingdom and which is supplementary to the Incoterm.

c.i.f.

The most frequently used term in international trade is the c.i.f. contract, with a named port of arrival. The initials stand for **Cost,**

Insurance, Freight (and *not* as T. S. Eliot appears to have believed, in *The Waste Land*, 'carriage and insurance free').

This means in essence that the seller has to pay all charges on the goods up to the point where they arrive at the port named. But in reality it means in commercial law much more than that.

It means that the seller must tender to the buyer:

(i) a clean **bill of lading** for the goods and no others. A bill of lading is a receipt by the shipowner that the goods have been received aboard his ship. Ever since the case of *Lickbarrow v Mason* 1794, [1775–1802] All E.R. Rep. 1, it has been accepted in law as a document of title to the goods. That is, whoever produces the bill of lading to the ship's master at the end of the voyage is entitled to take possession of the goods. Even the true owner is not entitled to the goods unless he can produce a bill of lading: *Truck and Spares Ltd. v Maritime Agencies*, [1951] 2 All E.R. 982.

It therefore fulfils three functions:

(a) it records the terms of contract of carriage between the shipper and shipowner.

(b) it records that the goods have actually been received aboard the ship.

(c) it enables the consignee of the goods, who has paid for them and received in return the signed bill of lading, to obtain possession of them on arrival.

The bill of lading and its terms are subject to the provisions of an Act of Parliament (see page 227), which in turn represents international agreements arrived at in The Hague in 1967 and 1968. A '*clean*' bill of lading is one which records that the goods are received in 'apparent good order and condition'. The opposite to this is a '*claused*' bill of lading when the shipowner has qualified this receipt.

(ii) an **insurance policy** on the normal form.

(iii) an **invoice** which shows the price and a deduction of the freight which the buyer pays beforehand.

Against tender of these three documents the buyer must pay the price.

It follows therefore that the seller's contractual obligation under a c.i.f. contract is to deliver to the buyer not the goods themselves but the documents of title to them. The buyer has two rights: the right to reject the documents when tendered, as not being 'clean' or in accordance with the contract, and a separate and distinct right to reject the goods later if on examination it is found that they do not conform to the contract: *Kwei Tek Chao v British Traders and Shippers Ltd.*, [1954] 1 All E.R. 779.

Variants of the c.i.f. clause are sometimes used, such as:

c.i.f. and c., which means cost, insurance, freight and commission, to indicate that the price includes the export agent's commission where goods have been ordered through an export agent.

c. and f., which indicates that the consignee is responsible for the insurance of the goods.

The f.o.b. Contract and Other Similar Terms

By f.o.b. is meant 'free on board'.

This refers to three things:

(i) the seller's responsibility for handling and carriage charges;
(ii) the seller's responsibility for the risk for the destruction or injury to the goods;
(iii) the customs declared value for export.

Generally speaking, under an f.o.b. contract, the seller is responsible for all charges and risk up to the moment when the goods pass over the ship's rail.

But this may not always be the case, as f.o.b. terms may vary with the port of shipment. In Southampton, for example, it would appear that by the custom of the port, the seller's charges end when the goods are on hook alongside the vessel, and the cost of cranage to the ship's rail is paid for by the consignee as part of the freight charges. But even there, the seller's risk only ends when the goods pass over the ship's rail. And where goods are consigned 'f.o.b. Belfast' the seller has discharged his responsibility both as to charges and risk, it would seem, when he has delivered the goods to a designated transit shed nominated by the shipping line for receipt of goods for foreign going vessels. To some extent this may vary with the exact expression used:

f.o.b. vessel. This usually means that both charges and responsibility for risk cease only when the goods pass over the ship's rail.

f.o.b. named port. This may mean that charges and responsibility end with delivery to the shipper's warehouse in the named port.

f.o.b. stowed vessel named port. This means that the seller's liability continues beyond the ship's rail to the very moment when they are stowed in the hold.

The Customs definition of f.o.b. for statistical purposes is:

'the cost to the nearest pound sterling of the goods to the purchaser abroad, including packing, inland and coastal transport in the United Kingdom, dock dues, loading charges and all other costs, profits and charges and expenses (e.g. insurance and commission) occurring up to the point where the goods are deposited on board the exporting vessel or aircraft . . . in all cases, outward freight and insurance should be excluded and cash and trade discounts to the purchaser abroad deducted.'

There is one exception to the general rule of the f.o.b. terms that the seller's responsibility for risk ceases when the goods pass over the ship's rail. This is that the seller is required to notify the buyer of the shipment in time for him to insure the goods. If he does not do so, and the goods are damaged after they have passed the ship's rail, the seller may be held liable as the result of s. 32 (3) of the *Sale of Goods Act, 1893*:

'Unless otherwise agreed, where goods are sent by the seller to the buyer by a route involving sea transit, under circumstances in which it is usual to insure, the seller must give such notice to the buyer as may enable him to insure them during their sea transit, and, if the seller fails to do so, the goods shall be at his risk during such sea transit.'

In addition to f.o.b. there are various other terms in use.

Ex works. In this case, the goods are to be made available to the buyer at the seller's works or warehouse. It is usually believed that the seller has to bear the cost of packaging the goods in a suitable form for the known method of transport.

f.o.r. The expression means 'free on rail' and in this country is construed as meaning the delivery of the goods to the collecting vehicle of British Rail and not the point in time when the goods actually arrive on a railway carriage.

f.a.s.—(named vessel)—'free alongside ship'. This is like the ordinary f.o.b. contract except that the seller's liability ceases when the goods are on the quayside waiting for craning aboard.

The Port of London has an arrangement with British Rail whereby certain goods can be carried at a quoted price to include service at the docks, so that an exporter can calculate exactly what he will have to charge to include this.

CHAPTER SEVENTEEN

HIRE PURCHASE AND SIMILAR TRANSACTIONS

The acquisition of goods by instalment payments (often at extravagant interest rates and subject to onerous conditions) has become an outstanding feature of modern life. The invention of these devices is commonly credited to the Mr. Singer, of sewing machine fame. Although all such transactions are commonly referred to as 'hire purchase', legally they may be one of three different contracts—true hire purchase contracts, conditional sale agreements or credit sale agreements.

True Hire Purchase Contracts

In the true hire purchase contract, the person who is usually called 'the buyer' goes to a shop or garage and 'buys' an article from them by instalments. That, at least, is the popular conception of the transaction.

In law, the situation is really quite different, in that:

(i) the shop sells the goods not to 'the buyer', but to a finance company;

(ii) the finance company thereby becomes the owner of the goods in question;

(iii) the finance company thereupon hires out the goods under a separate contract to the so-called 'buyer' over a fixed period at certain weekly or monthly 'rent'. This is, in essence, a **contract of bailment** (see page 263).

To illustrate it diagrammatically the transaction is:

Finance Company

Contract No.1. Sells To

Contract No.2. Hires To

Shop

Hirer

(iv) at the end of the period, the finance company will graciously allow the hirer either to return the goods or to become the owner of them for the payment of a nominal sum, usually £1 or thereabouts. An option to that effect is incorporated in the contract.

For a long time it was believed that there was no contractual relationship at all between the shop and the so-called 'buyer'. The result was that whatever promises and warranties were given by the shop to the 'buyer' to induce him to enter the transaction were not contractual obligations, and could be laughed off. And since the finance company was always careful to exempt itself in its contract with 'the buyer' from all responsibility of any kind for the condition of the goods, the 'buyer' was often saddled with shoddy rubbish for which he had no redress against anybody.

It was something of an event then when the law courts started to remedy this position. The credit for this must go to Mr. Justice McNair who, in spite of earlier judges who had in similar circumstances held garages not liable, in *Webster v Higgin*, [1948] 2 All E.R. 127, held that when a garage proprietor had assured a hire purchase 'buyer' that a car was 'a good little bus. I will stake my life you will have no trouble with it,' and the car proved to have, amongst a multitude of other defects, dangerous steering, the garage proprietor was liable on a **collateral contract of warranty**.

This was affirmed in *Karsales v Wallis*, [1966] 2 All E.R. 866. There, the plaintiff agreed to acquire on hire purchase from the defendants a Buick car which was described to him by them as being 'in perfect condition' and 'good for thousands of trouble-free miles'. Later the car was delivered outside his house in the dead of night, for the excellent reason that it was incapable of moving under its own steam and had to be towed there. The defendants disowned all responsibility. The only contract, they claimed, was between the plaintiff and the finance company and that excluded all liability for the condition of the vehicle. As for any contract of warranty, there was no consideration moving from the promisee (the plaintiff) to the promisor (the defendants).

The Court adopted the view expressed by McNair J. and held that there was in fact a collateral, unilateral, contract between the plaintiff and the defendant in these terms:

'If you enter into a contract with the finance company, I promise you that the goods are as I say they are.'

The defendants were therefore held liable not only for the cost of putting the vehicle into the condition they had warranted it to be, but also for loss of use during the period necessary.

The present position therefore can be represented diagrammatically as follows:

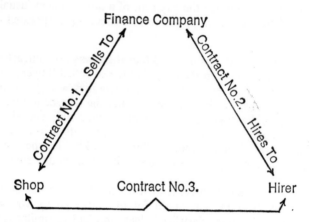

whereby in contract No. 3 the seller unilaterally warrants to the hirer that goods are as they are said to be if he will enter into contract No. 2.

And, quite apart from the *Hire Purchase Act, 1965,* even though there is no sale from the shop to the hirer, implied terms similar to those in the *Sale of Goods Act* may be contained in that collateral contract of warranty, quite apart from any express promises.

In the true hire purchase contract, therefore, the finance company remains the owner of the goods throughout and until the option to purchase is exercised.

Apart from various acts of Parliament (see page 208):

(i) The hirer has no right to part with goods without the consent of the owner;

(ii) If the hirer purports to sell them, 'a buyer', however innocent, can never become the owner—nor can any subsequent 'buyer';

(iii) In default of payment the owner has the right to take the goods back, however much has been paid on them. Repossession, or the 'snatch-back' as it became known, was a familiar feature of life in Britain and it was often immensely more profitable for a finance company to have customers who defaulted, than those who complied with their contractual obligations. The Courts not only gave the finance companies their pound of flesh but every drop of blood as well. It was a private Member of Parliament, Ellen Wilkinson, who began to alter this situation with her *Hire Purchase Act* of

1938 (now repealed) and, increasingly, Statute has restricted the terms of hire purchase agreements.

Conditional Sale Agreements

Such agreements differ from a hire purchase agreement in two respects:

(i) The person in possession of the goods has them under a **contract of sale** and not of **bailment**;

(ii) The ownership of the goods vests in the purchaser automatically when the terms of the contract have been fulfilled and not as the result of the exercise of an option right by him; until that moment the goods remain the property of the finance company. Apart from Statute the three conditions at the foot of the opposite page apply.

These contracts are sometimes also called **deferred sale agreements** or **suspensive sale agreements**. The essence of the contract is that the property does not vest in the buyer until a specific condition has been fulfilled. The *Sale of Goods Act, 1893*, s. 1 (2) contains a description of such agreements as does s. 1 (1) of the *Hire Purchase Act, 1965*, where it is defined as:

'an agreement for the sale of goods under which the purchase price or part of it is payable by instalments and the property in the goods is to remain in the seller (notwithstanding that the buyer is to be in possession of the goods) until such conditions as to the payment of instalments or otherwise as may be specified in the agreement are fulfilled'.

There is a further point to notice. If the conditional sale agreement is *not* subject to the *Hire Purchase Act, 1965* (e.g. at present, if the goods cost more than £2,000), since the customer is a person who has 'agreed to buy the goods', he can pass a good title to a purchaser by virtue of the *Factors Act, 1889* and s. 25 (2) of the *Sale of Goods Act*; but if the goods are subject to the *Hire Purchase Act, 1965*, he is deemed *not* to be a person who has 'agreed to buy the goods'.

Credit Sale Agreements

At common law the term credit sale means any sale where the purchase price is not payable either on completion of the contract or on the delivery of the goods. But the *Hire Purchase Act, 1965* has attached a special meaning to these words, as:

'an agreement for the sale of goods under which the purchase price is payable by five or more instalments, not being a conditional sale agreement'.

The chief differences therefore between credit sale, and hire purchase and conditional sale agreements, are that in credit sale:

(i) the buyer becomes the owner of the goods *immediately* the contract is agreed and not when all the instalments have been paid (unlike the conditional sale agreement).

(ii) the contract is subject to the provisions of ss. 12–15 of the *Sale of Goods Act, 1893*, unless these are expressly excluded—as they can be.

(iii) the buyer can sell the goods at any time and a purchaser from him will become the true owner.

(iv) the seller has at no time the right to re-possess the goods.

There are also considerable differences in the application of the statutes.

In practice, most credit sale agreements provide that in default of the payment of one instalment, the whole of the purchase price shall become immediately due and payable. In default of payment, a court judgment can be obtained for the whole of this sum and execution then levied on all the purchaser's goods, including the ones that are subject to the credit sale.

Acts of Parliament and Vendor Credit

Statute has interfered with the common law for four different reasons:

1. To control hire purchase and similar transactions for economic purposes—the so-called 'regulator'. This is outside the scope of this book, but the orders are made under the *Emergency Laws (Reactments and Repeals) Act, 1964*. It is a criminal offence to break such orders and it would appear that a finance house that is deceived by a collusive bargain between a dealer and a hirer is guilty of an offence under these Orders even though entirely innocent morally, and ignorant of the true facts.

2. To alter the common law about the title of the goods. Not infrequently, goods subject to hire purchase or other instalment contracts are wrongfully 'sold' to innocent third parties. The following statutory provisions concern this situation and will be explained in more detail later (see page 209):

(a) The *Sale of Goods Act, 1893*, section 25 (2) and, in almost identical terms, the *Factors Act, 1889*, section 9.

(b) The *Law of Distress Amendment Act, 1908*, section 4; the *Bankruptcy and Deeds of Arrangement Act, 1913*, section 15 and the *County Courts Act, 1959*, section 133.

(c) The *Hire Purchase Act, 1964*, Part III.

(d) The *Hire Purchase Act, 1965*, sections 53 and 54.

3. To control relationships between the parties. The *Hire Purchase Act, 1965* deals with principally this and is discussed in detail on page 212.

4. To control the advertising of hire purchase and similar transactions. The *Advertisements (Hire Purchase) Act, 1957* (which has been amended by the *Hire Purchase Act, 1964*) provides a whole set of regulations which apply to any advertisements (including those on film and television) for goods available for disposal by way of 'hire purchase or credit sale'.

The provisions of this Act apply to *all* hire purchase and similar transactions and not just those caught by the 1965 Act.

It lays down many specific details about what must be contained in a hire purchase advertisement, and also a formula for calculating the approximate true rate of interest:

$$\frac{200 \, md}{p(n+1) + \frac{d}{3}(n-1)}$$

where $m =$ the number by which the period in respect of which each payment must be multiplied in order to be equal to a period of 12 months.

$d =$ the difference between
(a) the sum stated in the advertisement as the total credit price and
(b) the cash price.

$p =$ the difference between
(a) the cash price and
(b) the amount of deposit,
or where no deposit is payable, the cash price.

$n =$ total number of instalments payable.

Presumably there are people who understand what it all means. A more convenient (and rough) rule of thumb is to double the nominal rate of interest and deduct 1, for one year.

There is also a set of regulations made under the *Hire Purchase Act, 1965* which lays down in detail the exact form and height of the smallest letter in the hire purchase documents, width of columns etc. etc., so as to promote legibility. There are not as yet, however, any regulations that require such documents, or regulations themselves, to be intelligible.

Transfer of Title

As we have seen, by the *Sale of Goods Act, 1893*, s. 25 (2), where a person has bought, or agreed to buy goods, and he comes into possession of them *with the consent of the seller*, even though by the express terms of the contract he has not become the owner of them, he can pass a title to an innocent buyer (see page 186).

This material alteration, and exception to the principle of *nemo dat quod non habet*, was first introduced into English law by s. 9 of the *Factors Act, 1889*, which is still on the Statute Book.

The credit sale transaction gives the purchaser a good title. In the early case of *Lee v Butler* 1893, [1891–4] All E.R. Rep. 1200, it was held that a purchaser under a conditional sale agreement was a person who had 'agreed to buy' the goods, and therefore could pass a good title by virtue of s. 9 of the *Factors Act*—even though, of course, there was an express provision in the contract that the property was not to vest until the last instalment had been paid. This rule has now been altered so far as conditional sale agreements which are subject to the *Hire Purchase Act, 1965* are concerned, i.e. those under £2,000 total credit price, and sold to private individuals. This was done by s. 54 which enacts that 'the buyer under a conditional sale agreement *shall be deemed not* to be a person who has bought or agreed to buy goods'.

The effect of this appears to be that in the case of **goods sold on conditional sale which are subject to the *Hire Purchase Act, 1965*:** the owner can recover them from an innocent purchaser.

In the case of **goods sold on conditional sale, but not subject to the *Hire Purchase Act, 1965*:** the owner cannot recover them from an innocent purchaser.

Hire purchase transactions are not affected by s. 25 (2) of the *Sale of Goods Act* or s. 9 of the *Factors Act*, since the hirer is not 'a person who has agreed to buy' but one who merely has an option to purchase at the end of the period of hiring: *Belsize Motor Supply Co. v Cox* 1914, [1911–13] All E.R. Rep. 1084. There is, however, an Australian case, not so far followed in this country, which suggests that if the option money is merely nominal (1s 6d in that case), then the transaction may in reality be a conditional sale and therefore subject to s. 25 (2).

Landlord's Distress. At common law, the landlord of premises may levy distress for the amount of any rent due on the premises by seizing any goods on the premises, whether they belong to the tenant or not. S. 1 of the *Law of Distress Amendment Act, 1908* altered this, by excluding goods belonging to people other than the tenant, provided the owners give notice in writing to the landlord; but this section does *not* apply to goods on hire purchase, by reason of s. 4. Section 4 expressly excludes:

(i) goods **'comprised in a hire purchase agreement'** made by the tenant.

(ii) goods **'in the tenant's possession with the owner's consent'**—a condition generally referred to as the 'reputed ownership clause'.

The result is that if the landlord seizes goods under hire purchase the distraint is a valid one, for both reasons. Various attempts have been made to avoid this consequence, the most effective being the clause found in *Times Furnishing Co. Ltd. v Hutchings*, [1938] 1 All E.R. 422: 'If any landlord of the hirer threatens or takes any steps to levy a distress for rent upon the furniture of or a possession of the hirer . . . this agreement . . . shall automatically determine and come to an end.'

This successfully got the goods out of section 4 (1) because they ceased to be goods 'comprised in a hire purchase agreement', but it did not avoid the reputed ownership clause; and it was not sufficient merely to terminate just the hiring, the whole agreement had to be terminated. The reputed ownership clause was, however, effectively barred, it was held in *Smart Bros. Ltd. v Holt*, [1929] All E.R. Rep. 322, by adding to the words above 'and the hirer shall no longer be in possession of the goods with the owner's consent'.

It has become common practice to write into hire purchase agreements a clause with an obligation to pay the rent to a landlord and a right to determine the whole agreement if the rent is not paid, together with what has come to be known as the *Smart v Holt* clause.

Apparently, written notice to determine the agreement is effective when posted, even if it arrives after the landlord has seized the goods. But, in goods subject to the 1965 Act, *if notice of default is served before the seizure*, the goods are deemed not to be 'comprised in a hire purchase agreement' (s. 53 (1) (a)); but they may still be in the 'reputed ownership' of the hirer.

It has been suggested that one way to defeat a landlord's lien is to allow the wife of a tenant to enter into the Hire Purchase agreement, with a contract of guarantee or indemnity by the husband; the goods then are never 'comprised in a hire purchase agreement' *by the tenant*, nor is he ever in possession with the consent of the owner—it is his wife who has the possession.

The *Hire Purchase Act, 1964*, Part III. The sections of the *Hire Purchase Act, 1964* which are not repealed deal with the protection of purchasers of motor vehicles. It applies only to:

(i) private purchasers, and not to car dealers or finance houses;
(ii) such private purchasers who buy in good faith and without knowledge that the car is subject to a hire purchase agreement or conditional sale agreement;
(iii) motor vehicles and not other goods; but it does apply to motor vehicles, even though the transaction is not subject to the *Hire Purchase Act, 1965*, i.e. if the credit price exceeds £2,000.

In such cases, a good title is obtained notwithstanding that the 'seller' has no right to sell the goods. The 1964 Act may also apply where the first sale by the hirer is to a garage or finance company. They get no title, but if they sell to a private individual, he will become the owner and therefore so will anybody who buys subsequently.

It is not commonly known, but members of the public can obtain information about whether a second-hand motor vehicle is the subject of a hire purchase agreement from **Hire Purchase Information Ltd.**, through the R.A.C., A.A. or any Citizens' Advice Bureau.

Other situations where the owner of the goods on hire purchase may find his title defeated.

(i) If the hirer becomes **bankrupt,** all his property vests in the trustee in bankruptcy; goods on hire purchase, or conditional sale, not being his property, do not rest in the trustee. But if they are in the hirer's possession *in his trade or business* they may vest in the trustee under the 'reputed ownership': s. 38 (c) of the *Bankruptcy Act, 1914.*

(ii) A repairer of goods has a **lien** on the goods so long as they are in his possession until his charges in respect of work done are paid. This is not affected even if there is a clause in the hire purchase agreement, whereby the hirer agrees not to allow such liens. The situation therefore commonly arises where a hirer takes a motor vehicle subject to hire purchase to a garage for repair and the repairer detains it until his bill has been paid. There is no practical way in which the owner can prevent this, where the hiring has not been determined before the hirer has parted with possession.

(iii) Goods subject to hire purchase or conditional sale agreements are not liable to have execution levied on them by the Sheriff's Office, in respect of a High Court judgment, or by the bailiff in respect of a County Court judgment. But if the Sheriff's Officer or the Bailiff does seize them, not knowing that they are subject to hire purchase, he is not liable to an action against him for conversion as the result of the *Bankruptcy and Deeds of Arrangement Act, 1913* and the *County Court Act, 1959.* If the goods are so seized and sold, the buyers get a good title to them. All that the owner is then entitled to is the proceeds of the sale as money 'had and received' to his use.

The *Hire Purchase Act, 1965*: the Form of the Agreement

This enactment applies to hire purchase agreements, conditional sale agreements and, to a more limited extent, to credit sale agreements where the purchase price is payable by five or more instalments. But it excludes:

(i) contracts where the total price—that is the cost of the goods plus the interest or 'service' charges—exceeds £2,000.
(ii) cases where the hirer or buyer is not a private individual but a corporation, such as a company.

The Act requires that *before* any agreement is entered into the owner must have stated in *writing* the cash price of the goods. It is sufficient if this is shown on a price tag or in a catalogue. This is intended to exclude the former popular price tag 'Only 9s per week', etc.

The Act then requires that the agreement should contain certain details. As a result of slovenly draftsmanship it does not in fact require that the agreement should be in writing, but this is implied by reference to the type, size and lettering of the agreement.

Such agreements must:
1. be signed by the hirer (the purchaser in the case of conditional sale or credit sale transactions) and not by any person as his agent.

In the case of hire purchase agreements, the agreement must bear the words in red:

This document contains the
terms of a hire purchase
agreement. Sign it only
if you want to be legally
bound by them.

Signature of hirer.

....

The goods will not become
your property until you
have made all the payments.
You must not sell them before
then.

H

In the case of conditional sale agreements the words:

This document contains
the terms of a conditional
sale agreement. Sign it
only if you want to be
legally bound by them.

Signature of buyer.

....

The goods will not become
your property until you have paid
.....................instalments.
You must not sell them before then.

In the case of a credit sale agreement:

This document contains
the terms of a credit
sale agreement. Sign it
only if you want to be
legally bound by them.

Signature of buyer.

....

2. be signed by the owner (or seller) or an agent on his behalf.
3. contain a description of the goods comprised in the agreement, sufficient to identify them.
4. state the cash price of the goods.
5. state the credit price or total price of the goods.

There is no requirement, as yet, that the interest rate has to be specifically stated.

Credit sale agreements do not have to bear a notice about no right to sell, since the instalment purchaser has already become the owner of the goods.

The effect of failure to comply with these requirements is that the owner is not entitled to enforce an agreement or a contract of guarantee; nor can he recover the goods.

However, if a court is satisfied that in any action failure to comply with any of these requirements has not prejudiced the hirer and that it would be just and equitable, the Court can dispense with the requirement.

But this provision does not apply to failure of the hirer to sign personally or the owner's failure to sign by himself or an agent.

Once again, credit sales are an exception. Those where the total purchase price is less than £30 are not subject to these provisions of the Act.

Dealers' Liability in Hire Purchase Transactions

Although there is no contract of sale between a dealer or retailer and a customer who is acquiring goods by any of the three usual contracts of instalment payments, the retailer may be liable to him in a number of different ways.

In the first place, if a statement is made fraudulently to induce the customer to enter into a contract with the finance company, an action for **deceit** will lie. Similarly an action for **negligence** may lie and it will also lie where the dealer or retailer supplies goods which have been negligently repaired as in *Hersch v Stewart and Arden Ltd.*, [1939] 4 All E.R. 123. The *Misrepresentation Act, 1967* also gives the customer a right to sue the dealer for false statements which amount to **innocent misrepresentation.**

In addition to all these, which are in essence actions in tort, an action will lie for breach of the **collateral contract of warranty**— *Andrews v Hopkinson*, [1956] 3 All E.R. 422 (see page 206).

Finance Companies' Liability to the Hirer

The finance companies are not liable vicariously for things said and done by retailers or dealers because such people are not their employees but are independent contractors. But for certain purposes the retailers or dealers may be the agent of the finance company so as to bind the company.

To what extent dealers are agents of the finance company is still somewhat uncertain, but they certainly are for the following purposes:

   (i) **Revocation of offers.** The completion of a hire purchase proposal form has been held to be the making of an offer which is capable of being accepted by the signature of, or on behalf of, the finance company.

   If the customer decides to withdraw his offer he is always at liberty to do so, provided he gives notice before the offer has been accepted. The retailer or dealer has been held to be the authorised agent of the finance company for this purpose, so that notice of revocation to them is notice to the company. In *Financings Ltd. v Stimson*, [1962] 3 All E.R. 386, the hire purchase agreement read that it was to be binding 'on acceptance by signature on behalf of the owner'. It was in fact signed on 25th March, but on the 20th March the customer had returned the car as unsatisfactory, which amounted to notice of revocation of his offer. On the night of the 24th/25th March, the car was stolen and badly damaged. It was held that the loss was to fall on the finance company since there was no contract between them and the customer. An offer which has been withdrawn cannot be accepted.

  (ii) **Notice of rescission.** If the customer claims to rescind the contract on any grounds such as misrepresentation, the dealer is the agent of the finance company for the purpose of receiving this notice of rescission. This is by virtue of section 31 (2) of the *Hire Purchase Act, 1965,* and it is not possible to exclude the operation of this section.

 (iii) **Antecedent negotiations.** The Act does not use the terms 'dealer' or 'retailer' but refers to the 'person who conducted antecedent negotiations'. These are defined 'as any negotiations, or arrangements with the hirer . . . whereby he was induced to make the arrangement or which otherwise promoted the transaction to which the agreement relates'.

The finance company is liable for any representation made by the person who conducts antecedent negotiations provided they are made 'in the course of a business carried on by him'; and this liability cannot be excluded by contract.

The Statutory Copies and the Right to Cancel

The *Hire Purchase Act, 1965* requires that copies of the contract be delivered to the instalment customer.

If the contract is signed at 'the appropriate trade premises' the customer must be supplied with *one* copy. For this purpose 'the appropriate trade premises' are defined by the Act as meaning the premises either:

(i) 'where the owner named in the agreement carries on his business'—i.e. the offices of the finance company, or
(ii) 'where goods of the description to which the agreement relates are normally offered for sale in the course of business'. From this it is clear that the premises do not have to be that of the dealer or retailer supplying the goods. Apparently other people's premises, provided they comply with the requirements, are sufficient.

If the contract is signed at the appropriate trade premises the contract is binding and the instalment customer has no opportunity of changing his mind.

But in cases where the instalment customer signs the contract elsewhere than at the appropriate trade premises, e.g. at his own house, he must be supplied with *two* copies, one at the time, the second sent by post within seven days. The contract itself must be signed by the hirer himself and not by any agent on his behalf.

All this is to prevent door-to-door salesmen pressurising housewives into signing agreements of which they later repent. The Act therefore provides for a 'cooling off' period in the form of a right to cancel the agreement, even after it is made and the goods have been delivered.

This right can only be exercised in writing and must indicate the hirer's intention to withdraw from the contract. This right must be exercised 'before the end of the period of four days beginning with the day on which he receives the second statutory copy'. For this purpose, the notice of cancellation is deemed to have been made at the time when the letter is posted.

The dealer is the owner's agent for the purpose of receiving this notice, so that if it is posted to him the owner of the goods is bound by it.

The effect of cancellation is that the parties have to be restored to the position they were in before the contract was made. If a deposit has been paid by the hirer it must be refunded. If goods have been given in part exchange, they must be restored. The hirer must return the goods if he has got them and he is under an obligation to take reasonable care of them for 21 days following the date of his notice of cancellation. He also has a lien on the goods in respect of the amount of his deposit or other payment and he is entitled to refuse to return the goods until he has got his money back. If this takes more than 21 days, his liability to take reasonable care of the goods ceases after the 21 days.

The Owner's Right to Terminate

The right to terminate the contract may arise:

(i) where the hirer dies or becomes bankrupt. Before the 1965 Act it was common practice to write a clause into agreements that the hiring should terminate with the death of the hirer. Any such clause is now void in accordance with s. 30. As a result, the rights of the hirer now vest in his estate, and his personal representatives, whether they be executors or administrators, have the right to continue the contract if they so wish and to exercise the same option to purchase the goods as the deceased had. But the owner can serve 'notice of default' on the personal representative of the deceased and seek to recover possession of the goods by means of a court order.

(ii) where there has been a breach of any of the stipulations of the contract other than those to pay money, e.g. failure to keep the goods on the premises or failure to insure them.

(iii) in the case of failure to keep up the instalment payments.

Goods subject to the *Hire Purchase Act, 1965* become **protected goods** if **one-third or more** of the hire purchase price has been paid. Once they have become that, the owner loses his traditional right to re-possess the goods without notice and can only do so with the leave of the Court.

Failure by the owner to obtain the leave of the Court to re-possess goods under the Act results in:

(i) the hirer being released from all future liability under the contract.

(ii) the hirer being entitled to repayment of the whole of the monies he has paid under the contract.

This does not apply however if a hirer agrees to return the goods, even if this comes about through his ignorance of his legal rights. If the hirer consents, there is no need for a court order.

At the court hearing, the Court may:

(i) order the goods to be returned to the owner, or

(ii) make an order for the return of the goods to the owner, suspended so long as the hirer pays the balance by such instalments as the Court sees fit, or

(iii) make an order vesting the title of part of the goods in the hirer and order the return of the balance.

In effect, the Court can in its discretion make a completely new contract for the parties.

The Hirer's Right to Terminate

At any time while a hire purchase or conditional sale agreement is in force, the hirer has the right to terminate it if the transaction is subject to the *Hire Purchase Act, 1965*. Section 7 of the Act says:

'At any time before the final payment, the hirer . . . shall . . . be entitled to terminate the agreement by giving notice of termination in writing . . .'

That is his statutory right; but commonly, such a right is also conferred by the words of the contract. In this event, any such term which seeks to impose on the hirer any greater liability than that contained in s. 28 is void. But the agreement may give the hirer more favourable terms than s. 28 and the clause is then good.

The right of s. 28 is subject to the goods being returned and to the payment by the hirer of:

(i) any instalments due up to the date of cancellation;
(ii) such an amount as will amount, with what he has already paid, to 50% of the hire purchase price of the goods (but the Court has the power to order a lesser sum to be paid if satisfied that such a sum represents the loss sustained as a result of the hirer's termination);
(iii) damages for failure to take reasonable care of the goods, if such damages can be proved.

BOOK IV: CARRIAGE AND INSURANCE

CHAPTER EIGHTEEN

CARRIAGE BY LAND

The Common Carrier

Normally a person who undertakes the carriage of the goods of another will only be liable for damages to them if it is proved that he has done something negligent or something which is a breach of his contract. Since these may be matters which are not easy of proof, the common law invented a category of carrier termed 'the common carrier' and these exist to this day, although in diminished numbers.

Essentially, a common carrier is one who, by law, is made the insurer of the goods he carries. If they are lost or damaged even without his fault or negligence, he is still liable for them.

To this absolute liability for the goods he is carrying there are five exceptions:

1. **Inherent vice in goods.** A railway company, then a common carrier, was held not liable when a bullock they were carrying escaped from a truck without their negligence and was killed.
2. **Fault of the consignor.** The common carrier is not liable for goods that are sent improperly secured, even if he knows they are. Nor is he liable, if the consignor has incorrectly addressed them.
3. **Act of God.** By that is meant any natural phenomenon such as an earthquake or a flood, which is not due to human intervention and which could not be reasonably anticipated.
4. **Acts of the Queen's enemies.** By this is meant hostile government forces, and not things like robbery or riot. If goods are lost or damaged as a result of either of the latter the carrier is liable.
5. **Acts of war.** The carrier is not liable where damage is done to the goods as the result of these.

The *Carriers Act, 1830* was introduced to modify the common law position of carriers. There can be common carriers by land, sea or air, but this Act applies only to those who carry goods overland. It allows the common carrier to restrict his liability at common law by a notice exhibited at his place of business making it clear that his contract of carriage limits his liability. If such a notice exists and the consignee accepts a contract on these terms:

the common carrier can limit his liability in respect of **articles of high value,** such as jewellery, to £10 per package unless the contents are declared to him and any increased charges paid.

If the value of the article is not declared, the carrier is not liable to any loss, even though it be caused by his own negligence.

But he cannot otherwise exclude his liability in respect of loss occasioned by the felonious acts of any servant of his or loss occasioned by his own personal default.

Being an insurer of the goods is not the only obligation laid on him by law. He is under an obligation to carry all goods offered him for the purpose unless the goods are not of the kind he professes to carry, or are consigned to a place to which he does not normally go, or he has no room in his vehicle.

He is also under a duty to carry goods by his accustomed route and not to deviate from it, and to deliver them in a reasonable time.

A carrier, however, only becomes a common carrier if he holds himself out as being one and as being willing to accept all goods of the class he normally carries unless his vehicle is full. A carrier who normally carries goods between two or more places may be a **private carrier** if he reserves to himself the right to accept or reject goods for carriage irrespective of whether his vehicle is full or not.

Carriage by Rail

The railways in Britain are no longer common carriers, as a result of the *Transport Act, 1962*; nor is London Transport.

British Rail, therefore, when it carries goods, does so under conditions of carriage which are merely contractual (or analogous to contractual). Nobody has yet raised the point as to whether British Rail is merely fulfilling a statutory obligation (see page 77) or entering into contracts.

Currently the railways limit loss of a whole consignment to £800 per ton of the goods weight or proportionately for partial damage or loss. It is also, at a lower rate, possible to have terms of carriage where the goods are at the owner's risk throughout.

One consequence of their change in status is that the railways are under no legal obligation to carry passengers; if they do, they are not allowed to exclude or limit liability for death or bodily injury to a passenger. But there is nothing preventing them from imposing any qualifications they like on the carriage of merchandise. One provision they do make is that notice of a claim must be made within three days of the **termination** of transport, and the claim itself within seven days. Non-delivery claims for loss of whole consignments or individual packages have to be made within 28 days from the **commencement of the transit.**

International traffic is carried by rail subject to the conditions contained in contracts prepared by **C.I.M.**—*Convention internationale concernant le transport des merchandises.* This convention has not been given the force of law in this country by Act of Parliament, but the terms are incorporated by a consignor who has the special form of consignment notes specified by the convention.

Carriage by Road

Carriers by road who are not in law common carriers can restrict their liability in any way they like; they can exempt themselves from any liability, including liability for their own negligence.

They cannot, however, contract out of liability for death or injury to passengers and any such provisions on their contracts is void: *Road Traffic Act, 1960*, s. 151.

International traffic is regulated by a convention called **C.M.R.**—*Convention relative au contrat de transport international des merchandises par route.* This has, unlike C.I.M., been incorporated into the domestic law of this country by the *Carriage of Goods by Road Act, 1965*. The terms of this Act cannot be avoided by contract for the carriage of goods internationally and any terms of a contract contrary to the Act is void.

Pipelines are governed by the *Pipelines Act, 1962*, which contains an unusual provision in that anybody who builds and uses a cross-country pipeline of more than 10 miles in length can be forced by the Department of Trade and Industry to allow other persons to use it on payment of charges.

CHAPTER NINETEEN

CARRIAGE BY SEA

The machinery whereby goods are carried overseas may be a document called **a charterparty**, that is the renting of a whole ship for the purpose; or it may be in the form of a bill of lading where the goods are carried by a shipping line, or form part of the cargo.

Charterparties

A contract of charterparty must deal with the whole ship and not just part of it.

There are two types of charterparty:

(i) Those that operate as a lease of the ship for a fixed period (a charterparty by **demise**), where the master of the ship and all the crew become the servants of the charterer.

(ii) A charter for a **voyage** when the master of the ship and all the crew remain in the employment of the shipowner.

The charters may also be a **time charter** or a **voyage charter.** The first are for a fixed period and the second specify the voyage or voyages for which the ship is engaged, and in this second type of charter it is necessary to stipulate the ports between which it shall sail.

In time charters, there is a stipulation as to when the charter shall begin and also a covenant that the ship is seaworthy. At one time both of these were regarded as conditions of the contract so that the charterer was released from any obligation to go ahead with the charter if either were broken. Since *Hong Kong Fir v Kawasaki*, [1962] 1 All E.R. 474, unseaworthiness on the day the time charter was due to begin does not necessarily discharge the charterer. It depends on the nature of the defect and the length of time it will take to put it right. The contract is only discharged if the breach is sufficiently fundamental to act as a frustration of the contract (see page 178).

The obligation on the charterer is to provide a **full and complete cargo,** since the remuneration is invariably based on the tonnage carried. If the charterer fails to provide a complete load he has to pay for what is termed **dead freight,** that is, for the unoccupied space.

The charter invariably provides for what are termed the **excepted risks,** i.e. restraints of princes and rulers, acts of God and the King's enemies, fire . . . and accidents of the sea.

In all charters, the shipowner has a lien (see page 196) over the goods for the amount of freight charges.

In some charters, a condition is inserted that the **Hague Rules on Bills of Lading** shall be incorporated. These rules were never intended to be applied to charterparties, but the object of the condition is to limit the owner's liability. It would appear that in this it may be effective because in *Adamston Shipping v Anglo Saxon Petroleum,* [1958] 1 All E.R. 725, a slip had been attached to the charterparty bearing the words: 'Paramount Clause. This bill of lading shall have effect subject to the *Carriage of Goods by Sea Act, 1936* of the United States.' That Act expressly stated that it was not to apply to charterparties.

The Court of Appeal held:

(i) that notwithstanding that the parties had used the words 'this bill of lading' in the typed document they had both meant 'this charterparty';

(ii) that notwithstanding that the Act excluded charterparties these could be treated as meaningless words, as in *Nicolene v Simmonds* (see page 71); therefore, there was a valid charter incorporating the other terms of the American Act.

Bills of Lading

The bill of lading is a document normally signed by the mate of a vessel, which fulfils three functions. It is a receipt for the goods shipped, i.e. evidence that they have been received on board. It is also evidence of the contract of carriage of the goods and, finally, and not the least important, it is the document of title enabling anybody who produces it at the ship on arrival at its destination to take possession of the goods. As such, its status in law is that of what is termed a *'quasi-negotiable' instrument.* As will be seen later (see page 252) a holder in due course of a negotiable instrument can obtain a better title in some circumstances than the person from whom he took the instrument. But in the case of the bill of lading, a person who acquires it even for a value and without notice of any defect in the title of the one who transfers it to him can never get a better title than the one from whom it has been taken. But it has some of the characteristics of negotiability in that it can be transferred from hand to hand by indorsement and delivery, and the person who ultimately produces it to the ship is entitled to take possession of the goods.

What normally happens in practice is that after the goods have been shipped and a receipt obtained, the top copy of the bill of lading is sent by post out to a bank abroad for release to the consignee against payment; and the second copy is forwarded by the next post.

The Bill of Lading as a Receipt for Goods Shipped

There are two kinds of bill of lading known as **shipped bills** (or 'on board' bills) and **received bills** ('alongside' bills).

On the first is the receipt that the goods have actually been:

'shipped in apparent good order and condition . . . on board the motor vessel. . . .'

The second states that the goods have been:

'received in apparent good order and condition . . . for shipment on board the motor vessel . . . or other ship or ships'.

By the first the shipowner certifies that the goods actually have gone aboard. The second merely records that the goods have been received into the custody of the shipowner.

The two are not the same thing, and if payment is arranged under documentary credit there is usually a provision that the bills tendered should be 'clean, on board, to order, and blank indorsed'. A tender of a 'received' bill does not comply with these terms (*Yelo v S. M. Machado and Co. Ltd.*, 1952), and the consignee is entitled to reject it as being in breach of the contract.

The distinction between clean bills and claused bills has been discussed earlier on page 201. A practice grew up of getting shipowners or their servants to issue clean bills when in fact they knew that the goods were not in apparent good order and condition, in return for an indemnity from the shippers. On the first occasion this practice came before the Courts, it was held that this indemnity was unenforceable since it was tainted with illegality in that the shipowners had committed the tort of deceit when they issued a clean bill well knowing that the goods were not in sound condition: *Brown Jenkinson v Percy Dalton*, [1957] 2 All E.R. 844.

Moreover, the shipowners will be estopped by an unclaused receipt, so that anybody who has relied upon that certificate of shipping when the goods were not in good order can sue the shipowner for damages. The effect of this can be seen in *Silver v Ocean Steamship Co.*, [1929] All E.R. Rep. 611. Frozen eggs were shipped under a bill of lading signed by the master, which stated that they were 'in apparent good order and condition'. The shipowner was not allowed to give evidence to show that, contrary to this assertion on the bill, the goods were already damaged when shipped; and he was therefore liable for the damage. If the goods were not in fact shipped in spite of the receipt, the shipowners will be liable on the basis again of estoppel. There is also statutory confirmation of this, contained in the *Bills of Lading Act, 1855*.

The *Carriage of Goods by Sea Act, 1971* replaces the *Carriage of Goods by Sea Act, 1924* and incorporates the rules amended by the Brussels Protocol of 1968.

The Act applies to all bills of lading for outward bound cargoes from British ports, with the exception of live animal and deck cargo, and also to the coastal trade, if the goods are carried under bills of lading. It also applies to all outward bound cargoes from countries which have adhered to the convention. By the Act, liability of carriers per package or unit is raised to 10,000 gold francs.

One of the most significant changes has been that the Act apparently reverses the decision of the House of Lords in *Scruttons Ltd. v Midland Silicones Ltd.*, 1962 (see page 99), in that a servant or agent of the carrier is entitled to rely upon this limitation clause, even though he is not a party to the contract of carriage in the bill of lading; but an independent contractor cannot.

Every bill of lading contains, as the result of Statute, implied terms:

(i) that at the beginning of the voyage due diligence has been used to make the ship 'seaworthy'. This expression includes crewing and the provision of proper holds, etc.
(ii) that the goods will be loaded carefully.
(iii) that in the event of loss or damage notice in writing will be given to the carrier before or at the time of their removal or if the loss or damage is not immediately apparent, within three days of discharge of the goods.

The Bill of Lading as a Contract of Carriage

Freight is the term used for the remuneration of a carrier for his safe carriage and delivery of the goods. The common law had two principles about freight, both of which are now commonly eroded by the express terms of a contract. The first is that no freight is payable unless the goods are actually delivered to their destination. 'It is payable only on the safe carriage and delivery of the goods. If the goods are lost on the voyage, nothing is payable.' The second really follows from the first. 'Freight does not become payable until the goods have arrived at their destination.' But bills of lading commonly contain a clause to the effect that 'freight shall be due and payable by the shipper on shipment at the port of loading in cash ... and shall not be repayable, vessel or goods lost or not lost' or 'freight deemed to be earned on shipment'. This makes the payment **advance freight.**

Usually the bill of lading is not the contract of affreightment but evidence of a prior agreement. By the time it is issued, the contract has been partly performed. If there is an inconsistency between an original oral agreement and the bill of lading the first in time prevails. So, in the case of *The Ardennes*, [1950] 2 All E.R. 517, a Spanish shipper made a contract with the shipowner whereby the latter guaranteed that the goods, oranges, would be in the United Kingdom before 1st December. The date was critical as on that day import duty on the goods was due to rise. The bill of lading, however, purported to confer on the shipowner the right to carry the goods by any route, directly or indirectly, and without regard to time. The Court held that the express warranty as to time of delivery given in the original oral contract was binding and took precedence over the written bill of lading; so that the shipper was entitled to damages. The contract was concluded before the bill of lading came into existence.

Non-shipment of goods, or 'shutting out' as it is called, is of frequent occurrence. Most export shipments are done through loading brokers who are the agents of the shipping company and these circulate a **sailing card** specifying the dates of anticipated sailing. If the shipper relies on this and sends his goods along to the quay, this constitutes an offer which the other party, the shipowner, can accept or reject as he chooses. No damages therefore lie for 'shutting out' in these circumstances, as there is no contract. But where the shipper had booked space in advance, to shut out the goods is a breach of contract. It is said, however, that even in these circumstances loss of profit in goods shut out cannot be recovered, presumably on the grounds that such damages are not reasonably foreseeable in the absence of express intimation.

The Bill of Lading as a Quasi-negotiable Instrument

As we have seen, the merits of a bill of lading as a document of title were recognised by the Courts as early as 1794; but the emergence of the bill of lading as something more than a document of title, as being almost negotiable, owes it origin to the *Bills of Lading Act, 1855*.

The holder of a bill of lading is, by virtue of production of that document, entitled to take delivery of the goods from the ship at their destination.

But if the bill is marked with the consignee's name and 'or his assigns', 'or order', it can be transferred from hand to hand like a pound note. The consignee may, on the strength of the bill, sell the goods to *A* by endorsing the bill accordingly, and *A* may sell them to *B*, who may sell them to *C*, who may go along and collect the goods represented by surrendering the bill to the shipowner.

If the shipper does not want this to happen and wants only the consignee to be the person who can collect the goods from the ship, he can effect this by *not* inserting the words 'or his assigns', 'or order' (or deleting them if they are already printed) and by deleting all words in the bill relating to its transferability.

Even where a bill is transferable as the result of bearing the words 'or his assigns', 'or order'—and is therefore in the common parlance of the trade described as 'negotiable' it is in reality not fully negotiable as is a bill of exchange (see page 251). The holder cannot get a better title than the one from whom he took it. He takes 'subject to the equities'. That is why, strictly speaking, bills of lading should be called 'quasi-negotiable instruments'.

The difference can be seen where a bill of lading has been obtained by fraud and indorsed to a man who has in all good faith given value for it. This latter does not get a good title to the goods.

Had the document been a bill of exchange, the indorsee would have got a good title—a better one than that of the person from whom he took it.

CHAPTER TWENTY

CARRIAGE BY AIR

The Warsaw Convention of 1929, as amended by the Hague Protocol of 1955, is the basis of our present law, the *Carriage by Air Act, 1961*. By an involved piece of legislation, section 10 of that Act retains part of the unamended Warsaw Convention.

Both the Convention and the Protocol made use of the expression 'carrier' without defining what was meant by it. In particular, neither explained whether by that word was meant the carrier who entered into contractual relationship with the shipper or some subsequent carrier who actually might carry the goods. English law, it may be recalled, underwent similar problems in connection with the railways when goods might start off on one particular company's lines, with whom the consignor had contractual relations, only to end up being delivered by a quite separate company with whom he had no contractual relationship. This failure to define carrier led to another Convention in 1961 at Guadalajara, Mexico, and to the *Carriage by Air (Supplemental Provisions) Act, 1962*.

The effect of these enactments is as follows:

1. Only the actual *consignor* and the *consignee* have any claims in respect of the loss, destruction or injury to goods consigned by air. The owner of the goods, if he be neither, has no course of action.
2. The carriers are liable without proof of breach of contract or negligence.
3. The carriers' liability, however, is limited to a maximum of 250 gold francs per kilogram; or the value declared by the consignor on which supplementary charges have been paid.
4. These limits are applied not only to the original **contracting carrier** but also to **successive carriers** and **actual carriers.** The contracting carrier is the one who accepts the goods for onward transit. You send a parcel by B.E.A. They are the contracting carriers and they may be the actual carriers if they do in fact load the parcel into one of their planes. But under pooling agreements, the goods may well be carried from first to last by Air France, who are the actual carriers. Or they may be

taken to Paris by Air France and then trans-shipped to Air Maroc, who become the successive carriers who fly them part of the way perhaps before transferring them for the final leg of the journey to T.A.P.

5. The limit of liability covers not only the companies but also all their servants and agents acting within the scope of their employment, in spite of the fact that there is no contractual relationship with them.

6. The principles on which liability is established are that the contracting carrier is liable for the whole of the carriage to the consignor, who may also, if he so pleases, bring action against the actual carrier responsible for the leg of the journey where the damage or loss occurred. The last carrier is liable to the consignee, who may also, if he so pleases, bring action against the actual carrier responsible for the leg of the journey where the damage or loss occurred.

Documentation for Air Freight

Carriage of cargo may be under one or more of three systems:

(i) The original Warsaw Convention;
(ii) The amended Warsaw Convention;
(iii) The non-Convention rules.

The United States of America, for example, has adhered only to the original Warsaw Convention; the United Kingdom has adopted the amended Convention. Air traffic between the two countries is therefore governed by the lowest common denominator, i.e. the original Convention. If reference is made to the *Carriage by Air* (*Parties to Conventions*) *Order* 1967, s. 1, No. 976, it is possible to discover which countries have adhered to the original and which to the original and amended Convention.

There are also countries which have not adhered to either Convention—for example, Turkey—so all flights between the U.K. and Turkey are governed by the non-Convention rules.

Under the **Original Warsaw Convention,** the document of carriage is called the **air consignment note,** or A.C.N.

This is in three parts: the first is for the carrier; the second for the consignee, and the third for the consignor. There are certain basic requirements to be shown on this document, including 'a statement that the carriage is subject to the rules relating to liability established by the Convention'. Without them the carrier loses his right to rely on the Convention.

Under the **Amended Warsaw Convention,** the document of carriage is called the **air waybill,** or A.W.B.

One major difference between this and the A.C.N. is that if goods are carried with the carrier's consent, without an A.W.B., then the carrier loses his right to rely on the amended Convention to limit his liability. A longer period than that in the original Warsaw Convention is stipulated for receipt of claims for damage or delay.

For non-Convention flights there is no agreed documentation, except where the carriers are members of the International Air Transport Association (I.A.T.A.), when they use the I.A.T.A. waybill. This provides that on non-Convention flights the carrier is liable only in proof of negligence or wilful default and unless there is a declared value the limit of liability is 250 gold francs per kilogram.

None of these documents has acquired the status of even quasi-negotiability.

CHAPTER TWENTY-ONE

CONTRACTS OF INSURANCE

The Insurable Interest

The essential difference between gaming or wagering contracts and contracts of insurance lies in their purpose. In insurance the assured seeks to protect himself against loss or to provide for his old age, or his family after his death. That is to say, all contracts of insurance fall into one of two classes. They are either **contracts of indemnity** by which an insurer undertakes to pay a money compensation for a certain loss, or they are **contracts for a sum of money payable on the happening of a certain event.** Even where there is an agreed sum stated as being payable on account of a loss (called a **valued policy**) these are still contracts of indemnity, and if the agreed value is grossly in excess of the real loss, the insurer can refuse to meet the claim on the ground that it was in reality a wager (see page 133).

All contracts of insurance require that the assured shall have an interest in the subject matter of the contract. In contracts of indemnity this is self evident. It is not insurance unless the assured stands to make a loss on the happening of the event insured against. In the case of other insurance contracts, they require **an insurable interest** as the result of Statute. The *Gaming Act, 1845,* to which reference has been made earlier (see page 135), also enacts that insurances are void where the assured has neither any interest when taking out the policy, nor any expectation of acquiring one. An even earlier Act, The *Life Assurance Act, 1774* (still in force), lays down that 'no insurance shall be made by any person on the life of any person or other event, wherein the person for whose benefit, or on whose account, such policy shall be made shall have no interest, or by way of gaming or wagering'. Every such insurance is null and void. So it is no good insuring the life of some foreign potentate in the expectation that he will be assassinated; in his life or death, you have no insurable interest.

The *Marine Insurance Act, 1906* repeats to some extent the *Gaming Act, 1845,* but also makes void any contract of insurance containing a term that the assured shall not be required to prove his insurable interest.

235

To define 'insurable interest' is not easy. It is easier to quote specific examples where an 'insurable interest' has been recognised by the Courts. Even so, an insurable interest may be **unqualified** or **qualified.**

Unqualified

1. By a man on his own life (though what pecuniary interest he can have is hard to see).
2. By a man on his wife's life (or a wife on her husband's).
3. By anybody for liability insurance, whether it be against a tort or a breach of contract.
4. By companies on the lives of their directors or employees.

Qualified

1. By a child on the lives of his parents—but only so long as he is dependent upon them; but (in spite of the vast number of policies of this nature which have been written) a parent has no insurable interest in the lives of his children.
2. A creditor in the life of a debtor—but only for the amount of the debt.
3. A servant on the life of his master—but only to the value of the employment.
4. Owners of property—but only to the extent of possible loss or consequential loss.

In most cases, it will be seen there has to be a direct pecuniary loss before there can be an interest.

An insurable interest has been held NOT to exist:

(i) by a father for the torts of his children (since he is not legally liable for these).
(ii) by a person who has a mere hope of an interest in property in the future.
(iii) by a shareholder in the assets of a company (but he can insure against resulting loss to his shares).

Formation of Insurance Contracts

Much business in insurance is done through brokers or insurance agents who in law are not the agents of the insurer, as is commonly supposed, but the agents of the assured. So that if he fills up a proposal form, as a broker commonly does, and fills it up incorrectly, the contract is voidable at the option of the insurers.

Even when brokers deal with claims under the policy they do not deal with them as agents of the insurers. It was argued at one time that they could be agents of both parties, but this view was rejected by Megaw J. in *Anglo-African Merchants Ltd. v Bayley*, [1969] 2 All E.R. 421. 'An agent may not at the same time serve two masters . . . in actual or potential opposition to one another, unless, indeed, he has the explicit informed consent of both principals. An insurance broker is in no privileged position in this respect.'

The formation of an insurance contract follows normal contractual principles, save that all contracts are *uberrimae fidei* (see page 138). Everything which would affect the mind of a prudent underwriter in determining whether or not he would accept the risk or in fixing the premium must be disclosed. Non-disclosure, or misrepresentation, does not make the contract void but voidable at the option of the insurer. The right to avoid the contract may be lost if, with knowledge of the matters, he affirms the contract either by meeting a claim on it or by accepting further premiums; and it may, in any event, be lost with the passage of time, if with knowledge he fails to repudiate it.

In the case of policies at Lloyds the moment when the contract becomes binding is when the broker has submitted **'a slip'** to the underwriter and he has initialled it. But it would appear that as a result of the *Marine Insurance Act, 1906,* section 22, the underwriter is not liable on the slip in the case of marine insurance and the contract does not become effective until the policy has been issued.

Cover notes are issued in some cases before there has been a concluded contract. They therefore form a separate, preliminary contract which, if reference is made in it to the insurer's usual form of policy, may be issued on the same terms as that policy. If there is no reference to any policy, the terms are not incorporated. The exact effect of the issue of a cover note pending renewal of the policy of motor car insurance was considered recently in a criminal case where the accused had in his possession a cover note from a company which had previously insured him but with whom he did not propose to re-insure. The Court held him to be uninsured. The case raises very difficult and unanswered questions about the formation of a contract in these circumstances, particularly as an uncommunicated mental assent is not enough to create a synallagmatic contract.

The policy is the document formally incorporating all the terms of the contract and it has to be issued within one month of the making of the contract by virtue of the *Stamp Act, 1891*. However, the contractual obligations exist independent of any policy and are actionable without one, except for policies of marine insurance where there is no contract without a policy.

Renewal of policies after the expiration of the period originally contracted for may take two forms, with different legal consequences. The renewal may be an extension in time of the existing policy or it may be a completely new contract. It is necessary to look at the terms of the policy to decide which it is.

If it is an extension, the renewal policy will be tainted with any defects of the original one, so that if there was non-disclosure or mis-representation the renewed policy will be voidable; but there is no further duty to make disclosures.

If it is a new contract, there is a fresh duty to disclose material factors at the date when the new policy is proposed.

Days of grace. There is no legal right to any days of grace before a policy is renewed. But many policies provide for it and the situation varies with the terms of each.

The **premium** is the money consideration for the promise to insure. Unless the contract expressly stipulates that the insurer shall not be on risk until payment of the premium—as many do—the insurer is liable from the date of the contract notwithstanding non-payment. However, he can treat non-payment as a repudiation which, if he accepts it, becomes a breach which discharges him from any further obligations.

The contract may be void if there is mistake (see page 163) as to the continued existence of the subject matter at the time when made. If the life of a person is insured at a time when, unknown to either contracting party, he is dead the contract is void and the premium therefore recoverable. In a 1912 case it was held that because the terms of the contract specified that if the contract was void the premium should be forfeit, the premium could not be recovered. But this appears to be a case which is wrong in principle and unlikely to be followed. If there is no contract there cannot be a term still standing, any more than a person who has committed a fundamental breach can rely on a protection clause (see page 171).

An insurance contract will be voidable at the option of the insurer for misrepresentation or non-disclosure. However, there is some authority that if he is allowed to rescind the contract on these grounds, Equity will put him on terms to refund the premium when he has not been on risk. If he has been on risk at all apparently no part of the premium is recoverable—at any rate at common law.

Conditions and warranties. To add confusion to an already confused situation (see page 178), in the law of insurance 'conditions' of the contract are termed 'warranties', i.e. they are terms of the contract breach of any of which is a matter of sufficient gravity to entitle the insurer to repudiate his obligations under the contract. The use of the word 'warranty' in an insurance contract is evidence that it is intended to be a condition: *Barnard v Faber* (1893); *Dawson v Bonnim*, [1922] All E.R. Rep. 85.

For what in the rest of the law of contract is termed 'a warranty' the usual term in insurance contracts is 'a stipulation'—the breach of it will give an insurer the right to claim damages but not to repudiate the contract. As perhaps we have remarked before it is a pity semantics are not compulsory study for lawyers.

Claims on Insurance Policies

There is no obligation imposed on an assured by law about how or when he should notify his insurer of loss or the happening of the event insured against. But all policies contain their own prescribed procedure for notifying claims. This procedure may be a condition precedent to the liability of the insured or it may merely be a collateral and subsidiary obligation on the assured; which it is will depend on the wording of the policy. If drafted with skill the words will enable the insurer to escape liability entirely, even if it is no fault of the assured that the procedure is not followed: *Adamson v Liverpool & London* (1953).

The burden of proving loss falls on the assured. But if the insurer wishes to set up that the claim is fraudulent or that—to take marine cases—the ship has been scuttled, the burden rests on the insurer; until recently by a rule of practice the insurer was allowed to make this allegation without furnishing further and better particulars of the allegation, but the Court of Appeal has now decided that particulars must be furnished.

Under insurance arises where the assured has not paid the premium for the full value of the risk insured against. If a man with a house worth £10,000 pays premiums on a value of £8,000 and part only is destroyed to the value of, say, £2,500, can he recover the whole of that sum? If it were a ship he could not, since in marine insurance the assured is deemed to be his own insurer for the uncovered value, so that he has to bear a proportionate part of the loss. For other insurances, the law is that he can recover the full amount. But this is subject to the express terms of the contract and if an Average Clause, as it is called, has been inserted in the policy—which nowadays it invariably is—he can recover only the amount that the proportion of the damage bears to the whole. That is, in the example given, he can recover only 8/10th of the £2,500.

Over insurance will not benefit the assured in any way. If he insures a house for £15,000 which is worth only £10,000 and it is totally destroyed he is entitled only to the actual value. Insurance of this kind is a contract of indemnity—he is entitled to recover only the loss actually suffered. This point is often overlooked by people insuring motor cars. If they are new, as soon as they are placed on the road, their value has depreciated substantially. If it is destroyed the next day, they are not, in the absence of an express term to the contrary, entitled to the price of a new vehicle.

An insurer who has paid out on a claim has various rights:

Salvage. In both marine and other sorts of insurance if the insurer has paid out a sum for total loss, the assured is deprived of all interest in the subject matter. In all cases of 'constructive total loss' (when the thing is repairable but not worth repairing) or 'actual total loss' the insurer becomes the owner of the subject matter. This includes things lost which are subsequently found.

Subrogation. This term has been explained earlier (see page 112), but it belongs particularly to the law of insurance. Essentially it means that the insurer who has paid under a policy is entitled to step into the shoes of the assured and enforce any rights he may have against a third party. The effect of this principle may be seen in *Castellain v Preston* 1883, [1881–5] All E.R. Rep. 493. A man contracted to sell his house, but between the contract being signed and the date for completion the house was burnt down. He received its value from the insurance company. Later, on completion he received the full sum from the purchaser and the Court held that he was liable to repay the amount of the insurance paid to him.

Subrogation only applies:

(i) where the whole and not just a partial loss falls on the insurer.
(ii) after the insurer has actually paid.

To enforce the right, the insurer must sue in the name of the assured. If the assured has released any third party from his obligation, the insurer is discharged from paying that part of the loss.

Contribution. A man may insure the same premises with several insurance companies against the same risk. But he cannot collect from all of them, and if he draws a full indemnity from one insurer, that insurer is entitled in equity to a *pro rata* contribution from the others.

Life Insurance

Life policies may be of two sorts: the ordinary type where the proceeds on the death of the assured becomes part of his estate; and contracts written expressly under the *Married Women's Property Act, 1882*. One spouse may insure his or her life for the benefit of the other or for the benefit of their children. If this is done a trust of the proceeds is created and the money forms no part of the deceased's estate, nor is it in any way liable for his debts. But if for any reason such a policy is surrendered for cash, the proceeds become saddled with the trust and can only be applied for the purpose specified. An assured is not entitled to treat the proceeds as his own monies.

A beneficiary can also be named by the assured under s. 56 of the *Friendly Societies Act, 1896*, and this also makes the proceeds not part of the estate of the deceased.

Assignment of life policies are governed by the *Policies of Insurance Act, 1867*, and the benefits of a life policy can be assigned to anybody either by endorsement on the policy or by the instrument set out in the Schedule to the Act. Written notice must be given to the insurer and the insurer is bound on payment of the fee prescribed by the Act, now 25p, to give a written acknowledgment of that notice.

Fire Insurance

This is a contract of indemnity, and while for a life policy it is only necessary to have an insurable interest at the time when the policy is taken out, for a fire policy to give effective cover there must be an insurable interest not only when it is taken out but when the claim is made. A tenant who is liable to pay rent after the destruction or damage of the house by fire has an insurable interest, so too has the owner and any mortgagee.

By virtue of that quaint Statute, the *Fire Prevention (Metropolis) Act, 1774* which, notwithstanding its title, applies to the whole of England, the insurer may be obliged to apply the insurance money to the restoration of the building. Anyone with an interest in the property—and this includes a mortgagee—can insist on this.

Marine Insurance

The insurance against 'maritime perils' is a vast subject which can only be touched on in passing in this book. The law centres principally around the *Marine Insurance Act, 1906.*

In the marine insurance case, the assured must have an insurable interest at the time of the loss and it is immaterial whether or not he had it when the policy is taken out. The definition of insurable interest is wide enough to include the ship's master and crew to the extent of their wages. Included also are those who have lent money on **bottomry**—that is a loan of money on the ship and her cargo to enable her to complete a voyage; and also on *respondentia*—the cargo alone as security.

The types of insurance normally granted include the following:

1. **Floating policies,** where the specific ship is not named at the time of the policy but is completed by declaration later.
2. **Voyage policies,** to cover a particular voyage.
3. **Time policies** to cover a specific period. By the *Stamp Act, 1891* policies cannot be issued for a period exceeding 12 months, but this is modified slightly by the *Finance Act, 1901*, which allows a continuation clause to extend the term to cover the end of a voyage or a reasonable period after the expiration of the original cover.

The policies issued can also be classed as **valued policies,** where the policy specifically applies to the value of the ship and this is binding on both parties; even if in excess of the actual value the policy is good in the absence of such gross over valuation as to amount to·

fraud. **Unvalued policies** are those where the value is to be ascertained after the loss, subject to the limitation of the sum insured.

The term **warranty** is used in the *Marine Insurance Act, 1906* with yet another different meaning (see page 178). It includes the affirmation of an existing set of facts and also undertakings as to future conduct. Whether it be material or non-material, fundamental or trivial, a warranty that is not complied with discharges the insurer from the obligation to pay, as from the date of the breach whether he knows of it or not. The Act also lays down a series of implied warranties that the ship is seaworthy at the start of a voyage policy, and reasonably fit to carry the goods to the destination envisaged by the policy. Deviation from the route specified by a voyage policy ends the insurers' liability even though the ship later resumes her notified voyage. But deviation for the purpose of saving life (but not saving property), for the safety of the ship, and various other reasons, are excusable.

Loss may be **actual total loss** or **constructive total loss,** as where the goods are repairable but the cost of repairing makes it not worth while.

From time to time, it becomes necessary to sacrifice cargo or make some abnormal use of the ship to rescue it and its cargo from the perils of the sea. If loss is so incurred, it has to be borne proportionately by all with an interest in the ship or the cargo or the freight and is called **general average loss.** For this to arise there must be a real danger and the sacrifice (e.g. throwing cargo overboard to lighten the ship) must be necessary.

Particular average loss is where the loss has to be borne by one of the three interests alone, e.g. ship, cargo or freight. If part of the ship is damaged by a storm, for example, this is a particular average loss and has to be borne by the shipowner.

CHAPTER TWENTY-TWO

ASSIGNMENTS OF CONTRACTUAL RIGHTS

The extent to which a person can dispose of a contractual obligation without the consent of the other party is limited. 'Neither at law nor in equity could the burden of a contract be shifted off the shoulders of a contractor on to those of another, without the consent of the contractee.' It is possible for one contracting party to get another to perform his obligations for him without the consent of the other party, but this **vicarious performance,** as it is called, is only possible where the obligations are not personal. Even where clothes are sent to a firm of cleaners, the Court of Appeal held in *Davies v Collins,* [1945] 1 All E.R. 247, that this was a personal obligation which could not be performed by anybody else, such as a sub-contractor. But the repair of railway wagons—'a rough description of work which ordinary workmen conversant with the business would be perfectly able to execute'—was held to be one that could be performed by somebody other than the party who had contracted to do it: *British Waggon Co. v Lea* 1880, [1874–80] All E.R. Rep. 1135.

But even where vicarious performance is possible, it is not the same thing as assignment, for the original party is still liable.

The **benefit** of a contract can, however, be freely assigned to a third party where there are no obligations which still remain to be performed by the original contracting party, who is the assignor. In the ordinary case of a sale of goods, if one party has fulfilled his obligation by delivering the goods, and there remains only payment by the other party to discharge all the obligations on both parties, the right to the payment can be freely assigned to a third party without the consent of the debtor.

There are some limitations on this right, as:

(i) where assignment is prohibited by Act of Parliament. Social security benefits cannot be assigned, for example;

(ii) where assignment is contrary to public policy. A married woman cannot validly assign to anybody else her right to maintenance from her husband nor can an officer or a servant of the Crown assign his salary;

(iii) where the contract expressly prohibits assignment.

Rights under a contract fall into the wider class of personal property known as **choses in action.** There is a distinction drawn between proprietary rights which can only be enforced by bringing an action in the Courts and proprietary rights, termed **choses in possession,** which can be exercised by taking physical possession of a thing. A debt or the copyright in this book is a chose in action since the right can only be enforced by an action; whereas a chair or a book or the manuscript of this book is a chose in possession since the right to possess any of them can be exercised without an action. The word 'choses' of course, means only 'things' and is a relic of the days before 1688, when the language spoken in the Courts was law French understood by nobody except lawyers.

As always, to understand the present position it is necessary to take a backward look. Before the *Judicature Act* of 1873 the only method at common law to effect a voluntary assignment of a chose in action was termed **novation.**

If Tom owes Harry £100 and Harry owes Bert £100, it may be agreed between the three of them that Tom shall pay Bert. Harry drops out.

In that case the consideration for Tom's promise to pay Bert is the discharge by Harry.

For Harry's discharge, the consideration is the substitution of Tom's liability for Harry's.

Novation is a new contract between the parties whereby both agree that a third shall replace one of the original two. This requires the consent of all three and this is the essential difference between assignment and novation. For there to be a transference of the right to a debt, there had to be the consent of the debtor; whereas, as we shall see, assignment is nowadays possible without the consent of the debtor. Novation can only take place by the discharge of one contract and the formation of a new one. Most of the modern cases about novation are therefore concerned with the changes which result in partnership by the retirement or death of one of the parties.

In the Court of Chancery the rules of equity were less rigid than those of the common law. Equity would enforce assignments of both legal and equitable choses in action.

Legal choses in action are such rights as were enforceable before the *Judicature Act* of 1873 by the Common Law Courts.

Equitable choses in action, on the other hand, are such rights, as for example to a legacy or an interest in a trust, which could only be enforced before the *Judicature Acts* by the Court of Chancery.

Chancery, when it enforced assignments of equitable choses in action, allowed the assignee to sue in his own name where the assignment was absolute without joining the assignor. But when it enforced legal choses in action it did so by making the assignor lend his name so that the assignee could bring an action in the assignor's name in the Common Law Courts.

Today, the rights under a contract and other choses in action, can be transferred to a third party by either:

(i) novation. As described above.
(ii) operation of law. As where the personal representatives of the deceased (i.e. his executors or administrator) become vested with all the rights that the deceased had. Similarly, in bankruptcy all the rights that the insolvent debtor had become vested in his trustee in bankruptcy.
(iii) legal assignment under s. 136 of the *Law of Property Act, 1925.*
(iv) equitable assignments where s. 136 is not complied with; for 'The Statute does not forbid or destroy equitable assignments or impair their efficacy in the slightest degree.'
(v) special statutory provision. Certain choses in action can only be assigned in accordance with special Acts dealing with them. They include copyrights, life insurance policies, shares in a limited company, patents and bills of lading, and negotiable instruments.

Legal Assignments

The *Judicature Act, 1873* first made provision for the legal assignment of choses in action. This is now replaced by s. 136 of the *Law of Property Act, 1925*:

'Any absolute assignment by writing under the hand of the assignor . . . of any debt or other legal thing in action, of which express notice has been given to the debtor, trustee or other person from whom the assignor would have been entitled to claim such a debt or thing in action, is effectual in law to pass and transfer from the date of such notice:

(i) the legal right to such a debt or thing in action.
(ii) all legal and other remedies for the same.
(iii) the power to give a good discharge for the same without the concurrence of the assignor.'

There are therefore four essential requirements for the legal assignment:

(i) It must be in writing.
(ii) It must be signed by the assignor.
(iii) It must be absolute and not by way of a charge (see below).
(iv) The debtor must be given notice of the assignment.

It will be noted that no consideration passing between the assignor and assignee is necessary in a legal assignment.

The situation can be reproduced diagrammatically:

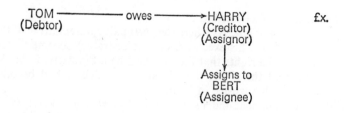

When the Act has been complied with, the situation becomes:

In spite of the wording of the section 'debt or other *legal* thing in action', which seems to suggest that only legal choses in action were contemplated by the draftsmen and equitable choses were intended to be excluded, the Courts have held that it includes the latter.

It is therefore possible to have:

    (i) a legal assignment of a legal chose in action, and also
    (ii) a legal assignment of an equitable chose in action,

where the expression 'legal assignment' is used in the sense of being made under the provisions of s. 136.

The word **'absolute'** needs some explanation. Absolute assignments do not completely exclude mortgages and charges and the test is said to be that if **the assignor has unconditionally transferred to the assignee for the time being the sole right to the debts in question, as against the debtor, it is an absolute assignment.** What may happen after the debt is paid is no concern of the debtor. Assignments of part of the debt, however, cannot amount to an absolute assignment.

The Statute does not in fact specify that written notice (though the assignment itself has to be in writing) must be given to the debtor. But one consequence of this has been that only one written document appears to be necessary, if the creditor has given written notice to the debtor to pay the debt to his assignee provided the assignee has consented: *Curran v Newpark Cinemas Ltd.*, [1951] 1 All E.R. 295. But the Courts have held that notice to the debtor must be in writing, even though it is known the debtor cannot read: *Hockley and Papeworth v Goldstein*, [1920] All E.R. Rep. 480.

Finally, an assignee only steps into the shoes of his assignor, so that he takes the right to the choses in action subject to any counter claims or defences the debtor would have had against the original creditor. The legal jargon for this is that the assignee 'takes subject to the equities existing between the creditor and the debtor'.

Section 136, it has been said, 'is merely machinery; it enables an action to be brought by the assignee in his own name in cases where previously he would have sued in the assignor's own name, but only where he could so sue'.

Equitable Assignments

Equity will enforce both legal and equitable choses in action even where section 136 of the *Law of Property Act, 1925* is not complied with. There is, however, one important distinction between equitable assignments of legal choses in action and equitable assignments of equitable choses in action.

The first does not have to be in writing to be enforceable, whereas the second does, for it is caught by s. 53 (1) (c) of the *Law of Property Act, 1925*:

'a disposition of an equitable interest or trust subsisting at the time of the disposition must be in writing signed by the person disposing of the same, or by his agent thereunto lawfully authorised'.

For an equitable assignment what is essential is an intention to assign and it can be done by telling the assignee that the debt or other chose has been assigned to him, or by telling the debtor to pay the debt to the assignee. Notice to the debtor is therefore not essential to an equitable assignment. However, if the debtor pays the assignor before he learns of the assignment, he gets a good discharge. For this reason in practice it is desirable to advise the debtor.

Another good reason is what is known as the rule in *Dearle v Hall* (1823). If there are successive assignments of the same debt, the first assignee to give notice to the debtor takes priority over the rest provided he did not know of their claims at the time of his assignment. In one case a debt due to a partnership was assigned in writing by one partner to the defendants and afterwards another partner assigned it by deed to the plaintiff. Since the plaintiff advised the debtor first, he took the debt even though his assignment was subsequent in time to the defendant's.

Consideration is not necessary for the equitable assignment of an existing debt. 'A person can make a gift of a chose in action no less than of a chose in possession.'

There can also be an assignment in equity of part of a debt.

The machinery by which the Courts will enforce equitable assignment of equitable choses in action is simply by the assignee suing in his own name as assignee.

Where the debt is a legal one, it is commonly said that the assignor has to be joined as a party, i.e. as co-plaintiff if he is willing or as co-defendant if he is not. But it would appear that the debtor may dispense with the right to have the assignor joined and the Court could even, without the consent of the debtor, proceed to adjudicate where the assignor is not joined, since the Rules of the High Court now provide that no cause of action is to be defeated through non-joinder of a party: *Order 15, rule 6 (1)* 'No cause or matter shall be defeated by reason of the misjoinder or non joinder of any party; and the Court may in any cause or matter determine the issues or questions in dispute so far as they effect the rights and interests of the persons who are parties to the cause or matter.'

The matter can perhaps be summarised in the following table.

Necessary?	Statutory Assignments of		Equitable Assignments of	
	Legal Choses	Equitable Choses	Legal Choses	Equitable Choses
1. Writing	Yes	Yes	No	Yes
2. Signed by Assignor	Yes	Yes	No	Yes.
3. Notice to Debtor.	Yes	Yes	No	No
4. Whole of Debt	Yes	Yes	No	No
5. Joinder of Assignor	No	No	Perhaps	No
6. Subject to Equities	Yes	Yes	Yes	Yes

CHAPTER TWENTY-THREE

NEGOTIABLE INSTRUMENTS

The Nature of Negotiability

The assignments so far discussed proceed on two fundamental premises:

1. That the party chargeable, the debtor, is only bound to pay the assignee when notice is given to him to do so.
2. This is also subject to the rule of *nemo dat quod non habet*—a man cannot give a better title than he has got, so that an assignor can only transfer to an assignee the same choses in action which he possesses and the assignee takes it subject to the equities existing between the debtor and the assignor.

The *Bills of Exchange Act, 1882* expressly says that a bill of exchange or cheque drawn on a banker is not an assignment of the amount for which the bill or cheque is drawn even if it be for the exact amount of the debt the bankers owe the drawers. This is a legal technicality, though there is good reason for it (see page 249). But the essence of the transaction is exactly the same:—

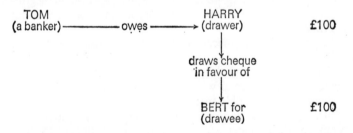

Negotiable instruments differ from other assignments, firstly on the two vital points mentioned above:

1. No notice of any kind need be given to the debtor. You do not have to advise your bank manager before you draw a cheque on him if your account is in credit, i.e. if the bank owes you money.
2. The transferor of a negotiable instrument can give a better title than he himself has got. The transferee does not take 'subject

to equities'; if he is a *bona fide* holder for value he is not prejudiced by any defects in title of the person from whom he took it.

Negotiable instruments also differ from other assignments of choses in action in two other respects:

3. They are transferable by delivery of the actual piece of paper in the case of 'bearer' instruments, or by delivery and indorsement in the case of 'to order' instruments; that is, the rights can be transferred from person to person.
4. The rights embodied in the instrument cannot be transferred without the instrument. It follows, therefore, that notice to the debtor does not create priority and that the rule in *Dearle v Hall* has no application to negotiable instruments (see page 249).

As we have seen on page 99, only persons who are privity to a contract can enforce rights under it, unless there is a novation or an assignment. But in the case of a negotiable instrument, any holder who is in possession of it can bring an action to enforce it, and he becomes a party to it.

A negotiable instrument therefore is a document which the law has recognised as having this quality of negotiability. Originally, this negotiability was acquired by the customs and practice of merchants, but some, such as promissory, notes have been made negotiable by Act of Parliament. The category is not closed and in 1898 the Court recognised that bearer debentures issued by an English company in England had, by mercantile custom, acquired the characteristics of negotiability.

A man cannot sit down and create a new form of negotiable instrument. Recognition must come from usage or with statutory authority.

The instruments at present recognised as possessing this quality are:

Bills of exchange and cheques, promissory notes (but not I.O.U.s), exchequer bills, dividend warranties, debentures payable to bearer, and some bonds payable to bearer.

But any of these cease to be negotiable if it is restricted, as for example by the crossing 'a/c payee only' on a cheque, or by marking it 'not negotiable'. In that event they are still transferable from hand to hand, but they have lost the magic quality of negotiability. A holder in due course gets no better title than the man from whom he took it.

What is a Bill of Exchange?

The most familiar form of negotiable instrument is the cheque. It is, by the definition contained in section 73 of the *Bill of Ex-*

change Act, 1882, '**a bill of exchange drawn on a banker, payable on demand**'.

So, before discussing cheques, it is necessary to take a look at bills of exchange. A bill of exchange is defined by section 3 (1) of the Act as:

1. —'an unconditional order in writing
2. —addressed by one person to another
3. —signed by the person giving it
4. —requiring the person to whom it is addressed to pay on demand or at a fixed or determinable future time
5. —a sum certain in money
6. —to or to the order of a specified person
7. —or bearer'

1. 'an unconditional order in writing'

There has to be an imperative order. An authority to pay, or a polite request, is not a bill of exchange. 'Please to let the bearer have seven pounds and place it to my account and you will oblige' was held not to constitute an order. 'We hereby authorise you to pay on our account . . .' was, likewise, not a bill of exchange.

If the order is conditional on the happening of a certain event or payable out of a certain fund or on the giving of a receipt, it is not a bill of exchange. 'Pay out of my rents in your hands' and 'out of X's money as soon as you receive it' were held to be conditional; so too was a bill which included the clause 'provided the receipt at the foot hereof is signed'. The order must be unconditional or the instrument is not a bill of exchange.

Such documents may take effect as a valid assignment but they cannot constitute a bill of exchange.

But the Act itself does allow, provided the order itself is unconditional, for it to be linked with an indication out of which fund the drawee is to reimburse himself, as where a cheque bears under the signature 'No. 2 account'. Even if the document carries details of the transaction which gives rise to the bill, it is unconditional.

2. 'addressed by one person to another'

A man cannot draw a bill on himself, although he can perfectly well draw a bill in favour of himself. Bankers' drafts, drawn by one branch on the head office, are not therefore bills of exchange.

But by section 5 (2) if a bill is drawn where the drawer and the drawee are the same person or the drawee is a fictitious person, the holder may at his option treat it as a bill of exchange or as a promissory note.

3. 'signed by the person giving it'
The signature can be by printing or some other form of reproduction such as a rubber stamp, provided it is affixed with the intention of being the drawer's signature.

4. 'requiring the person to whom it is addressed to pay on demand or at a fixed or determinable future time'
On demand includes bills payable on sight or on presentation. A cheque does not cease to be payable on demand just because it is post-dated. When that time comes, it is payable on demand.

A determinable future time depends entirely on whether it is an event which is certain to happen or is one which may not happen.

'Ten days after Tom's death' is a determinable future time.
'Ten days after Tom's marriage' is not; for he may never marry.
'On or before 13th December 1956' was held invalid because of lack of certainty about the day on which it should be paid.

If the figure and the words disagree, the sum payable is the amount in words (section 9 (2)), though banking practice is to return cheques so drawn. A bill is not invalid, because it is ante-dated or post-dated; or drawn on a Sunday, in spite of popular opinion to the contrary.

5. 'a sum certain in money'
It must be money and nothing but money. An order for money and a canary is not a bill of exchange. But it does not cease to be a bill because it is expressed as payable with interest—for the interest can be calculated and is therefore certain; or if it be payable by instalments.

6. 'to or to the order of a specified person'
Difficulty sometimes arises when the space has been left blank in a printed form of cheque so that it reads

Pay.............or order,

because the Act requires that it should be payable to a specified person. However, in at least one case this was construed as meaning 'Pay myself or order'. It cannot be construed as payable to bearer as the use of the words 'or order' negatives that. The holder in any event is entitled to complete it by filling in a payee.

Section 7 (3) of the Act deals with the situation where the named payee is a fictitious or non-existent person. The bill then becomes payable to bearer. So where a clerk invented a person called John Brett and got his employer to draw cheques in favour of John Brett, on the pretext that work had been done, the bills were valid bills of exchange payable to bearer.

The Act does not require that the words 'or order' shall be inserted.

If there are no words restricting transfer, then it is automatically payable to the payee's order and he can indorse it to anybody.

7. 'or bearer'

The bill is payable to bearer:

(a) if it is expressly drawn in this fashion, i.e. 'Pay bearer';
(b) if the last indorsement is in blank, i.e. no further person has been named as to one to whom the bill is payable, and the indorser has merely signed his name;
(c) if it is payable to a fictitious or non-existent payee. This may also, apparently, be the effect if the payee does in fact exist but the name is written with no intention of his being a party to the bill: *Bank of England v Vagliano Bros.* 1891, [1891–4] All E.R. Rep. 93. Vagliano Bros. were in the habit of accepting bills drawn on them by Vucina and payable to P. & Co. One of their clerks forged such a bill and it was accepted by Vagliano Bros. payable at the Bank of England. The clerk then forged the indorsement of P. & Co. and obtained payment from the bank. It was held the bank was entitled to debit Vagliano Bros.' account because the bill was payable to a fictitious person since P. & Co. were never intended to take under the bill, and it therefore became a bill payable to bearer.

Whether the payee is fictitious or not depends on the state of mind of the drawer; if the payee named is never intended to benefit, he is fictitious.

Bills of exchange are usually to be found in these forms:

Order Bill on demand

£1,000	London 1st. April 1980

On demand pay Harry Jones or order the sum of one thousand pounds for value received.

To Bert Brown.	Tom Smith

Bearer Bill on demand

£1,000	London 1st. April 1980

On demand pay bearer the sum of one thousand pounds for value received.

To Bert Brown.	Tom Smith

Order Bill payable at time

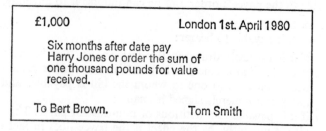

£1,000　　　　　　　　　　London 1st. April 1980

Six months after date pay
Harry Jones or order the sum of
one thousand pounds for value
received.

To Bert Brown.　　　　　　　Tom Smith

The parties are known as **the drawer** (Tom Smith in the examples above), **the drawee** (Bert Brown) and **the payee** (Harry Jones).

Acceptance and Non-Acceptance of Bills of Exchange

The person on whom the bill has been drawn is called the 'drawee'. But when he has agreed to pay the bill he is said to become the **acceptor.** The acceptance is by writing his signature on the bill, or by writing the words 'Accepted payable at X bank' with his signature. The drawer of the bill may have transferred it to another person before it has been accepted and it is then for the transferee to present the bill for acceptance.

Acceptance may be either **general,** i.e. unqualified, or **qualified** by conditions.

The holder is entitled to treat the bill as dishonoured by non-acceptance unless he gets an unqualified acceptance; but he may, if he please, take an acceptance qualified as to amount, time or place. If he does so, the drawer and any previous indorsers are released from liability unless they have expressly assented to the qualified acceptance.

A holder does not *have* to present a bill for acceptance though it will be to his advantage to make the drawee liable on the bill as well as the other parties. But there are three circumstances in which a bill must be presented for acceptance:

(i) If the bill expressly requires that it shall be.
(ii) If it is a sight bill—i.e. 'Pay ten days after signed'—since only this fixes the time when payment will become due.
(iii) When it is payable elsewhere than at the place of business or residence of the drawee.

If a bill has been dishonoured by non-acceptance or by a qualified acceptance which the holder is not prepared to accept, **notice of dishonour** must be given.

This is done by informing the last indorser and anybody else whose name is on the bill, within a reasonable time.

What is a reasonable time has been the subject of legislation. When the parties live in the same place, notice must be given on the day after the bill has been dishonoured. Where they do not live in the same place, the notice must be on the day after the dishonour of the bill. It cannot be sent off before the bill has actually been dishonoured, even if it is known that the bill will be.

The bill may be dishonoured by non-payment as well as non-acceptance, but if it has not been accepted and is therefore dishonoured, then no further notice is required if it is also dishonoured by non-payment.

Foreign bills—that is any bills not both drawn and payable within the British Isles or drawn within the British Isles upon some person resident here—must also be protested.

'The protest' is a formal document drawn up by a notary public to establish that the bill has been dishonoured. It must contain details of the person on whose behalf the bill is protested, the date and place and reason why the bill is being protested, the demand made and the answer given. The protest must incorporate a copy of the bill.

If no notary public is available at the place where the bill is dishonoured, a protest can be certified by any householder in the presence of two witnesses.

The Holder in Due Course

This is a technical term which represents the holder who is in the strongest position of all in law to enforce the bill.

A **holder** of a bill is any person who is in possession of a bill. It includes payees as well as indorsers of order bills, as well as the person in possession of a bearer instrument. The term is wide enough to include those who have acquired the bill wrongfully, e.g. a thief or a receiver. But it does not include somebody who is holding in his lawful possession a bill indorsed or payable to somebody else. A holder can sue on the bill in his own name but his rights can be defeated by the equities.

A **holder for value** is the holder of a bill for which value has been given at some time in its history. This is a confusing term because it suggests that the holder must have given value for it himself. That is not so. The holder for value has not necessarily given value for it himself. The Act says that where value has at any time been given for a bill, the holder is *deemed* to be a holder for value as regards the acceptor and all parties who became parties to the bill prior to such time. A holder for value is not a holder in due course and against him prior parties can raise a defence of fraud or duress, though not one of want of consideration.

A **holder in due course** is a holder who:

(i) takes a bill which is completed and regular on the face of it.

    (ii) takes a bill before it becomes overdue.

   (iii) takes a bill without notice of any defect in the title of the person who negotiated it to him.

   (iv) takes a bill without notice that it has previously been dishonoured, if such be the fact.

    (v) must himself have given value for it.

Since the Act refers to a 'holder who has taken a bill' the Courts have construed these words to mean that the **original payee** can never become a holder in due course.

A holder in due course takes the bill completely free from any defects in the title of any of the parties and can enforce payment against all the parties to the bill. Anybody who takes after a holder in due course, whether he gives value himself or not, has the same rights. So if a holder in due course gives the bill to his wife as a birthday present, she has the same rights as he, although she is only a holder for value.

All holders are presumed to be holders in due course until the contrary is proved.

Liabilities of the Parties to a Bill of Exchange

The drawee is liable only if he signs the bill as **acceptor.** The drawing of the bill does not constitute an assignment of any monies that may be in his hands owed by the drawer.

An acceptor who has signed is estopped from denying to a holder in due course (but not to any other holder):

    (i) the existence of the drawer and the authenticity of his signature.

   (ii) if the bill is drawn to the drawer's order, the capacity of the drawer to endorse it.

   (iii) if the bill is payable to somebody other than the drawer, the existence of the payee and his capacity to indorse.

The drawer. By drawing the bill, the drawer promises that it will be honoured by the drawee when presented and that he will recompense any holder or indorser who has had to pay on the bill.

The indorsers. Each indorser promises any subsequent indorser or holder that he will recompense any holder who has to pay on the bill.

An indorser is estopped from denying to a holder in due course the authenticity of all signatures prior to his indorsement, i.e. the drawer and every previous indorser.

Transmission without indorsement. An indorsement in blank makes the instrument a bearer one, so that it can pass from hand to hand without further indorsement. A **transferor by delivery,** as a person who does not indorse the bill but passes it on, is called, cannot be sued on the bill. He does, however, impliedly promise to his immediate transferee, provided he is a holder for value, that the bill is what it claims to be and that he has a right to transfer it.

Cheques and the Bankers

The relationship of a banker and his client is that of a debtor and creditor, in that the banker whose customer's account is in credit owes this money to his client. It is also a contractual relationship whereby the banker undertakes to maintain his customer's account confidential, and also to honour all cheques drawn on the account for which there are funds or for which an arrangement has been made to meet them. For breach of this contractual obligation, the banker will be liable for substantial damages to a customer who is in trade (or, possibly, a profession), but a private individual will be entitled only to nominal damages unless he can prove loss has actually been incurred and was reasonably foreseeable: *Gibbon v West-minster Bank*, [1939] 3 All E.R. 577. That decision was some time ago and the situation may have to be looked at again by the Courts in the light of the changed circumstances caused by the prolification of agencies reporting on the credit of individuals. But the banker who wrongfully dishonours a cheque for which funds are available may also be liable to damages for libel. The words 'refer to drawer' or 'R.D.' on a returned cheque have by now acquired a significance which undoubtedly conveys the innuendo that the cheque has been drawn when funds were not available. In an unreported case, the Post Office Giro system settled an action of this nature by paying damages for libel.

But a banker is not bound to honour a cheque where the customer has made a cash deposit but the banker has not had reasonable time to credit it to his account; nor where the customer has paid in other peoples' cheques for collection by his bank and the cheques have not been collected. But once an item has been credited to a customer's account, he is entitled to draw against it, even though some cheques have not been cleared. If a banker credits an account wrongly and the customer changes his position by drawing on the account, the banker is estopped from denying that is the customer's money.

By s.75 (1) of the *Bills of Exchange Act, 1882*, a banker is under a duty not to honour a cheque if the customer has 'stopped' it. If the banker should honour such a cheque he is not then entitled to debit his customer's account. Mr. Barnett had accounts with the Westminster Bank at two different branches. He drew a cheque on one account by altering the printed address on the cheque form supplied to him by the other branch, then gave instructions to the branch on which the cheque was drawn to stop payment. The computer gaily identified only the metallic lettering on the cheque form and therefore debited the account in the branch for which the printed form had been supplied, ignoring the handwritten alteration on the cheque. It was held that the bank were not entitled to debit Mr. Barnett's account. The request printed on the cover of the cheque book that customers should use cheque forms only for the account for which they were printed was not a contractual term: *Barnett v Westminster Bank*, [1965] 3 All E.R. 81.

At the same time, the customer owes a duty to the banker to take care. He may be estopped by his conduct if he allows somebody to operate his account without his consent, as in *Greenwood v Martins Bank* 1933, [1932] All E.R. Rep. 318, where a husband failed to tell the bank that his wife had forged his signature to cheques and cashed them. So, too, if a customer is negligent in drawing a cheque so that the fraud of a third person is facilitated, the customer is estopped from setting up that the cheque is a forgery. In *London Joint Stock Bank v Macmillan* 1918, [1918–19] All E.R. Rep. 30 a cheque was signed as drawn by a clerk, without any words and only the figure £20. The clerk then changed the £20 to £120 and wrote in the words, 'One hundred and twenty'. The drawers were held to be estopped by their negligence and could not therefore allege successfully that the bank had no authority to pay the cheque.

As A. P. Herbert has amusingly pointed out, a cheque does not have to be written on the printed form supplied by the bank, and provided it is in writing, it matters not that it is written on a cow, an egg or, as happened in one Edwardian case, in lipstick on a pair of French knickers. The banks much prefer customers to draw cheques on their printed forms and their computers are ill equipped to deal with cows, eggs or French knickers *et hoc genus omne*. But so long as it is a written mandate, the bank is bound to honour it, no matter what form the writing takes.

Protection of the Paying Banker

The *Bills of Exchange Act, 1882* affords the banker paying cheques some protection against loss of the right to debit a customer's account.

'When a banker on whom a cheque is drawn pays it in good faith and in the ordinary course of business, it is not incumbent on the banker to show that the indorsement of the payee or any subsequent indorsement was made by or under the authority of the person whose indorsement it purports to be, and the banker is deemed to have paid it in due course, although such indorsement has been forged or made without authority' reads section 60.

This covers the banker when paying on a cheque where the indorsement has been forged and the cheque is otherwise regular.

The ordinary course of business means during normal banking

hours and in the manner adopted generally by bankers. It has been held that if he gives cash over the counter for a crossed cheque he is not paying in the ordinary course of business.

Section 80 of the same enactment provides a similar protection to a banker who pays a *crossed* cheque in accordance with the manner of the crossing and in good faith and 'without negligence'. Whether this affords any greater or less protection to a paying banker than s. 60 has been disputed and it has been suggested that this section is entirely unnecessary since it does nothing that s. 60 does not already do.

Section 1 of the *Cheques Act, 1957* protects a banker who in good faith and in the ordinary course of business pays a cheque which is not indorsed or is irregularly indorsed. With the mania for legislation by reference which so disfigures the English Statute Book, this section enacts that a banker who pays such a cheque is deemed to have paid it in due course within the meaning of section 59 of the *Bills of Exchange Act, 1882*. The result is to abolish the need for indorsement where cheques are being paid into the account of the payee. But in spite of the legislation, which would appear to obviate the need for indorsement of any kind, the bankers have apparently decided that it is in the ordinary course of their business that indorsement should be required for cheques cashed over the counter.

Nothing in these, or any other Statutes, exonerates a banker who pays out on a forged drawer's signature. He is expected to recognise the signature of his own customers.

Protection of the Collecting Banker

When you pay cheques into your bank account, your bank has to collect these on your behalf. If you have no title to the cheque because it has been stolen or obtained by fraud, the banker could be liable to action for the tort of conversion by the true owner.

The *Cheques Act, 1957*, section 4 enacts:

'Where a banker in good faith and without negligence receives payment of a cheque (whether crossed or otherwise) or other document issued by a customer and intended to enable a person to obtain payment from that banker of the sum mentioned in the document, or having credited a customer's account with the amount of such an instrument, receives payment thereof for himself; and the customer has no title, or a defective title to the instrument, the banker does not incur any liability to the true owner of the instrument by reason only of having received payment thereof.'

It will be noted that the protection of this section is lost if the banker acts negligently. Negligence in this connection can be either in opening the account or in the circumstances in which the instrument was accepted for collection.

It is negligent for a banker to open an account for a customer without taking up reference, or without finding out by whom the customer is employed.

It is negligence in collection if the bank collects for a customer's account cheques drawn in favour of his employer or even cheques purporting to be drawn by the employer; or where the cheques collected are much larger than the known resources of the customer. It has been held to be negligence where a cheque crossed 'a/c payee only' has been collected for an account other than that of the named payee.

Promissory Notes

'A promissory note is an unconditional promise in writing made by one person to another, signed by the maker, engaging to pay, on demand or at a fixed or determinable future time, a sum certain in money, to, or to the order of, a specified person or to bearer': section 83, *Bills of Exchange Act, 1882.*

This is the classic definition of the Act. By that definition, I.O.U.s are excluded because they do not contain any promise to pay, but merely record the existence of a debt; but an I.O.U. that does contain a promise to pay and complies with the terms of the Act is a promissory note.

'*To Johnny Jones—I.O.U. £50 and promise to pay by 1st December 1980*'—is a promissory note if signed by the maker.

Promissory notes are fully negotiable in the true sense of the word but differ from bills of exchange in that they do not have to be presented for honouring. The maker of the note is deemed to be the same as the acceptor of a bill, and the first indorser is treated as the drawer of an accepted bill payable to his order. Protest is not required when a foreign bill is dishonoured.

By section 84 a promissory note is inchoate and incomplete until its delivery to a payee.

On demand, promissory notes have to be presented for payment within a reasonable time.

CHAPTER TWENTY-FOUR

BAILMENT, LIENS AND SECURITIES

The Nature of Bailment

Bailment is the nearest thing we have in English law to the old Roman 'real' contracts in which contractual obligations were imposed not because of a promise, express or implied, but because of a course of dealing with property. Indeed in the leading case of *Coggs v Bernard* 1703, [1558–1774] All E.R. Rep. 1, Holt C.J. based himself almost entirely on the Roman law on the subject.

The classic definition of bailment in English law is that of Pollock and Wright:

'Any person is to be considered a bailee who, otherwise than as a servant, receives possession of a thing from another or consents to receive or hold possession of a thing for another upon an undertaking with the other person either to keep and return or deliver to him the specific thing according to directions, antecedent or future, of the other person.'

But, as will be seen, that is anything but simple and it is necessary to break it down into its elements:

1. Bailment applies only to personal chattels, 'things'.
2. It is an obligation imposed by law on anybody who comes into possession of the goods of another.
3. Bailment may come about as the result of a contract, but it equally well may not. For example, as we have seen the 'hirer' in a hire purchase contract is the bailee of the goods in question until the moment comes when he exercises his option and becomes the owner.

But a person who finds the goods of another is equally a bailee of them.

Similarly, there is bailment where you are lent a book. In most cases, where you borrow a book from a friend, it is impossible to find contractual obligations because of a want of intent. (See page 75.) But the law imposes certain obligations on the bailee, the borrower.

The fact that bailment can exist apart from the assumption

of contractual obligations can clearly be seen in *Gilchrist Watt v York Products Ltd.*, [1970] 3 All E.R. 825. The plaintiffs in Australia ordered two cases of clocks from Germany and these were carried out to Sydney by the M.V. *Regenstein*. In Sydney the two cases were discharged from the ship by the defendants, who were stevedores, and lodged in a shed under their control. When the plaintiffs came to collect them, one case had disappeared.

It was argued on behalf of the defendants that there was no liability on them because there was no contract between them and the plaintiffs. It was evident that there was in fact no contract, but in spite of that the defendants were held liable for the loss. The defendants by voluntarily taking possession of the plaintiffs' goods had become bailees of them and therefore liable.

4. There is, however, no bailment unless there is a handing over of possession. So, if you hang a hat on a coatstand while you have your hair cut, the barber is not liable because he has never been put in possession of your hat. On the other hand, where a man went into a restaurant to dine and his coat was taken by a waiter and hung on a hook, it was held that the restaurant proprietor was liable as a bailee, since the coat had been placed in his possession: *Ultzen v Nicols* 1894, [1891–4] All E.R. Rep. 1202. But it has been held, somewhat surprisingly, that when you put a car in a car park for which there is an attendant, and for which a charge is made, that is a mere licence and not a bailment. In *Ashby v Tolhurst*, [1937] 2 All E.R. 837, when the plaintiff went to collect his car, he was told by the attendant that somebody else had taken it away. He could not recover because there was no duty of care owed him by the licensor. This was followed in *Tinsley v Dudley*, [1951] 1 All E.R. 252.

The Bailee's Obligations

For very many years it was believed that there was in law a difference between the obligations imposed on a bailee for reward and one who either voluntarily or even unwillingly became the bailee of another's goods. However, this view was decisively rejected in the case of *Houghland v R. R. Low (Luxury Coaches) Ltd.*, [1962] 2 All E.R. 159 by the Court of Appeal. The standard of care is the same whether the bailment be for reward or is gratuitous.

The duty of a bailee can be summarised as follows:

1. To take **reasonable care** of the goods in question. What is reasonable depends entirely upon the facts and circumstances of any

particular case. But the burden of proving that reasonable care has been taken falls upon the bailee. If the goods are lost or returned damaged it is for the bailee to show that this happened in spite of the fact that he had taken reasonable care of them. If he cannot explain how the loss or damage came about he fails to discharge the burden of proof on him to show that it happened without his negligence.

2. The bailee's duty goes beyond that. He is also under a duty to take **reasonable steps to recover** them if they pass out of his possession. Cattle were sent to a farmer's pasture for agistment and by that contract he became bailee of them. Without any neglect on his part, they were stolen. He did not, however, inform the police or the owner or make any effort to recover them because he thought it would be a waste of time. It was held he was liable for the loss unless he could satisfy the Court that the cattle would not have been recovered if he had taken the appropriate steps: *Coldman v Hill* 1919, [1918–19] All E.R. Rep. 434.

3. The duty of the bailee extends not only to the bailor but also to the **owner of the goods** where he knows that the bailor is not the owner. Customs and forwarding agents entrusted goods to a carrier on behalf of the owner. Part of the goods were stolen while the driver of a vehicle left it unattended. Even though there was no contractual relationship between the carrier and the owner, since the carrier knew of the ownership, he was liable to the owner: *Lee Cooper v C. H. Jenkins & Sons Ltd.*, [1965] 1 All E.R. 280.

4. To return the goods to the bailor when called upon so to do or in accordance with the contract. If the bailee fails to do this he is liable for detinue or conversion.

Once a demand has been made for re-possession, the bailee ceases to be in lawful possession of the goods and is therefore liable for their loss or damage **even if he can prove it happened without negligence on his part.** Books were delivered to a binders to be bound. The binder took an unreasonably long time and the customer demanded them back. The bookbinder failed to comply with the request and a fire broke out, with the result that the books were burnt. The bookbinder was held liable even though he could show that the fire was not in any way due to his want of care: *Shaw v Symmons & Sons* 1917, [1916–17] All E.R. Rep. 1093.

5. To store the goods in the place agreed, if there is a contract and if this contract so required. A warehouseman contracted to store goods in his warehouse in a particular place. He, however, stored them elsewhere and they were destroyed by fire. He was liable for them in spite of terms in the contract exonerating him from all liability and in spite of the fact that he was not negligent: *Lilley v Doubleday* 1881, [1881–5] All E.R. Rep. 406.

Hotels and Guests' Property

Although an hotel proprietor is not strictly a bailee of all the goods brought on his premises by guests, apart from those expressly committed to his care, he has special obligations laid upon him.

The common law recognised, the 'common innkeeper' in a special way and with special obligations, not unlike those of the common carrier (see page 223).

The present position is governed by the *Hotel Proprietors Act, 1956*. By that Act an hotel means:

'an establishment held out by the proprietor as offering food, drink, and if required, sleeping accommodation, without special contract, to any traveller presenting himself who appears able and willing to pay a reasonable sum for the services and facilities provided and who is in a fit state to be received.'

That definition is virtually the same as at common law for the 'common innkeeper'. It excludes lodging houses, private residential hotels, public houses and restaurants; but it may include taverns and a temperance hotel. What a place is called is not decisive: the important factor is how it is used and what it holds itself out to do.

A traveller is anyone 'who uses the inn . . . in order to take what the inn can give'; it therefore includes local residents who go for meals or a drink.

The obligations laid by common law and Statute upon the hotel proprietor are as follows:

1. To receive and, if called upon so to do, to lodge all travellers who come to him. In this he is unlike the ordinary public house which would more aptly be termed 'a private house' since the landlord there has the right to exclude anybody with or without reason (subject to the provisions of the *Race Relations Act*). The hotel under the Act, like the common innkeeper, cannot turn away guests while he has food and accommodation available.

2. To be strictly liable for loss or damage to the property of the guest while staying in the hotel. This strict liability cannot be excluded by contract: *Williams v Linnitt*, [1951] 1 All E.R. 278.

But it can be limited in accordance with the provisions of the *Hotel Proprietors Act, 1956*, provided a notice framed in accordance with the Schedule to that Act is exhibited near the reception desk or, if there is no reception desk, near the entrance.

The limitation is:

(a) £50 for one article or
(b) a total of £100 in the case of one guest.

But this does not apply if the property was stolen or damaged through the neglect of the hotel proprietor or his servants; nor does it apply to goods deposited for safe custody with the hotel proprietor—in these two cases he is fully liable.

The 1956 Act excludes from the strict liability loss or damage to any vehicle or any property left therein. So motor cars left in an hotel's car park are now excluded as the result of the Act.

Even where there is strict liability, the hotel proprietor is not liable if the loss or damage was caused by the guest's negligence. He does not appear to be liable either for damage by fire, as a result of the *Fire Prevention (Metropolis) Act, 1774* except where the fire is caused by his negligence; nor is he liable if the damage or loss is caused by an Act of God or by the King's enemies.

Liens

A lien is a right to retain goods which are the property of another person. It does not of itself confer a right to dispose of them by sale or otherwise, nor does it confer a right to claim for their storage while they are being detained.

The most common example is that where a motor car is taken into a garage for repair. Once the repairs are completed the garage proprietor is entitled to keep the car until his proper charges have been met. As stated earlier (see page 212), this right can triumph over the owner's interest in a motor vehicle subject to hire purchase. The innkeeper or hotel proprietor has a similar lien over the goods of guests brought on to his premises until his proper charges are paid. And an unpaid seller has a right to retain goods sold until payment, in spite of the fact that as a result of the contract of sale the buyer has become the owner (see page 196).

This type of lien is described as a **possessory lien** and is a **particular lien,** i.e. it applies only to certain goods and until the charges in respect of them have been paid.

There are also possessory liens which are **general liens.** That is a right to retain all goods belonging to the debtor whether the debt relates to those goods or not. Solicitors are entitled to detain any papers in their possession belonging to a client in respect of any professional charges. Bankers are entitled to a similar right over all securities in their possession whether charged against the debt or not, even where they are deposited solely for safe custody. The banker's general lien also entitles him to combine accounts unless such an act is expressly contrary to the contractual agreement, as it was in *Halesowen Presswork & Assemblies Ltd. v Westminster Bank,* [1970] 3 All E.R. 473.

The possessory lien is lost when:

   (i) the goods pass out of the possession of the holder unless they are wrongfully removed.

(ii) the sum due is paid or offered in cash.

(iii) other security is accepted in place of the lien.

A maritime lien is different from a lien of the nature described above because it does not depend upon possession, and can be exercised only by taking proceedings against the property in question. A ship, for example, can be arrested and detained by an order from the Court. Persons entitled to such action include those who have suffered damage as the result of a collision with the ship, the holder of a bottomry bond (see page 241) and the master and seamen for wages and disbursements.

An equitable lien is the right to have a specific part of some property —whatever its nature—put against some specific payments. It has nothing to do with possession of property. An unpaid seller of land, for example, is said to have an equitable lien over the land in respect of the purchase price.

Statute may confer a right on a person who has a lien to sell the goods. Examples are:

(i) The unpaid seller of goods (see page 196).

(ii) Warehousemen under the *Merchant Shipping Act, 1894*.

(iii) Repairers under the *Disposal of Uncollected Goods Act, 1952*.

(iv) Hotel proprietors under the *Hotel Proprietors Act, 1956*.

In the absence of such authority a person has no right other than to detain the goods, and cannot dispose of them.

Pledge or Pawn

A pledge or pawn arises where one person parts with the possession of a chattel he owns to another as security for a debt or loan. There is an implied undertaking by the pledgee (as the recipient is sometimes called) to return the goods when the debt has been paid at the stated time or, if no specified time has been stated whenever the pledgor pays, within a reasonable time.

A duty is laid by law on the pledgee to take reasonable care of the goods put in his possession, and if he cannot restore them when payment is made, he is liable to compensate the pledgor unless he can prove the goods have been lost without his negligence.

The common example of pledge are the pawnbrokers, and transactions with them are now governed by the *Pawnbrokers Act, 1872* and the *Pawnbrokers Act, 1960*. The Acts do not apply to loans over £50. The effect of the Acts is that:

(i) pawn tickets must be given in every case.

(ii) every pledge is redeemable within six months of the pledging, after seven days of grace.

(iii) after this period:

goods under £2·00 become the absolute property of the pawn-broker.

goods over £2·00 have to be sold by auction and until so sold are redeemable by the pledgor. If sold by auction anything over the loan and interest charges must be paid to the pledgor.

(iv) if the goods pledged are destroyed by fire, the difference between the value and the loan plus interest must be paid to the pledgor by the pawnbroker.

LIST OF ABBREVIATIONS

[1891] A.C. .. .. The Law Reports, Appeals to the House of Lords and the Judicial Committee of the Privy Council and Peerage cases, from 1891 onwards.

Ad. & El. .. .. .. Adolphus and Ellis's Reports, Queen's Bench. 12 volumes. 1834–40.

[1936] All E.R. .. .. All England Law Reports from 1936 onwards.

[1923] All E.R. Rep. .. All England Reports Reprint.

App. Cas. .. .. .. The Law Reports, Appeals to the House of Lords and the Judicial Committee of the Privy Council. 15 volumes. 1875–90.

B. & Ad. .. .. .. Barnewall and Adolphus's Reports, King's Bench. 5 volumes. 1830–4.

B. & Ald. .. .. .. Barnewall and Alderson's Reports, King's Bench. 5 volumes. 1817–22.

B. & C. .. .. .. Barnewall and Cresswell's Reports, King's Bench. 1822–30.

B. & S. .. .. .. Best and Smith's Reports, Queen's Bench. 10 volumes. 1861–70.

Beav. .. .. .. Beavan's Reports, Rolls Court. 36 volumes. 1838–66.

Bing. .. .. .. Bingham's Reports, Common Pleas. 10 volumes. 1822–34.

C.B. .. .. .. Common Bench Reports. 18 volumes. 1845–1856.

C.B.(N.S.) .. .. .. Common Bench Reports, New Series. 20 volumes. 1856–65.

C. & P. .. .. .. Carrington and Payne's Reports, *Nisi Prius*. 9 volumes. 1823–41.

C.P.D. .. .. .. The Law Reports, Common Pleas Division. 5 volumes. 1875–80.

[1891] Ch. .. .. .. The Law Reports, Chancery Division, from 1891 onwards.

1 Ch.D. .. .. .. The Law Reports, Chancery Division. 45 volumes. 1875–90.

Cho. Ca. .. .. .. Choice Cases in Chancery. 1558–1605.

Cl. & F. .. .. .. Clark and Finelly's Reports, House of Lords. 12 volumes. 1831–46.

Co. Rep.	..	..	.. Coke's Reports. 13 parts. 1572–1616.
Cox C.C.	..	..	.. Cox's Criminal Law Cases. 1843–1945.
Digest	..	..	.. English and Empire Digest.
De G.M. & G.	..	..	.. De Gex, Macnaghten and Gordon's Reports, Chancery. 8 volumes. 1851–7.
Dowl.	..	..	.. Dowling's Practice Reports. 9 volumes. 1830–41.
E. & B.	..	..	.. Ellis and Blackburn's Queen's Bench Reports. 8 volumes. 1852–8.
Eq. Case. Abr.	..	..	.. Abridgement of Cases in Equity. 2 volumes. 1667–1744.
Exch.	..	..	.. Exchequer Reports (Welsby, Hurlstone and Gordon). 11 volumes. 1847–56.
Ex.D.	..	..	.. The Law Reports, Exchequer Division. 5 volumes. 1875–80.
H. & C.	..	..	.. Hurlstone and Coltman's Exchequer Reports. 4 volumes. 1862–6.
H. & N.	..	..	.. Hurlstone and Norman's Exchequer Reports. 7 volumes. 1856–62.
Hob.	..	..	.. Hobart's Reports, Common Law. 1613–1625.
H.L.C.	..	..	.. Clark's House of Lords Cases. 11 volumes. 1847–66.
Hy. Bl.	..	..	.. Henry Blackstone's Reports, Common Pleas. 1788–96.
Jur. ..	..	..	.. Jurist Reports. 18 volumes. 1837–54.
[1901] K.B.		..	.. The Law Reports, King's Bench, from 1901 onwards.
Ld. Raym. ..	..	..	.. Lord Raymond's Reports, Common Law. 1694–1732.
L.J.Ch.	..	..	.. Law Journal Reports, Chancery. 118 volumes. 1831–1949.
[1951] Lloyd's Rep.		..	.. Lloyd's List Law Reports, cited by date from 1951 onwards. 84 volumes from 1919 to 1951.
L.J.C.P.	..	..	.. Law Journal Reports, Common Pleas. 1831–1875.
L.J.Ex.	..	..	.. Law Journal Reports, Exchequer. 1831–75.
L.J.P.	..	..	.. Law Journal Reports, Probate, Divorce and Admiralty. 1875–1946.
L.J.P.C.	..	..	.. Law Journal Reports, Privy Council. 1865–1946.
[1947] L.J.R.		..	.. Law Journal Reports. 1947–9.

L.R.Ex.	..	..	..	The Law Reports, Exchequer. 10 volumes. 1865–75.
L.R.Q.B.	..	..	..	The Law Reports, Queen's Bench. 10 volumes. 1865–75.
L.T.	..	..	..	Law Times Reports. 1859–1947.
L.T.(o.s.)	..	..	..	Law Times, Old Series. 34 volumes. 1843–60.
Leon.	..	..	..	Leonard's Reports, Common Law. 1522–1615.

M. & W. .. .. .. Meeson and Welsby's Exchequer Reports. 16 volumes. 1836–47.

Moore K.B. .. .. Sir F. Moore's Reports, King's Bench, Folio. 1 volume. 1485–1620.

[1891] P. .. .. .. The Law Reports, Probate, Divorce and Admiralty Division, from 1891 onwards.

P.D. .. .. .. The Law Reports, Probate Division. 15 volumes. 1876–90.

Ph. .. .. Phillips's Reports, Chancery. 2 volumes. 1841–9.

Q.B. .. .. .. Queen's Bench Reports (Adolphus and Ellis, New Series). 18 volumes. 1841–52.

[1891] Q.B. .. .. The Law Reports, Queen's Bench Division, from 1891 onwards.

Q.B.D. .. .. .. The Law Reports, Queen's Bench Division. 25 volumes. 1875–90.

Russ. .. .. .. Russell's Reports, Chancery Appeals. 1824–1829.

Salk. .. .. .. Salkeld's Reports, King's Bench. 1689–1712.

S.J. .. .. .. Solicitor's Journal, from 1856 onwards.

T.L.R. .. .. .. *The Times* Law Reports. 1885–1952.

T.R. .. .. .. Terms Reports (Durnford and East). 8 volumes. 1785–1800.

Vent. .. .. .. Ventris's Law Reports. 1688–91.

W.Bl. .. .. .. Sir William Blackstone's King's Bench Reports. 1746–80.

[1953] W.L.R. .. .. Weekly Law Reports, from 1953 onwards.

W.N. .. .. .. Weekly Notes. 1866–1952.

W.R. .. .. .. Weekly Reporter. 54 volumes. 1852–1906.

Yelv. .. .. .. Yelverton's King's Bench Reports. 1602–1613.

TABLE OF CASES

(References to pages on which some account of the facts of a case are given are printed in **bold** type)

TABLE OF STATUTES

(Page numbers in **bold** type indicate that the section referred to,
or a part of it, is set out verbatim in the text)

Index